Civic identity and public space

Manchester University Press

Civic identity and public space

Belfast since 1780

**Dominic Bryan and S. J. Connolly,
with John Nagle**

Manchester University Press

Copyright © Dominic Bryan, S. J. Connolly and John Nagle 2019

The right of Dominic Bryan, S. J. Connolly and John Nagle to be identified as the authors of this work has been asserted by them in accordance with the Copyright, Designs and Patents Act 1988.

Published by Manchester University Press
Oxford Road, Manchester M13 9PL

www.manchesteruniversitypress.co.uk

British Library Cataloguing-in-Publication Data
A catalogue record for this book is available from the British Library

ISBN 978 0 7190 8636 6 hardback
ISBN 978 1 5261 6366 0 paperback

First published 2019
Paperback published 2022

The publisher has no responsibility for the persistence or accuracy of URLs for any external or third-party internet websites referred to in this book, and does not guarantee that any content on such websites is, or will remain, accurate or appropriate.

Typeset in 10.5 on 12.5 pt Bembo Std Regular by
Servis Filmsetting Ltd, Stockport, Cheshire

Contents

List of figures	*page* vi
Preface	viii
List of abbreviations	ix
Introduction	1
1 The origins of public space	16
2 Lord Donegall's town	36
3 The making of a municipal culture	62
4 Freedom and order	92
5 Public space and civil conflict	114
6 Public space and the Protestant state	133
7 New directions? The 1960s	158
8 Violence and carnival: renegotiating public space 1970–2008	180
9 Shared space or divided future?	203
Conclusion: public space – past lessons and future strategies	228
Index	234

Figures

Cover credit: Engraving of Belfast and Northern Counties Railway Terminus, by Robert John Welch (1859–1936) (© National Museums NI Collection Ulster Museum BELUM.Y.W.10.21.270)

1. Belfast in 1757 as depicted in a contemporary map (courtesy of the Linen Hall Library) — page 17
2. Belfast Poor House (c.1785–90), by John Nixon, c.1750–1818 (© National Museums NI Collection Ulster Museum BELUM.P1.1983) — 21
3. Victoria Street in the 1880s, view northwards from Victoria Square, by Robert John Welch (1859–1936) (© National Museums NI Collection Ulster Museum BELUM.Y.W.10.21.259) — 64
4. Map showing the route of Queen Victoria's progress through Belfast, 11 August 1849 — 72
5. Royal Avenue by Robert John Welch (1859–1936) (© National Museums NI Collection Ulster Museum BELUM.Y.W.10.21.228) — 79
6. Belfast City Hall, by A. R. Hogg (© National Museums NI Collection Ulster Museum BELUM.Y1967) — 81
7. Belfast Public Library, by A.R. Hogg (© National Museums NI Collection Ulster Museum BELUM.Y2655) — 82
8. Plan of the city of Belfast, from *The Emerald Isle Album of Belfast and County Down* (1897). The Linen Hall was replaced soon after by the new City Hall (1906)
9. Sunday evening at Custom House Square, c.1900–5, by Alexander Robert Hogg (© National Museums NI Collection Ulster Museum BELUM.Y15389) — 116
10. The security gates at the entrance to Donegall Place, 1977 (Pacemaker Press International) — 183
11. The Lord Mayor's Show, 2008 (photo Dr Dominic Bryan) — 192

12 City Hall, St Patrick's Day, 2015 (photo Dr Dominic Bryan)   210
13 Giro d'Italia, 9 May 2014 (photo Dr Dominic Bryan)   212
14 Belfast Pride parade, 30 July 2011, and counter-demonstration,
    Royal Avenue (courtesy of Dr Neil Jarman)   217
15 Twelfth of July parade, 2010 (photo Dr Dominic Bryan)   219

Preface

The research for this book was begun as part of the Economic and Social Research Council (ESRC) project 'Identities and Social Action', directed by Professor Margaret Wetherell and supported by ESRC grant RES-148-25-0054. Chapters 1–6 are the work of Professor Sean Connolly, Chapter 7 of Dr John Nagle and Chapters 8 and 9 of Dr Dominic Bryan. Chapter 6 incorporates some material prepared by Dr Gillian McIntosh as part of her work as a research officer on the project.

Sean Connolly would like to thank Dr Paul Harron, Dr Catherine Hirst, Dr Alice Johnston, Mr Stuart Irwin and Dr Jonathan Wright, former research students who have worked with him on Belfast topics, and from whom he has learned a great deal. He would also like to thank the members of the informal Queen's University discussion group on urban history – Dr Kieran Connell, Dr James Davis, Dr Elaine Farrell, Dr Tom Hulme, Professor Sean O'Connell, Dr Olwen Purdue – who assisted him in getting to grips with the initially unfamiliar process of theorising space. Dr Vivienne Pollock of the Ulster Museum provided invaluable assistance with illustrations for the volume. Mavis Bracegirdle was, as always, an acute critical reader.

Dominic Bryan would like to acknowledge colleagues who worked on two other related ESRC projects. Preliminary work was undertaken under ESRC grant L219252112 with Dr Gillian McIntosh and work continued under ESRC RES-062-23-1140 in the project 'Embodying the Imagined Community: The role of collective participation in the transformation of Irish identities' with Professor Steve Reicher, Professor Orla Muldoon, Dr Clifford Stevenson, Dr Sam Pehrson, Dr Aisling O'Donnell and Dr Danielle Blaylock. He would also like to recognise the contribution and friendship of Dr Gordon Gillespie and Dr Neil Jarman, who have accompanied him to many events. Staff at the Institute of Irish Studies at Queen's University, particularly Catherine Boone, Valerie Miller and Joan Watson, carried much of the administrative load.

Abbreviations

BCC	*Belfast Commercial Chronicle*
BL	British Library
BNL	*Belfast News Letter*
CND	Campaign for Nuclear Disarmament
CRM	civil rights movement
CSORP	Chief Secretary's Office, Registered Papers
DUP	Democratic Unionist Party
ICTU	Irish Congress of Trade Unions
IRA	Irish Republican Army
NAI	National Archives of Ireland, Dublin
NICND	Northern Ireland Committee of the Campaign for Nuclear Disarmament
NILP	Northern Ireland Labour Party
NW	*Northern Whig*
PP	Parliamentary Papers
PRONI	Public Record Office of Northern Ireland, Belfast
PSNI	Police Service of Northern Ireland
RUC	Royal Ulster Constabulary
SDLP	Social Democratic and Labour Party
UDA	Ulster Defence Association
UUP	Ulster Unionist Party
UVF	Ulster Volunteer Force

Introduction

'This Protestant town'

In July 2006 Ian Paisley, Jr, a member of the Democratic Unionist Party (DUP), called for the banning of a proposed nationalist parade in the town of Ballymena, County Antrim. Such a parade, he argued, could have only one purpose: to provoke 'public disorder and tension around this Protestant town'.[1] The casual definition of an urban space in religious terms might at first sight seem to be no more than another illustration of the crippling inability of the chosen spokesmen of Ulster unionism to articulate its allegiances and values in terms comprehensible to members of a secular, liberal democracy. Looked at more closely, however, his words summarise two long-standing features of the political culture of modern Northern Ireland. The first is a propensity to define civic life in exclusive terms: a sphere in which only certain aspirations and allegiances can legitimately claim recognition. The second is the frequency with which these issues of legitimacy are expressed through disputes over access to public space. A celebrated early incident in the prehistory of the recent Northern Ireland conflict, for example, was the mobilisation of Protestants in Dungannon, County Tyrone – backed by the paramilitary Ulster Volunteer Force – for the purpose of blocking a planned civil rights demonstration, on the grounds that its proposed destination, the market square, was 'unionist territory'.[2]

The Dungannon civil rights march, rerouted by the police despite the protests of the organisers, passed off peacefully. But over the next few years similar disputes over marches and demonstrations in public places, and the confrontations that resulted, were central to the political crisis that culminated in the collapse of the Northern Ireland state and the commencement of the Irish Republican Army's long campaign of violence. Later, following the paramilitary ceasefires of 1994, parading emerged as one of the main threats to a fragile truce. Between 1995 and 1998 attempts to negotiate a political settlement were complicated by the annual confrontations that took place as

Orange lodges marching to Drumcree church near Portadown asserted their right to pass down the mainly Catholic Garvaghy Road. Later, as the initial jubilation surrounding the agreement achieved in 1998 died down, it became increasingly clear that a literal war of murder and intimidation was to give way to what many observers have labelled a 'culture war',[3] focussed on public expressions of identity and allegiance and on competing claims to control the narrative of the recent past. In this new context parades, along with the display of flags or portraits in public places, the status of the Irish language and of Ulster Scots, and the official commemoration of historical events, have remained central to a continuing contest for power and legitimacy within Northern Ireland. Space and its meaning to contending groups has also been central to a long-running dispute – at the time of writing still unresolved – over whether the site of the former Maze prison, where ten Republican prisoners died on hunger strike in 1981, should be preserved as a museum, converted into a peace centre, adapted to strictly non-political uses, or, in the view of some unionists, bulldozed into oblivion.[4]

The public debate on these issues has been passionate yet superficial. Where parades are concerned, in particular, defenders of Protestant marching rights have appealed to what they present as an unqualified and historically grounded constitutional right, frequently summed up, with spurious archaism, in references to walking 'the queen's highway'.[5] Opponents assert the right of 'nationalist areas' to refuse admission to parades deemed offensive, thus replicating the exclusive claims to space earlier articulated, at Dungannon and elsewhere, by their political opponents. For their part, policy makers and public authorities, charged with adjudicating between irreconcilably conflicting claims, have often floundered as they have sought to reconcile hazily defined notions of individual and collective rights, of public order and of the claims of tradition.

With these points in mind, this book has two main purposes. First it seeks to give a historical dimension to current debates on the representation of identity and the use of public space. Historians have long recognised that the claims to legitimacy based on long-standing continuity that are advanced from both the unionist and the nationalist camps are to be treated with scepticism; in reality both of these present-day political self-definitions are the product of processes of invented tradition and selective historical memory familiar to students of identity politics everywhere in the modern world.[6] But it is also important to recognise that the modern concept of public space, and the conventions generally seen as governing its use, are likewise the products of specific historical developments. Indeed, it will be argued here, the whole pattern of identity politics in contemporary Northern Ireland can be understood in terms of the flawed adoption of what elsewhere proved to be a largely successful development, in response to the needs of an urban industrial society, of new ideas of collective identity and new ways of regulating behaviour in public space. The

Introduction

second aim is to ask how far such a historical perspective can contribute to the understanding and possible resolution of current contests over flags, parades and other symbols of identity. In both cases the focus will be on a case study of Belfast, whose emergence as a major industrial city, and the metropolis of unionist Ulster, has made it the site of some of the most intense and revealing episodes in the working-out of these contentious questions.

The nineteenth-century city: civic pride and the invention of public space

Between 1800 and 1901 the population of Belfast rose from just over 20,000 to 349,000. Its growth from a modest provincial port to a major industrial centre thus took place during what is now recognised as a golden age of urban culture and civic achievement. The starting point was the radical reform of municipal government that was introduced in Great Britain in 1835, and extended five years later to Ireland. The Reform Acts replaced the former chaotic patchwork of corporations, parish vestries and boards created by local improvement Acts with a uniform system of mayors and corporations elected by the votes of ratepayers.[7] What this meant in practice was that responsibility for managing the rapidly expanding towns of an industrialising United Kingdom passed into the hands of what has been called an urban squirearchy. The landed class of the eighteenth century had dominated the public life of their localities through their prestige as a social elite, their economic power as landlords and employers and their control of the key office of justice of the peace. Now a new urban elite, dominated by wealthy business leaders and wielding a similar combination of cultural, economic and institutional power, came to the fore. Working through the structures created by municipal reform, and empowered by the still limited functions of the central state, it took charge of the management of Britain's towns at a time when both the demands on urban administration and the resources at its disposal were expanding beyond all precedent.[8]

Progress was not immediate. In many towns, shopkeepers and other lesser commercial rate payers strenuously opposed improvement projects involving an increase in expenditure. There was also a natural reluctance to interfere with profitable businesses: measures to limit emissions from factory chimneys, in particular, lagged significantly behind action on other threats to public health. Over time, however, self-evident and urgent need, along with the confidence and dynamism of the commercial and manufacturing elite, inspired substantial improvements, especially after the extension of the municipal franchise in 1867 had diluted the voting power of the 'shopocracy'. Giant integrated schemes for the provision of clean water and the removal of waste, along with by-laws setting minimum standards for house building, reversed what had been a calamitous drop in urban life expectancy. Streets were lit, paved and widened, in the process clearing some of the worst inner-city slums. Amenities such as domestic gas, water supply and tramway systems (initially horse drawn, later powered by electricity) became giant enterprises owned and managed by the municipality.[9]

Sanitary and other reforms removed the environmental horrors that for a time had made the new industrial town a byword for dehumanised squalor. In its place there developed an assertive pride in the achievements of these newly created urban giants, and a confidence in their potential as centres both of social progress and of cultural achievement. The pride was evident above all in civic building. Imposing town halls provided a symbol of the status and prosperity of the urban community, and a workplace for the growing army of municipal employees that attended to its needs. Alongside them other edifices – museums, art galleries, libraries and concert halls – sought to demonstrate that the industrial city could be a centre not just of wealth creation but of high cultural achievement. The architecture of this boom in civic building made its own statement: classical styles asserted a parity with the stately homes of the great landowners and the palaces of royalty, while at the same time recalling an earlier great age of urban civilisation in the city states of ancient Greece; the new vogue for Gothic recalled the free cities of the Middle Ages, and in particular the thriving urban republics of northern and central Italy.[10]

The new and exalted self-image evident in civic architecture was also reflected in the development during the same period of an elaborate body of civic ritual. Dressed in newly invented official costumes, members of the municipal elite assembled and processed to welcome visiting dignitaries, to mark royal birthdays and other national events, to dignify local civic occasions such as the installation of a new lord mayor and to celebrate a range of real and invented traditions. The ostentatious ceremonial, the gold chains and other trappings of office superficially resembled the pomp affected by royalty and aristocracy. But the meaning was different. What was on display was not the individual, elevated by royal or noble birth, but the office, a transitory status in which those serving as mayor and councillor became for a fixed period representatives of the imagined community of the town or city.[11]

One striking consequence of this massive programme of rebuilding and improvement was that the spatial arrangement of the British town was, in effect, turned inside out. Traditionally it had been the wealthy who had lived in town centres, while the poorer classes gathered on the outskirts. Already by 1845, on the other hand, the German socialist Friedrich Engels, describing Manchester, outlined a wholly different urban geography: a town centre of offices and warehouses, 'lonely and deserted at night', traversed by more lively main thoroughfares lined with shops; around it, 'stretching like a girdle', the houses of the working class; and, beyond this again, streets of middle-class housing, from which horse-drawn omnibuses regularly carried passengers into the city.¹² The pace of change in other towns varied according to topography, occupational structure and the development of public transport. But the long-term pattern of development was everywhere the same: a non-residential town centre devoted to commerce and retailing; an inner zone of housing for a working class required to live in close proximity to places of work; and outer suburbs where the more affluent could find relief from the bustle of the centre and enjoy the company of their social equals.

The most obvious consequence of this changing urban landscape, with major implications for social and political life, was the establishment of a new, more rigid pattern of social segregation. Almost equally important, however, was the creation of a wholly new relationship between public and private space. The streets of the city centre, formerly the dwelling place of the rich and powerful, were no longer exclusive to any particular social group. Instead they were open to all, in part for purposes of business, but also, as warehouses and offices were joined by shops, public houses, theatres and clubs, as sites for consumption, leisure and sociability. Retail in particular was transformed, as the small specialist shop gave way to the department store, deliberately conceived as a place to wander and browse rather than simply to complete a predetermined purchase.¹³ Large-scale urban planning exercises also permitted the creation of other public spaces: squares offered space and an opportunity for display in a grid of congested streets, while public parks gave urban dwellers access to grass, trees and water. The new working-class suburbs, meanwhile, brought their own transformation of space. The courts and alleys that had previously accommodated the urban poor had constituted areas wholly controlled, for normal purposes, by the inhabitants. In their new environment, by contrast, the private space of the working-class family was located inside one of a row of small terraced houses, while beyond lay what was now the public space of the open street.¹⁴

Nineteenth-century urban development, then, created large areas that were in new ways open to all. Public, however, did not mean free of restraint. On the contrary, the principle from the start was that space, precisely because it was public, had to be kept clear of obstructions; if all were to be able to avail of it, then some potential uses could not be tolerated. In place of the restrictions formerly imposed by private ownership or social privilege, there were to be new, and often highly intrusive, forms of regulation. The transition was particularly clear in the case of the new public parks. These were an undoubted amenity. But where they were laid out on what had previously been waste ground or common land, there were losses as well as gains. From 1839 onwards, for example, Brandon Hill outside Bristol was developed as a public park, with gravel walks, trees, shrubbery and rock gardens, later further embellished by two cannon from the Crimean War and, at the end of the century, an ornamental tower. The result was to create an attractive site for decorous walks and family outings. But the transformation also ended Brandon Hill's long history as a site for popular political meetings.[15] Elsewhere a similar transformation of open ground into regulated space, subject to by-laws and patrolled by keepers, was in part responsible for the sharp decline of boisterous popular sports such as prize fighting and the baiting or fighting of different types of animal.

Blood sports and bare-knuckle boxing were practices that quite possibly would not in any case have survived the changes in culture and sensibility that took place during the early and mid-nineteenth century. In other cases, too, new restrictions were matters of clear necessity. In what were now heavily congested city centres, drivers of vehicles had to keep to one side of the road, to remain within the permitted speed and to observe a growing body of traffic regulations. Householders could no longer dispose of their waste, or butchers slaughter animals, where they chose. Pedlars and vendors could no longer lay out their goods on busy pavements. Other restrictions, however, were less clearly a response to practical necessity. Pedestrians, too, became subject to new rules. To be loud or boisterous or visibly under the influence of alcohol was to become subject not just to disapproval but to criminal sanctions. Above all, one had to keep moving: one of the most common, and most resented, aspects of the police that now began to appear in growing numbers in towns across the United Kingdom was the constant barked instruction, directed at supposed 'loiterers', to 'move on'. The same concern with keeping the streets clear of obstruction, and enforcing decorous behaviour, was evident in other petty forms of regulation, such as the frequent prosecutions of children playing games in the street, or of adults engaged in casual games of chance on street corners or at other natural gathering places.[16]

The creation of a new type of public space also had implications for the conduct of politics. The remodelled town centre, with its monumental civic buildings, straightened and widened boulevards and open squares provided a much improved venue for processions and assemblies. Indeed a vigorous exploitation of these new opportunities was an important means by which the municipal authorities that were created under the reformed system consolidated their own place in urban life. Access to these spaces for other groups was initially much less straightforward. Between the 1790s and the 1840s, the era of the great European revolutions and of the first and most brutal phase of large-scale industrialisation, British governments responded to political disaffection and social discontent with repressive legislation and the curtailment of traditional freedoms. As part of this process radicals and labour activists were repeatedly denied access both to traditional places of assembly, such as commons or open fields, and to the streets and squares of the remodelled urban landscape. Even where central government, mindful of long-standing tradition, was willing to accept a limited right to assemble and petition, Loyalist vigilantes still acted to prevent it. At the notorious 'Peterloo' at St Peter's Fields in Manchester in 1819, for example, it was the locally raised volunteer yeomanry that charged a peaceful crowd of men, women and children, killing about eighteen and wounding many others.[17]

From the 1850s, however, a more prosperous and stable Britain was able to accept that public space was indeed for all. By the late nineteenth century the presumption of a right of assembly in public space was being extended even to gatherings that were technically illegal. The Catholic Emancipation Act of 1829, while giving Catholics the right to sit in Parliament and removing a range of other restrictions, had made it a criminal offence to appear in clerical vestments, or to perform any distinctively Catholic ritual, outside a church or private house. In Cardiff, the marquis of Bute, a convert to Catholicism and still a dominant figure in the town's commercial and civic life, was able from the 1870s to sponsor an elaborate annual celebration of the festival of Corpus Christi. However, this remained within the law, the public event consisting of a procession of girls and young women carrying banners and bunches of flowers, while the priests in their vestments waited with the consecrated host inside the private grounds of the marquis's residence, Cardiff Castle.[18] By the 1890s, on the other hand, Catholic parishes in London felt able to go further, organising formal ecclesiastical processions through the streets, while the government explicitly told ultra-Protestant organisations who protested that it was not disposed to take action.

Against this background the archbishop of Westminster, Francis Bourne, accepted the invitation to host a major international event, the Eucharistic Congress of 1908, in London. The Congress was intended to conclude with a procession through the streets surrounding the city's Catholic cathedral, headed by the consecrated host carried in a gold monstrance and followed by visiting ecclesiastical dignitaries in their most elaborate religious vestments. The Commissioner of the Metropolitan Police raised no objection. The Prime Minister, H. H. Asquith, privately expressed his irritation at having 'this gang of foreign cardinals taking advantage of our hospitality to parade their idolatries through the streets of London: a thing without precedent since the days of Bloody Mary'. Yet neither he nor his colleagues were inclined to intervene. At the last moment, however, rumours of potentially violent counter demonstrations by militant Protestants panicked the government into asking Bourne to curtail the planned procession. The archbishop was able to claim a moral victory, loyally obeying the government's instructions while announcing publicly that it had demonstrated to the world that Catholics 'do not enjoy the same liberties as other Englishmen'. The reality was, rather, that Asquith and his colleagues had blundered into an ill-considered action that was widely seen, by Protestants as well as Catholics, as having violated the central principles governing access to public space.[19]

Ireland, in this context as in others, presented particular problems for the liberal conception of popular rights and freedoms that took shape in the nineteenth century. Recurrent outbreaks of violent agrarian agitation, and successive movements of revolutionary nationalism, repeatedly forced governments to abandon cherished legal principles. Ireland, alone among the regions of the United Kingdom, was policed by an armed constabulary, under central government rather than local control. This paramilitary force was regularly supplemented by the deployment of soldiers. And Irish chief secretaries, year after year, returned to the House of Commons to apply for legislation giving the authorities extraordinary coercive powers. At least as striking as these deviations, however, are the limits within which government continued to operate. The reason why so many coercion Acts had to be introduced, after all, was that no one wanted to make the transition from supposedly temporary suspensions of normal practice to an admission that it was not in fact possible to rule Ireland under normal British law. The special powers involved included provisions such as the suspension of habeas corpus and the replacement of juries by panels of judges. But trials of offenders continued to follow the usual rules of evidence, and to demand the usual standard of proof. When a watchman accused of facilitating the escape from a Dublin prison of the Fenian leader James Stephens in 1865 was found to have a copy of the organisation's oath in his room, the trial judge ruled that it would be dangerous to the liberties of the subject 'to convict a man from the simple fact that a treasonable document was found in his possession'. Newspapers were in some cases prosecuted as seditious, but for the most part the government allowed the nationalist press considerable latitude. Police monitoring the postal service were told that they could examine the outside of envelopes for handwriting and postmarks, but could not open any letter without a warrant.[20]

A similar hesitance about departing from the permissive norms that by this time were well established in the rest of the United Kingdom was evident in relation to public meetings. The rise to prominence of the Irish Republic Brotherhood or Fenians, explicitly committed to the overthrow of British rule in Ireland, began in November 1861, when its leaders organised a massive public procession, seven or eight thousand strong, to mark the transfer to Dublin's Glasnevin cemetery of the remains of Terence Bellew McManus, a veteran of the Young Ireland rising of 1848, who had died in political exile in San Francisco. In 1867, even larger numbers turned out for a mock funeral procession for the 'Manchester Martyrs', three Fenians hanged in England for their part in the killing of a policeman. In neither case did government try to intervene. In 1869, during a series of mass meetings calling for an amnesty for other imprisoned Fenians, the Lord Lieutenant, Earl Spencer, refused to suppress the gatherings, on the grounds that 'no free government [could] object to public meetings for any legitimate object'. Two years later, during a visit by the Prince of Wales, the police did intervene, with what was considered undue violence, to prevent a rally on the same issue from taking place close to where the royal party were staying. Their action was widely condemned and the government, faced with criticism in Parliament, felt obliged to give assurances that there would be no further interference with public meetings.[21]

Later, in the tense period preceding the First World War, the principle of free use of public space was to be carried to extraordinary lengths, when the government permitted uniformed and armed Volunteers, unionist and nationalist, to organise, drill and parade in plain view, with no attempt to curtail their activities. When the nationalist Irish Volunteers staged a deliberately provocative importation of guns at the small harbour of Howth, a few miles north of Dublin, police and army did intervene, leading to a disastrous outcome when soldiers taunted by a hostile nationalist crowd opened fire, killing three people. The aftermath, however, was revealing. The next day the authorities formally returned to the Volunteers the nineteen rifles they had managed to confiscate, while the Assistant Commissioner of the Dublin police, who had authorised the seizure, was suspended from duty.[22]

Where politics is concerned, then, the picture, with only the partial exception of Ireland, is at first sight of a progressive widening of access, creating a genuinely public space open to all. But the widening of access must be placed in the broader context of the nineteenth-century reform of political life. Superficially what took place was progress towards improved representation: archaic local oligarchies gave way to elected councils; constituency and municipal boundaries were revised to reflect the distribution of population; the franchise was progressively widened. Yet movement was not always in the direction of greater participation. Some of the institutions of the unreformed municipal system, such as the ad hoc town meetings or parish vestries, had been loosely defined entities, managed according to custom and practice. The clearly defined municipal electorates that replaced them, based on rigid formulae tying representation to property, were in some places more exclusive than the less formal structures they replaced. The rituals of the unreformed electorate system, too, had provided for a degree of mass participation. Those voting may have been a small, often arbitrarily selected, body. But the hustings at which candidates formally announced themselves, the poll extending over a period of days, the triumphant chairing of the victorious candidate, could all provide an opportunity for much larger numbers to feel themselves to be a part of the process. One part of the reform process, however, was to eliminate these rowdy by-products of the casting of votes. Electoral politics moved from the streets to the assembly room and the ticket-only meeting. Debate was conducted primarily in the columns of the press rather than by the spoken word.

The same new decorum was evident in the use of public space. By the late nineteenth century, public processions were one of the ways in which campaigners on a range of issues, as well as trade unions, friendly societies and other interest groups, maintained solidarity in their ranks, advertised their cause and provided evidence of popular support. But entry to the new spaces remained conditional. Participants were expected to be well dressed and orderly, to follow routes negotiated in advance with the authorities and to submit to the direction of accompanying police. Bonfires, the parading of effigies and other carnivalesque elements of the traditional public political culture were now unacceptable, as was the consumption of drink. Banners might still be carried, but what they displayed was the work of specialised craftsmen, as opposed to the crude but expressive folk art of an earlier era.[23] Once again greater freedom, and the opening up of public space, were inseparably linked to the acceptance of new controls on behaviour.

This apparent contradiction between liberation and constraint was no superficial anomaly. It was in fact the defining characteristic of the wider ideology, nineteenth-century liberalism, that had underpinned these changes in urban landscape and popular politics. Liberalism took as its central principle the freedom of the individual to pursue his (or, within a more limited sphere, her) inclinations and interests, unfettered by tradition, inherited status, ecclesiastical authority or government regulation. But this left the problem of how such freedom was to be prevented from degenerating into socially dangerous forms of disorder. The liberal answer was to combine an insistence on individual freedom with a corresponding insistence on the need for self-discipline. The liberal citizen was autonomous, yet ruled by an internal censor of words and actions. Those without this censor were not legitimate claimants to freedom. This in turn permitted the emergence of a powerful new abstraction. Where earlier systems of social regulation had sought to protect the wealthy or privileged, liberalism imposed its restrictions in the name of 'the public', an imagined self-disciplined majority whose enjoyment of liberty and of access to public space were legitimately protected from the potential misuse by others of those same liberties and rights.[24] In Great Britain, the resulting concept of a 'rule of freedom' was to prove highly effective, providing what are still widely accepted principles for the regulation of public behaviour. In Ulster, however, the same rhetoric of 'the public' was subordinated to religious and political sectionalism, with results that quickly laid bare the inner contradictions of the liberal synthesis of freedom and order.

Space and place

The concept of public space, then, is more complex than it appears at first sight. It emerged out of a very specific set of historical circumstances, and in the form in which it has developed it contains within it a built-in contradiction between freedom and restraint. In recent years a growing body of theoretical work has sought to explore this contradiction within the context of a wider discussion of the concepts of space and place.

This 'spatial turn', as it has been called, has not been universally welcomed. Historians have pointed out that they have not required an elaborate apparatus of theory to make them aware, for example, that large-scale building projects are more often than not an architecture of power, or that urban planning and redevelopment can be a form of social control. (Who has not heard of Baron Haussmann's cavalry-friendly Parisian boulevards, driven through what had been neighbourhoods of narrow, easily barricaded streets?) It is also painfully obvious that, despite the proliferation of theoretical papers, practitioners of the spatial turn have been unable to arrive at a coherent set of terms and definitions. One attempt, in 2013, to survey the current state of the field, produced thirteen different definitions of space.[25] Nevertheless, some key ideas have emerged that put the narrative of the changing shape of the nineteenth-century city given above into a broader context.

At the centre of the spatial turn is an insistence that space must be seen not just as a location where things happen but as a socially constructed context that shapes what can and cannot take place within it. The attraction of such an approach to the study of modern urban life is obvious. Indeed Henri Lefebvre, whose *The Production of Space* (1974) is a key text in the spatial turn, argued that the concept acquired a new importance in the modern era, when developments in cartography, technology and government made space something to be mapped and planned, to be considered in the abstract as well as physically inhabited. Lefebvre went on to develop what has become an influential tripartite model. 'Spatial practice' refers to the everyday routines through which people inhabit space. 'Representational space' refers to the way space is conceptualised, in the work of scientists, urban planners and similar groups. Lefebvre, a Marxist, took it for granted that such conceptualisations would necessarily represent the relations of production within the society. Others, less wedded to a classic model of base and superstructure, have identified 'representational space' more explicitly with the conscious use by elites of buildings and planned space to represent and consolidate their power.[26] Finally, and in opposition to the official conceptions of representational space, there are 'spaces of representation', where the population inhabiting a location invest it with meaning by the way in which they move, assemble or behave. Lefebvre's distinction is echoed in another influential text, Michel de Certeau's essay on 'Walking in the city'. Taking as his starting point the contrast between Manhattan as seen from above, from the 110th floor of the World Trade Centre, and the city as experienced at street level, de Certeau emphasised the contrast between the rational, formal design of the urban planner and the behaviour of individuals, who realised, subverted or by-passed different elements of that design by the choices they made of where and how to walk.[27]

The ideas of Lefebvre and de Certeau have been highly influential. For some, however, their value is weakened by their concentration on the conceptual. Lefebvre's celebrated tripartite model, it has been pointed out, offers 'one system of people doing things, and … two systems of people representing things. But no things!' Yet things have their own stubborn existence, independent of any process of social construction. A civic elite may let ideology run riot as it plans a town hall or a street-widening scheme. But large buildings and broad streets, once constructed, cannot be easily altered. An analysis, according to this line of argument, may begin with the processes by which spaces came to be configured as they are. But it must also identify a tipping point, where spaces 'become a material cause, producing effects beyond their symbolic functions'.[28]

An alternative approach is to focus not on space but, rather, on place.[29] Civic elites used the built environment to create images of their own power and authority, to offer representations of communal identity, to encourage or discourage certain types of behaviour. In some cases this involved the manipulation of space — the development of a processional route, the arrangement of significant buildings in relation to one another (as with the parish church and the big house at opposite ends of the traditional village), the planning of a residential district. But in many cases the focus was rather on place. Even in complex societies, it has been argued, there are sites of social centrality, places in which a dominant group's hegemonic power is inscribed; the point of such spaces is to naturalise the group's control over the political and cultural institutions of the state. There is, accordingly, often a strong aura of the sacred imbued in such sites, which can make them seem timeless, unchanging and even beyond rational scrutiny and contestation.[30] At a different social level, innumerable studies have shown how important place has been in the history of popular protest. Over and over again what has been involved is not the defence of abstract rights, but customary entitlements — rights of access, freedom to graze animals, collect wood, hunt or fish — tied to particular places.[31] Places could also become significant through their liminal or marginal status. The peripheries of cities, on a border between two separate jurisdictions, commonly became zones of relative freedom. The sites of fairs, markets and other gatherings could become places where, at specific times, the normal rules of behaviour were relaxed or suspended, permitting those attending to enjoy a degree of carnivalesque liberty.

From all this it should be clear that the theoretical literature that constitutes the spatial turn does not provide a clear blueprint for the discussion that follows. What it does do is to highlight the complexities involved in any attempt to explore the changing and often violently contested use of public space in Belfast since the late eighteenth century. The extraordinary growth of Belfast during the nineteenth century, as a modest provincial port expanded to become one of the United Kingdom's great industrial centres, created exceptional opportunities for its ruling elite to engage in the purposeful creation of urban space. They did so, however, against a background of acute religious and political conflict, where the spaces they had created were appropriated and invested with meaning in ways that were beyond their control. If engineers and architects used maps and plans to give form to their vision of an orderly, improving urban centre, the city's working-class inhabitants carried in their heads a different, but even more influential, map, of an urban landscape defined by a rigid pattern of residential segregation. Meanwhile urban space, once created, helped to reshape the ways in which people behaved. Suburbanisation both reflected and reinforced a widening separation between social classes; the increasingly lethal character of sectarian conflict was directly related to the disappearance of open space beneath a grid of densely packed terraces of working-class houses.[32] Place, too, was important as specific locations acquired a symbolic and emotional meaning that made them central to the maintenance of communal identity, and on occasion to conflict between communities, and as particular districts became territory to be invaded and defended. In all of these ways space and place were at one and the same time both social product and material actor.

Notes

1. *Ballymena Times*, 26 July 2006.
2. This was how their claims were summarised in the subsequent report of the royal commission chaired by Lord Cameron: *Disturbances in Northern Ireland* (Cmnd 532, 1969), chap. 3, para. 31. The actual language may well have been closer to that of Mr Paisley in 2006.
3. For example, Henry McDonald, 'Culture war is sticking point in Northern Ireland power-sharing talks', *Guardian*, 28 June 2017.
4. Laurence McKeown, 'Bulldozing history?', *History Ireland*, 6 (2005), 5–6.
5. E.g. *Belfast Telegraph*, 19 February 2010, quoting DUP councillor and Orangeman John Finlay.
6. For an incisive overview see R. V. Comerford, *Inventing the Nation: Ireland* (London: Bloomsbury, 2003). See also S. J. Connolly, 'Culture, identity and tradition: changing definitions of Irishness', in Brian Graham (ed.), *In Search of Ireland: A Cultural Geography* (London: Routledge, 1997), pp. 43–63.
7. Derek Fraser, *Power and Authority in the Victorian City* (Oxford: Blackwell, 1979); Matthew Potter, *The Municipal Revolution in Ireland* (Dublin: Irish Academic Press, 2011).
8. John Garrard, *Leadership and Power in Victorian Industrial Towns 1830–80* (Manchester: Manchester University Press, 1983), chap. 2; Garrard, 'Urban elites: the rise and decline of a new squirearchy', *Albion*, 27:3 (1995), 583–621.
9. Bill Luckin, 'Pollution', in Martin Daunton (ed.), *The Cambridge Urban History*

of Britain, Vol. 3: *1840–1950* (Cambridge: Cambridge University Press, 2000), pp. 207–28; Robert Millward, 'The political economy of urban utilities', in *ibid.*, pp. 315–50.

10 Simon Gunn, *The Public Culture of the Victorian Middle Class: Ritual and Authority in the English Industrial City 1840–1914* (Manchester: Manchester University Press, 2000); Tristram Hunt, *Building Jerusalem: The Rise and Fall of the Victorian City* (London: Weidenfeld and Nicolson, 2004); Kate Hill, '"Thoroughly imbued with the spirit of ancient Greece": symbolism and space in Victorian civic culture', in Alan Kidd and David Nicholls (eds), *Gender, Civic Culture and Consumerism: Middle-class Identity in Britain, 1800–1940* (Manchester: Manchester University Press, 1999), pp. 99–111.

11 David Cannadine, 'The transformation of civic ritual in modern Britain: the Colchester Oyster Feast', *Past & Present*, 94 (1982), 128–9.

12 Friedrich Engels, *The Condition of the Working Class in England* (Harmondsworth: Penguin Books, 2009), pp. 85–6.

13 E. D. Rappaport, *Shopping for Pleasure: Women in the Making of London's West End* (Princeton: Princeton University Press, 2000).

14 M. J. Daunton, 'Housing', in F. M. L. Thompson (ed.), *The Cambridge Social History of Britain 1750–1950*, vol. 2: *People and their Environment* (Cambridge: Cambridge University Press, 1990), pp. 195–250, at p. 204.

15 Steve Poole, '"Till our liberties be secure": popular sovereignty and public space in Bristol, 1780–1850', *Urban History*, 26 (1999), 40–54.

16 Robert D. Storch, 'The policeman as domestic missionary: urban discipline and popular culture in northern England, 1850–1880', *Journal of Social History*, 9:4 (1976), 481–509.

17 Katrina Navickas, *Protest and the Politics of Space and Place 1789–1848* (Manchester: Manchester University Press, 2016).

18 Paul O'Leary, 'Processions, power and public space: Corpus Christi at Cardiff 1872–1914', *The Welsh History Review*, 24:1 (2008), 77–101.

19 G. I. T. Machin, 'The Liberal government and the Eucharistic procession of 1908', *Journal of Ecclesiastical History*, 34:4 (1983), 559–83; Carol A. Devlin, 'The Eucharistic procession of 1908: the dilemma of the Liberal government', *Church History*, 63:3 (1994), 407–25. For Asquith's comment see Machin, 'Liberal government', 565, and for Bourne, see Devlin, 'Eucharistic procession', 424.

20 Brian Jenkins, *The Fenian Problem: Insurgency and Terrorism in a Liberal State 1858–74* (Liverpool: Liverpool University Press, 2008), pp. 41, 116. See also Virginia Crossman, *Politics, Law and Order in Nineteenth-century Ireland* (Dublin: Gill and Macmillan, 1996).

21 Jenkins, *Fenian Problem*, pp. 280, 317–18.

22 Charles Townshend, *Political Violence in Ireland: Government and Resistance since 1848* (Oxford: Oxford University Press, 1983), pp. 260–1, 274–6.

23 James Vernon, *Politics and the People: A Study in English Political Culture c.1815–1867* (Cambridge: Cambridge University Press, 1993). See also Frank O'Gorman, 'Campaign rituals and ceremonies: the social meaning of elections in England 1780–1860', *Past & Present*, 135 (1992), 79–115.

24 Patrick Joyce, *The Rule of Freedom: Liberalism and the Modern City* (London: Verso, 2003). See also Andy Croll, *Civilizing the Urban: Popular Culture and Public Space in Merthyr, c.1870–1914* (Cardiff: University of Wales Press, 2000), pp. 3–11.
25 The count is by Leif Jerram, 'Space: a useless category for historical analysis?', *History and Theory*, 52:3 (2013), 400–19, in a discussion of Gerd Schwerhoff, 'Spaces, places and the historians: a comment from a German perspective', *History and Theory*, 52:3 (2013), 420–32.
26 See, for example, the presentation of Lefebvre's model in Katrina Navickas, '"Why I am tired of turning": a theoretical interlude', History Working Papers Project, 2011, www.historyworkingpapers.org/?page_id=225 (accessed 14 February 2018).
27 Michel de Certeau, 'Walking in the city', in *The Practice of Everyday Life* (Berkeley and Los Angeles: University of California Press, 2011), pp. 91–110.
28 Jerram, 'Space: a useless category', 411, 417–18. For the transition from planned space to a material environment that structures social action see also Thomas Gieryn, 'What buildings do', *Theory and Society*, 34 (2002), 43.
29 Navickas, 'Why I am tired of turning'.
30 Kevin Hetherington, *Expressions of Identity: Space, Performance and Politics* (London: Sage, 1998). See also Roger Friedland and Richard Hecht, 'The Bodies of Nations: A Comparative Study of Religious Violence in Jerusalem and Ayodhya', *History of Religions*, 38:2 (1998), 101–49. This part of the discussion is contributed by Dr Nagle.
31 Navickas, *Protest and the Politics of Space*; E. P. Thompson, *Customs in Common: Studies in Traditional Popular Culture* (London: Merlin Press, 1991).
32 See below, pp. 85–6.

1

The origins of public space

The pre-industrial town

Belfast began as an outpost of the Ulster plantation, strategically important because of its position at a ford across the River Lagan, but overshadowed by the longer-established Carrickfergus to the north.[1] As the regional economy developed, however, this crossing point between the counties of Down and Antrim became of increasing economic importance. By the 1680s the trade was sufficient to warrant the construction of the celebrated Long Bridge, whose twenty-one arches and almost half-mile length made it the most ambitious structure of its kind in Ireland. Geography also conferred other advantages. The river mouth offered an indifferent harbour, its shallow waters obstructed by mud deposits and sandbanks. But the Lough provided a sheltered haven for shipping, and the sea passage to Scotland and northern England was a short one. Most important of all, Belfast stood at the head of the corridor of rich agricultural land formed by the valley of the River Lagan, providing the natural outlet both for its exports of pork, beef and butter and for the linen cloth that began to be produced there from the late seventeenth century. By the mid-1720s Belfast, with a population of around 8,000, was Ireland's third-busiest port, and possibly its sixth-largest town.[2]

Despite this rapid growth in wealth and population, the Belfast of the early and mid-eighteenth century retained the characteristic spatial layout of an early modern town. The core of the town consisted of three parallel streets: Waring Street, site of the original plantation settlement; High Street, developed originally as quays along both sides of the River Farset, but now culverted for part of its length; and Bridge Street (later Ann Street), carrying traffic to and from the celebrated Long Bridge. Between them shorter connecting streets formed a rough grid pattern. To the west three other roads, Mill Street and North Street, both already lined with houses, and the more recent Linenhall Street, radiated outwards to join the main road to Carrickfergus. But the whole town

The origins of public space

was still comfortably enclosed by the line of the defensive earthen ramparts that had been erected as far back as 1642.

In such a confined space there was limited scope for zoning by function. High Street, Waring Street and the connecting Broad Street were the town's prime residential areas. A map drawn up in 1757 for use by the Donegall estate (Figure 1) described them as being lined with houses that were 'handsome, several stories high and chiefly composed of brick'. High Street, however, was also a commercial artery, broadening at its western end to provide a market square, while at the other end the river emerged and the street remained a quay, with stalls erected in front of the houses on market days.[3] The lower end of Waring Street also reached the docks, and archaeological evidence indicates that here the street became a primarily industrial area, home at different times to a pottery, a salt-panning enterprise established on the mud flats of the tidal Lagan and a tannery.[4] Residential segregation was likewise limited. Some of the poor lived on the outskirts. The roads leading out of town to the north and west, the same map recorded, were lined with 'low thatched dwellings of a mean appearance'. Others, however, lived in the town centre itself, in an increasingly dense complex of side streets and alleyways, referred

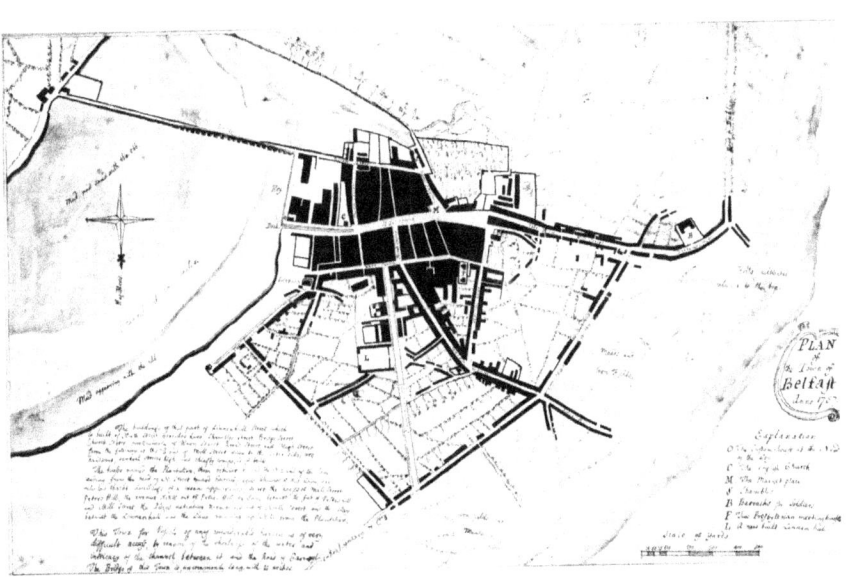

1 A contemporary map of Belfast in 1757. The orientation is, unusually, south at the top, so that the River Lagan is shown to the left. The River Farset is visible running down the centre of the lower part of High Street. The map was probably drawn in connection with plans for the redevelopment of the Donegall estate (see p. 19), and some of the black shading on North Street may indicate planned rather than actual buildings.

to as 'entries', created by infill building behind the main streets. To Richard Pococke, Protestant bishop of Ossory, visiting in 1752, Belfast appeared to consist 'of one long broad street & of several lanes in which the inferior people live'.[5]

A corollary of the compactness of the urban centre was that open space for social gatherings or amusement was sought outside its boundaries. In the first half of the century the Long Bridge, at that stage presumably less busy than it later became, served as a fashionable promenade. At the other end of town, the grounds of the former Donegall Castle, abandoned by the family after a fire in 1708, provided an alternative place of resort, until they were swallowed up by new building during the 1790s. In 1785 Martha McTier described a friend returning down Linenhall Street – by now renamed Donegall Street – from a 'country walk', presumably having strolled along one of the main roads that led away from Belfast to the towns of Antrim or Carrickfergus.[6] Another walk, along a raised causeway – identified on a map of 1791 as the Mall – that ran through the waterlogged lowlands to the south of the town, was clearly an important amenity. In 1788 two men were paid for keeping watch over the trees along the walk, to prevent their being cut down to provide decorative bushes on May Day.[7] There were also sites for more robust entertainments: the Point Fields, to the north of Linenhall Street, were a venue for cock fighting, dog fights, bare-knuckle boxing and other blood sports, while the slopes of Cave Hill, above the town, emerged as a gathering place on holidays, in particular Easter Monday.[8]

Already in the first half of the eighteenth century Belfast had a role as a social centre, providing entertainment and meeting places both for its own citizens and for the middle and upper classes of the surrounding countryside. A visiting army officer in 1738 noted condescendingly that there was an assembly every fortnight in the town hall, 'where you shall see a fine appearance of ladies and gentlemen, so trade don't always spoil politeness'.[9] Yet its amenities were, by later standards, modest. The combined town hall and market place, erected in 1663, was by the mid-eighteenth century seriously dilapidated, and was used for a miscellaneous range of purposes. The Methodist leader John Wesley, who preached in the lower of its two levels in 1762, noted that the floor above was occupied by a dancing master 'till at twelve the sovereign put him out by holding his court there'.[10] The parish church in High Street, meanwhile, appeared to Pococke to be 'a very mean fabric for such a considerable place'.[11] A visitor in 1780 complained of the piles of dung swept up following Friday's markets but then left to decorate the main streets of the town during the whole of Sunday. There were also repeated complaints of the reckless speed with which drivers of carts propelled their vehicles through the town.[12]

Social life likewise had a boisterous quality. In 1759 a public notice condemned 'several idle and disorderly persons' who had made a practice of firing

The origins of public space

guns from the Long Bridge, 'by which several ladies, gentlemen and passengers in carriages and on horseback have met with accidents'.[13] Even significantly later, in the 1790s, the memoirs of Theobald Wolfe Tone and Thomas Russell, young radicals at large in the growing town, testify to a culture of heavy drinking. Tone's celebrations in 1792 of the fall of the Bastille, for example, ended with 'dinner at the Donegall Arms. ... Generally drunk. Broke my glass thumping the table. Home, God knows how or when.'[14] Russell, in April 1791, was even more frank: 'Very drunk. Fall in the gutter and spoil my coat, bend my sword, etc.'[15] Russell (though not the married Tone) also confided to the diary his encounters with 'all the whores in town', although here it was claimed that what had been a modest vice trade had greatly increased with the recent influx of soldiers into what government perceived as a centre of subversive politics.[16]

Aristocratic patronage and urban development

Belfast also resembled other early modern towns in that its fortunes were closely tied up with those of an aristocratic proprietor. The entire ground area was the property of the earls of Donegall, descendants of the town's founder Sir Arthur Chichester (1563–1625). In the seventeenth century the Chichesters had occupied a substantial residence, generally called a castle though more properly a fortified house, in the south-west corner of the town. In 1708, however, the house was destroyed by fire, and the family moved to England. More seriously, the fourth earl of Donegall, who succeeded to the estate in 1706 at the age of eleven, had only narrowly avoided being classified as mentally unfit, and his estate was entangled in a web of lawsuits and legal settlements as trustees and relatives competed for control of its management. The resulting paralysis, lasting several decades, brought a serious check to what had been the town's rapid expansion. There was no authority capable either of investing in Belfast's infrastructure or of granting leases of sufficient length to encourage private building. By the 1750s the number of houses was in fact slightly lower than that recorded in 1725, and the number of vessels using the port had fallen from 14 to 9 per cent of total Irish shipping.[17]

The first steps towards escape from this cycle of decline came in 1752, when a private Act of Parliament empowered the earl's trustees to grant leases for up to ninety-nine years. By 1757, as is indicated by the map in Figure 1, work had begun on new schemes of urban improvement. The main focus of attention was Linenhall Street, projecting into an area of open fields to the north-west and anchored by the erection there in 1754 of a new Brown Linen Hall, centre of the town's most important commercial activity. These early plans for a new phase of urban investment, however, were fairly quickly superseded by something far more ambitious. The fourth earl of Donegall died in September 1757.

His nephew and successor, the fifth earl (promoted in 1791 to first marquis of Donegall), was, like his uncle, an absentee, with residences at Fisherwick in Staffordshire and on St James's Square, London. But he was nevertheless a highly active proprietor, who used his authority as landlord and patron to embark on a major programme of urban improvement.

This programme had three main elements. The first was a refurbishment and extension of the built-up area. In 1765 Donegall visited the town for the first time, and supervised a general releasing of almost the whole urban estate. The new leases were for realistic terms – the duration of three named lives, with a minimum of ninety-nine years – but they contained detailed specifications as regards the size and quality of the houses to be built. Those for High Street and Waring Street required tenants to build to a height of twenty-four or twenty-five feet. Meanwhile Donegall also used building leases to complete the building of Linenhall Street, now renamed Donegall Street and extended as far as the line of the road north to Carrickfergus, with further lines of brick terrace houses along side streets to right and left. A second phase of development, commencing in the 1780s, focussed on what had been the poor quarter to the west of the town centre. The market square at the end of High Street was redeveloped as the Parade (later Castle Place), lined with houses whose building leases required them to be three to four feet higher than those in High Street itself. Beyond this again there appeared a wholly new residential street, a broad avenue initially named Linen Hall Street, but later known as Donegall Place.

Donegall's second contribution to the urban landscape was to provide an impressive new set of public buildings. Here he was particularly generous along the line of his major project, Donegall Street. At its start, on the corner with Waring Street, he financed the construction in 1769 of a new market house. Above this, seven years later, he provided spacious Assembly Rooms, elaborately decorated with mahogany and ornamental plasterwork. Further along Donegall Street the earl provided the sites for a new Brown Linen Hall, replacing an earlier structure erected in 1754, and, at the top of the street, neatly closing off the vista, for the elegant poor house erected in 1774 by the Belfast Charitable Society (Figure 2). His final contribution to the street, a new parish church financed entirely by himself, was a significant choice. The poor state of the existing building reflected the modest size and circumstances of the Anglican congregation in a mainly Presbyterian town. The construction of St Anne's parish church, with its spire and dome 'forming an interesting and conspicuous object for many miles around', was thus a testimony both to Donegall's support for the established Church of Ireland and to his continued proprietorial control.[18]

The third feature of this new phase of landlord-inspired development was the first steps towards a pattern of zoning by function and social status. From

The origins of public space

2 The Belfast Charitable Society's elegant Poor House on North Queen Street, designed by the local manufacturer Robert Joy and opened in 1774, testified to the determination of an emerging middle-class elite to tackle the social problems of the growing town, while at the same time making a distinguished addition to the urban landscape. John Nixon's drawing, c.1785–90, conveys, and possibly exaggerates, the building's rural setting. The road in the foreground is in fact the upper end of what was to become the marquis of Donegall's showpiece, Donegall Street.

1788 the town's principal market was relocated to new purpose-built premises at Smithfield Square, west of the town centre and well away from the shops and coffee houses of High Street and Castle Place. Meanwhile the newly laid out Donegall Place became the preferred residence of the town's elite. An English lawyer, visiting in 1792, noted approvingly that its houses were 'uniformly built of good red brick on a modern London plan' and that one, belonging to the cloth merchant William Sinclair, was 'equal to many in Grosvenor Square'.[19] A later account described the street as 'the St James's of Belfast'.[20] At the other end of the social scale was the development of the town's first specifically working-class residential district. The area to the west of the town was already characterised by the ribbon development of low-quality housing along Mill Street and Peter's Hill. From the 1780s, however, developers leasing plots of land in this area began to lay out a more dense network of streets, with houses designed for occupation by weavers and other artisans, and also for the first generation of workers in the new factory-based industry that was over the new few decades entirely to transform the character of the town.

Lord Donegall's decision to unite commerce and sociability, by topping an Exchange intended to facilitate the transaction of business with an Assembly Room where the better class of inhabitant could meet for balls and other entertainment, reflected a prominent contemporary preoccupation. In the urban commercial society of Georgian Britain politeness and sociability, easing the necessary everyday intercourse of persons not bound to one another by ties of kinship or close neighbourhood, had come to be seen as central civic virtues. Alongside the amenities provided by Donegall, other institutions appeared, reflecting the same concerns. A theatre opened in 1768, replaced by a better-furnished building in 1793. Inns and coffee houses provided the venues for a range of social clubs and associations. These included card-playing clubs, freemasons' lodges and an Adelphi club linked to the theatre, as well as other associations, like the Patriot Club of the 1750s and the Amicable Society of the 1780s, that combined support for political reform with regular displays of alcohol-fuelled good fellowship.[21] Lower down the social scale a Reading Society established in 1788 by a group of self-improving artisans and tradesmen became the basis of one of the town's enduring cultural institutions, the Linen Hall Library.[22]

Ireland's Manchester

The first marquis of Donegall's programme of improvement commenced at an opportune moment. The Irish economy in the first half of the eighteenth century had suffered from weak trade and recurrent crises of subsistence. From the 1740s, however, conditions improved dramatically. One engine of growth, benefitting Belfast along with other ports, was the massive expansion in exports of agricultural produce, first to the West Indies and later, by the end of the century, to the new and hungry urban centres of industrialising Britain. The other, affecting Belfast in particular, was the runaway growth in exports of linen cloth, the great bulk of it produced in Ulster. Initially much of this trade had been conducted, despite the lengthy overland journey involved, through Dublin. In 1785, following a dispute between Dublin and Ulster business interests, Belfast merchants invested in their own White Linen Hall, erected on land donated by Donegall but paid for by a public subscription of £17,550.[23] Meanwhile Donegall himself invested a reported £60,000 in the completion of the canal works that converted the River Lagan into an effective conduit for the transport to Belfast port of a growing volume of both linen and agricultural produce from the town's rich hinterland.

This successful capture of the Ulster linen trade, like the parallel rise of its provisions exports, confirmed Belfast's standing as a major port and commercial centre. Through a network of local markets, its merchants collected up linen cloth spun and woven by male and female workers throughout rural Ulster for finishing and export. Another development of the late eighteenth century, by contrast, pointed to the town's future as a manufacturing centre. Commencing in the 1770s manufacturers began to apply the new technology, just developed, of spinning cotton thread by water- or steam-powered machinery. In the long run, the Irish cotton industry was to prove unable to compete effectively with its larger and more efficient English and Scottish rivals. In Belfast, however, further technological advances in the mid-1820s made it possible to apply the same techniques of powered machine spinning to the finer fibres of the flax plant, thus allowing for a transfer of capital and resources into an industry where the town enjoyed a substantial historical advantage. As the number of cotton mills slowly declined, their place was taken by an expanding number of linen-spinning factories. By this time the town had also become the base for a range of smaller but still significant manufacturing enterprises: iron foundries, glass making, chemical works. A small-scale ship-building business established in 1791 also grew rapidly. There are press reports of the launch of forty vessels from two yards between 1802 and 1825, including the first steam-powered vessel in 1820. Meanwhile the volume of shipping passing through the port tripled between 1815 and 1835.[24] To the Scottish traveller Henry Inglis, visiting in 1834, Belfast did not seem really to belong in Ireland. Instead, 'round and round, scores of tall chimneys, and their clouds of utilitarian smoke, remind one of Manchester, Glasgow, or Leeds'.[25]

With industrial development came a dramatic acceleration in the growth of population. In 1800 Belfast had an estimated 20,000 inhabitants. By the time of the first official census, in 1821, this had risen to 37,000, rising again to 53,000 in 1831 and to 75,000 by 1841. Growth of this magnitude in turn required a significant expansion of the physical area of the town. George Benn, writing in 1823, noted that in the previous fifteen years the number of streets had risen from 114 to 150, a figure that did not take in 'some small rows or lanes' lately given names as part of the continued ordering of public space within the town.[26] The construction boom received a significant boost from 1822 as the second marquis of Donegall, crippled by debt, began granting perpetually renewable leases for the entire area of the town and surrounding district in exchange for ready money.[27] Inglis, in 1834, believed that 'at least one-third of the town has been built within the last fifteen years'. And indeed the number of houses had risen from just under 6,000 in 1821 to 8,700 ten years later.[28]

Much of this new building was designed to house a hugely expanded industrial workforce. The zone of working-class housing erected from the 1780s to the west of the town centre, where water power from the Farset and Blackstaff had encouraged the establishment of the first spinning mills, continued to expand. To the east, on the other side of the Long Bridge, the district of Ballymacarrett became home to a foundry, rope-works and glass and vitriol works, as well as to a colony of handloom weavers. Contemporary estimates suggest that the population of this industrial suburb rose from 1,208 in 1791 to over 5,000 by 1831. Meanwhile a third industrial district had begun to appear to the north of the town centre, where a new thoroughfare, York Street, was laid out from 1803 through what had previously been a mixture of agricultural land and the area of waste ground known as the Point Fields. A fourth district, Cromac, to the south-east, was less an extension of the town than a small adjacent settlement where access to the River Blackstaff had encouraged the location of a range of enterprises, notably the paper mill owned by the Joy family, proprietors of the *Belfast News Letter*. The erection there of the gasworks in 1823 confirmed its status as a centre of low-status workers' housing.

The expansion of the town also had implications for the residential patterns of the better-off. The town centre, congested, noisy and disorderly, became increasingly unattractive. The very wealthy, able to maintain their own coaches, could withdraw to villas on the rising ground of the Malone Ridge to the south, along the Antrim Road to the north, or across the Long Bridge, on the County Down shore of Belfast Lough.[29] It was presumably they who created the congestion complained of in a newspaper report of 1813 on the 'coaches, post chaises and jaunting cars' that on a Sunday converged from all directions on the town's oldest and most prestigious Presbyterian meeting house, in Rosemary Street.[30] The less affluent, however, had no choice but to remain within walking distance of their place of work or business. The result was the further expansion, in what has been described as a process of 'peripheral suburbanisation', of the socially exclusive district immediately south of the town. Donegall Place remained the town's most prestigious address. But beyond it the lines of large, terraced town houses began to spread round the four sides of the square surrounding the Linen Hall, now renamed Donegall Square, along Chichester Street to the east and Wellington Place to the west. At the end of Wellington Place the area gained a second focus with the construction during 1807–14 of the Academical Institution, set up to provide a third-level education for the town's expanding middle class. During the 1820s and 1830s further solid, four-storey terraces appeared on the uncompleted square surrounding the college and on the adjoining streets.[31]

If High Street remained the commercial and retailing centre of the town, the area between Donegall Square and College Square thus became its fashionable quarter. At its heart stood the White Linen Hall, a commercial establishment but also a meeting place and the site of the library that had grown out of the Belfast Reading Society. Meanwhile the ground immediately surrounding the Linen Hall had been developed to give Belfast its first true urban park, a place of resort that was neither wholly public nor wholly private. Railings surrounded the walkway around the building, while 'small gates for ingress and egress' regulated entry to the promenade. A local newspaper in 1812 acknowledged the novel character of the area when it proposed that two or three benches be provided there for the use of 'infirm persons, or nurses with children'.[32] A much later account, recollecting the Belfast of the 1840s, confirmed that the promenade around the Linen Hall had become the resort of 'the belles and swells of that remote period'.[33]

The Belfast of the 1820s and 1830s was thus a considerably more substantial place than the improved town that had emerged in the late eighteenth century. But it was also, it seems, a somewhat less elegant one. The second marquis of Donegall was never in a position to attempt the close supervision over building that had been exercised by his father. He had entered on his inheritance burdened by the debts built up in a decade of gambling and reckless extravagance, and his estate had almost immediately been placed in the hands of trustees appointed to deal with his creditors. Any residual possibility of influence disappeared when he went on to grant perpetual leases, reducing himself to a mere receiver of ground rent. In the absence of proprietorial control, the builders of the new upper-class streets opted for quantity over quality. Inglis in 1834 wrote favourably of the 'fine broad streets, and handsome rows and squares' he had encountered on the outskirts of the town, 'evidently but of yesterday, and as evidently the residences of wealthy persons'. But he also commented harshly on the 'liny hungry look of the modern streets of Belfast [...] streets and rows present unbroken lines of buildings, uniform in height, and unrelieved by the least architectural ornament'.[34] The novelist Thackeray, visiting the town eight years later, conveyed a similar image of neat but rather dull uniformity. The houses 'have no attempt at ornament, for the most part, but are grave, stout, red bricked edifices, laid out at four angles in orderly streets and squares'.[35]

One further consequence of this rapid growth of population was the first stage in what was to be one of the most distinctive features of nineteenth-century Belfast, the development of a pattern of religious segregation. Belfast, established by British settlers and located in an overwhelmingly Protestant hinterland, was traditionally a solidly Protestant town. In the 1770s and 1780s its Catholic population numbered around 1,000, less than 10 per cent of the total. The homes of this minority may already have been concentrated in the area round Hercules Street. This was an old street that had originally connected the top of High Street to one of the gates in the town's ramparts, and was the centre of the butchering trades, a low-status occupation in which Catholics were disproportionately represented. Over the next five decades, as the growing town sucked in migrants, not just from Antrim and Down, but from the religiously mixed counties of south and central Ulster, this Catholic population began to expand, rising to 16 per cent in 1808, and to 32 per cent by 1834.[36] By the 1820s Hercules Street was clearly identified as a Catholic district. There was also by then a second area of Catholic settlement, a new cluster of streets that had grown up on one side of an old road that had continued the line of High Street and Castle Place into the countryside beyond the ramparts, and that took its name, the Pound, from the pen for impounded cattle formerly located there.

A pattern of segregation by religion did not in itself necessarily reflect sectarian hostility or aggression. The ethnic neighbourhoods that were a standard feature of nineteenth-century American cities, like the Jewish districts in some of their British counterparts, testify to the natural tendency of new arrivals in a harsh and impersonal urban environment to settle close to familiar accents, habits and institutions. In addition, both Hercules Street and the Pound were close to what was until 1815 Belfast's only Catholic place of worship. And in fact the limited evidence suggests that the emergence of the Pound as a distinctive Catholic quarters had already taken place by 1820, before serious violence between Catholic and Protestant first became a regular occurrence.[37] When a pattern of sectarian feuding did develop, on the other hand, the existence of residential segregation both contributed to the intensity of the violence and was itself reinforced by the climate of intimidation that resulted.

Managing public space

In Belfast, as elsewhere, administrative structures were slow to catch up with the sudden spurt of urban growth that took place in the late eighteenth and early nineteenth centuries.[38] In a manner typical of the unreformed municipal system, responsibility for providing basic amenities was divided between a range of bodies. The Grand Jury of County Antrim, selected by the sheriff from among the leading landed proprietors, levied county cess on the inhabitants and provided, up to 1800, for the upkeep of roads and bridges. The parish vestry of the Church of Ireland, despite the weakness of the established church in a predominantly Presbyterian town, remained a significant unit of local government, empowered to levy church rates for both ecclesiastical and public purposes. It was the vestry, for example, that finally implemented a plan for street lighting in 1765. Other aspects of local government were the responsibility of a Corporation comprising a Sovereign and twelve other members. However, this body, appointed by nomination, and so in no real sense accountable to a wider public, paid only limited attention to the day-to-day affairs of the town. From time to time the Sovereign made a formal progress through the town's markets, checking the weights and measures used by traders and confiscating meat and other produce unfit for consumption. In a celebrated incident in 1768 he sought to highlight the ordinance against allowing pigs to wander unattended in the street by appearing in person to shoot two of the offending animals. But these were occasional gestures from a body whose main function was to elect the two MPs that Belfast returned to the Irish Parliament.[39]

A further important aspect of urban government was even more clearly rooted in the practices of a small and intimate urban community. On receipt of a 'requisition' from a body of inhabitants of appropriate standing, the Sovereign could summon a town meeting to discuss specific matters of public concern. In March 1791, for example, the Sovereign convened a meeting to discuss proposals for a public coal yard. In August of the same year, 'in compliance with a requisition from a number of respectable inhabitants of Belfast', he summoned a second meeting, to set up a subscription to finance the prosecution of felons.[40] The procedure for these gatherings to some extent compensated for the oligarchic nature of other administrative agencies, in that there was no formal qualification for attendance. Martha McTier, widow of one of the town's businessmen, attended a meeting in 1795 on the subject of political reform, although she noted that she was the only woman present.[41]

By the last quarter of the eighteenth century, this combination of traditional institutions and ad hoc meetings was already proving inadequate to deal with the problems of a growing town that was also an emerging centre of factory-based industry. A full-scale reconstruction of municipal institutions, however, had to await the reform-minded 1840s. Earlier, in a society less disposed to challenge proprietorial and corporate rights, provincial towns had two main ways of dealing with the problems of growth. The first was to create new administrative structures that would discharge necessary functions while leaving the traditional corporate structures intact.[42] The first such innovation in Belfast was in 1752, when leading citizens, concerned at the growing problem of vagrancy, created a Charitable Society. In 1774 the society received a parliamentary charter of incorporation, and later the same year it opened its poor house at the top of the new Donegall Street. From the 1790s, as a means of providing an income, it took over responsibility for the town's water supply, formerly delegated to individual contractors, leasing springs from the Donegall estate and constructing a reservoir and a network of wooden pipes. In 1783 merchants in the town established a Chamber of Commerce. In 1785 a petition to Parliament from the Chamber led to the creation of a new chartered body, the Ballast Board, elected by merchants and ship-owners and empowered to maintain and develop the town's harbour.

A more radical expedient open to a growing town hampered by inadequate municipal institutions was to apply to Parliament for a local Act creating an elected board empowered to levy rates for purposes such as the paving, cleaning and lighting of streets. Belfast's 'police act', passed just prior to the dissolution of the Irish Parliament under the Act of Union and apparently designed to protect the interests of the Donegall family, created a somewhat cumbersome two-tier Police Board, comprising an oligarchic Police Commission and a more representative Police Board.⁴³ For the next four decades, however, it was this body that took the lead in maintaining and developing the infrastructure of the expanding town. The amount raised in police tax rose at a steady rate, from £1,567 in 1802 to around £5,000 in the mid-1820s and to over £7,000 a decade later. A large part of its work concerned the paving of streets, the provision of raised footpaths along their edges and their regular cleaning, all of which the Board took over from the Grand Jury. It also sought to provide other basic amenities, including the first public 'necessaries', erected in 1820–24. Street lighting was another major expense. The initial system of lamps burning whale oil was replaced in 1823 by gas lighting throughout the town, provided by a private company under contract to the Police Board. Local newspapers hailed the technological innovation, with fourteen miles of pipe carrying gas distilled from coal, and the contrast with the 'gloomy twilight' of the system they replaced. In practice, once the grand opening was over, the Board, and later the reformed Corporation, continued for several decades to order thrifty reductions in lighting on summer nights and during the full moon.⁴⁴

In addition to maintaining streets and providing other basic amenities, the Police Board sought to impose a new level of order on the expanding urban space for which it was responsible. One of its first acts was to have name boards erected at street corners, and to have houses numbered. The numbering initially began on the right-hand side of each street as it led away from the Exchange or from a principal thoroughfare; a move in 1816 to place odd and even numbers on opposite sides was to involve the Board in prolonged conflict with householders unwilling to adopt the new system. Meanwhile by-laws introduced in 1808 required householders, on pain of a fine, to have the footpath in front of their dwellings swept before nine in the morning. Moreover, no person was to shake or dust carpets or mats in any street or lane between eight in the morning and ten at night.⁴⁵ Other regulations governed behaviour in the town's increasingly congested streets. Drivers of carts had to display their name and licence number, to keep to the left and to travel at 'no quicker pace than a walk', replaced in 1814 by a speed limit of four miles per hour 'within the precincts of the lamps'.⁴⁶ Butchers too were no longer to be permitted to clog gutters or alleyways with blood and offal. Instead they were permitted to slaughter animals or dress meat only inside their shops or in designated slaughterhouses.

Regulations of this kind came under the contemporary definition of 'police'. Police in the sense of a specialist agency of law enforcement remained a controversial novelty, in part because some saw it as an undesirable extension of state power, but also on grounds of cost. Belfast's first experiment in this direction was a voluntary scheme, introduced at a town meeting in 1812. Respectable householders, chosen by ballot from a register of those willing to serve and authorised by the sovereign to act as 'special constables', were to patrol the streets each night, accompanied by soldiers from the local garrison. By November the scheme had collapsed due to a lack of volunteers. The Police Committee on 2 December presented plans for a paid nightly patrol of a chief constable and twelve constables, at an annual cost of £120. The Police Commissioners, however, rejected the scheme. Instead, in a revealing backward glance to practices more appropriate to the small-scale and intimate urban communities of the past, where shame could be a powerful sanction, they instructed their clerk to enquire into the price of cast iron and wooden stocks.[47] The voluntary watch scheme was briefly revived in February 1816, but ended in May of the same year.

The establishment of a voluntary watch indicates a rising level of anxiety about crime and public order on the streets of the expanding town. A patrol by uniformed soldiers following a predictable route, however, was unlikely seriously to interfere with the activities of the determined criminal. Instead the main business of the patrols, in both years, was with lesser offences against public order. Many of these involved men seriously the worse for drink, indicating that the culture of alcoholic sociability earlier chronicled by Tone and Russell remained strong. Here the response in many cases was to escort the men concerned safely to their homes. Others were temporarily detained, but then released. Even Hamilton Clark, who declared that 'he would knock the face off Mr Farrel that was taking him to his said home', was released on giving security for his future good behaviour.

The other recurring problem was prostitution. By 1812 the main gathering place for the town's sex workers had become the Assembly Rooms and Exchange on Waring Street, in the very heart of the commercial centre, where they attracted 'a number of drunken and profligate men and boys'. The watch repeatedly minuted their concern at their 'noisy and offensive' behaviour, a 'great disgrace of an otherwise well regulated town'.[48] Arrests, however, were once again rare. In July 1812, for example, 'three unfortunately profligate women' were detained for rioting but dismissed 'after being some time confined, and receiving a serious lecture on their improper and disorderly conduct'. The following month the patrol was provoked into arresting all the members of a particularly disorderly gathering of men and women round the Exchange. 'After some time', however, 'they were all dismissed on promise of returning home.'[49] The opening in September 1812 of a 'black hole' removed one apparent barrier to effective action, the lack of suitable place of confinement. Four years later, however, the reconstituted watch once again complained of 'idle women, who made much noise, which of course must annoy the neighbourhood greatly'.[50]

The hesitant approach to the imposition of public order that is evident in these proceedings probably reflected the amateur status of the agents involved. In September 1816, having successfully insisted on a radical overhaul of the rating system, the police commissioners at last agreed to the creation of a paid police force.[51] Initially the force of thirty men, almost immediately increased to forty, constituted a night watch, patrolling between the hours of 9 p.m. and 6 a.m. Two day constables were appointed in October 1817, and by 1834 there were eleven day police out of a total force of eighty. Their duties extended not just to the preservation of public order and the pursuit of criminals, but to the enforcement of the growing body of by-laws and regulations governing the movement of traffic on the streets, the disposal of refuse or the obstruction of pavements. They were expected to prevent illegal trading, enforce the licensing hours in public houses, shoot stray dogs and deal with other public nuisances.

Alongside these as yet imperfect attempts to impose a more effective system of law enforcement, there were also signs of a new concern for the protection of what has been called 'polite space': areas that were formally public, but were in practice intended for the decorous recreations of the propertied classes. In the case of the walk around the Linen Hall the gates and railings presumably served as a guarantee of social exclusiveness. In the case of the Exchange and Assembly Rooms, on the other hand, the Police Commissioners were forced to turn to their new police force. A resolution in 1820 recalled that when the first marquis of Donegall had erected the Exchange on Waring Street he had offered the public free access to the building on condition that unsuitable persons were excluded. Accordingly, constables were directed 'to devote their free time in attending to the Exchange, to prevent the resort of improper persons there'. The porters who gathered at the same site awaiting employment were likewise to be required to move to the other side of North Street.[52] A second development in the same year was more problematic still. In August the *Belfast News Letter* reported indignantly that soldiers from the garrison

> are beginning to infest the favourite walks of this neighbourhood in company with idle women. The very appearance of those abandoned women, independently of their obscene conversation, is sufficient to disgust females of delicacy.

In this case the solution found was to approach the officers of the garrison, who put a stop to their subordinates' promenades.[53]

The limits of public space

The first decades of the nineteenth century thus saw the beginnings of a major reordering of urban space, along lines similar to those of Engels's Manchester or of the other new industrial cities of the period. In place of the traditional residential town centre, dominated by the wealthiest inhabitants, a distinction was now beginning to emerge between a town centre dominated

The origins of public space

by commerce and retail and the residential districts, segregated by class, that lay beyond. Increasing size had also brought with it the first steps towards more formal and far-reaching regulation of movement and behaviour in the different quarters of the town. Both developments, however, were still in their early stages. The very wealthy could travel in their coaches from villas in the County Antrim or County Down countryside. For most, even among the relatively affluent, it remained necessary, in the absence of any form of public transport, to remain within walking distance of the centre. The solid terraces of College Square and Donegall Place were at most a few hundred yards from the smoking chimneys and cramped terraced houses of the industrial district to the west. In the traditional town centre, meanwhile, middle-class families continued to live above offices and commercial premises, while behind the large buildings fronting the main streets were the densely packed courts and entries of the inner-city poor.

In other respects too, the transition to a more closely regulated urban environment was a gradual process. Reports from the Police Office in the late 1820s include instances of the enforcement of civic by-laws. In January 1828, for example, several householders were fined for failing to have the pavement in front of their houses swept by ten in the morning. In August of the following year nearly thirty persons from the Sandy Row area were convicted for allowing heaps of manure to stand on the road in front of their houses.[54] Other occasional prosecutions hinted at the beginnings of a move towards new standards of decorum in public places: 'a disorderly ballad singer' and 'a pretending fortune teller', for example, were each committed to the House of Correction for a month at hard labour.[55] The *Belfast News Letter* in 1833 claimed to detect a significant improvement. 'In all our principal streets we observe constables at their post, actively and vigilantly attending to their duty', so that 'gangs of juvenile thieves' no longer pilfered from vehicles passing through High Street and the pathways and entries were no longer obstructed by boys playing marbles and other games.[56] Other accounts, however, were less favourable. The liberal *Northern Whig*, less sympathetic to the Police Board, insisted in 1825 that it failed to provide value for the large sums raised in rates. Roads were so badly maintained as to be unfit for sprung carriages, pavements were obstructed by illegal vendors of fruit and herrings, 'filth of every description is permitted to accumulate', and 'the inhabitants are frequently annoyed by servants shaking carpets at an early hour in the morning'.[57] The son of one of the town's leading businessmen, looking back much later to his childhood in the 1830s, recalled that even High Street 'was not always orderly in the evenings', and that young ladies attending St George's church 'went in a company ... for mutual protection'.[58] And the records of the Police Board itself, abounding as they do with instances of constables disciplined or dismissed for sleeping on duty, neglecting their responsibilities and accepting bribes, suggest that enforcement of the new regulations would have remained uneven.[59]

The almost four-fold increase in numbers that took place between 1800 and 1840 meant that Belfast was no longer the face-to-face society evident in the accounts of Tone and others during the 1790s. But it was still by most standards an urban centre of modest proportions. The 75,000 inhabitants recorded in 1841 were less than a quarter of the population of Manchester, less than one third that of Liverpool and Glasgow, under half that of Birmingham, Edinburgh or Leeds. What this meant in practice can be glimpsed in the brief notes in which, during 1837 or 1838, a young Belfast woman, apparently the daughter of a shopkeeper, recorded fragmentary details of what appears to have been her awkward relationship with a family friend named Greer. On a single day in late March the two met and spoke in Bridge Street, then ran into one another twice more as she walked about the town. Later the same day, she 'saw him on our way home in Donegall St go into a shop to avoid seeing us'. A month later, meeting her in Bridge St, he 'immediately turned the corner of the street' to avoid her, only to come face to face with her soon after. Three days later they again met twice, in High Street and Donegall Street. Three days later again, it was the young lady's turn to be embarrassed.

> 2nd May. I was standing in Miss Murray's shop and saw Mr G and FE passing on the opposite side of the street. Afterwards I came out of the confectioners' in Bridge Street. I was surprised by David Patterson coming forward to stop me by saying had I got all the little things out of his book. At that instant I caught a glimpse of the gentlemen coming up, and if I had been killed upon the spot for the crime I could not turn round to recognise them at the time and just let them pass at my back as if I had not known they were there at all.[60]

The full story behind these tantalising fragments is lost forever. But they serve as a reminder that Belfast, at the end of several decades of rapid growth, was still some distance from the true anonymity of large-scale urban living.

Notes

1 For early urban development see Raymond Gillespie, *Early Belfast: The Origins and Growth of an Ulster Town to 1750* (Belfast: Ulster Historical Foundation, 2007); Raymond Gillespie and S. A. Royle, *Belfast, Part 1, to 1840* (Dublin: Royal Irish Academy Historical Towns Atlas, 2003). For the changing physical geography of the town, Emrys Jones's pioneering *A Social Geography of Belfast* (London: Oxford University Press, 1960) remains an outstanding overview.

2 Calculated from the figures in Arthur Dobbs, *An Essay on the Trade and Improvement of Ireland* (Dublin: A. Rhames, 1729), pp. 6, 16.

3 Thomas Gaffikin, *Belfast Fifty Years Ago* (2nd edn, Belfast: Belfast News Letter, 1885), p. 8.
4 Gillespie, *Early Belfast*, pp. 138–41.
5 John McVeagh (ed.), *Richard Pococke's Irish Tours* (Dublin: Irish Academic Press, 1995), p. 38.
6 Jean Agnew (ed.), *The Drennan-McTier Letters* (3 vols, Dublin: Irish Manuscripts Commission, 1998–99), i.217.
7 R. M. Young (ed.), *Town Book of the Corporation of Belfast* (Belfast, 1892), p. 339.
8 Gaffikin, *Belfast Fifty Years Ago*, pp. 5, 13.
9 T. G. F. Patterson, 'Belfast in 1738', *Ulster Journal of Archaeology*, 3rd series, 2 (1939), 112.
10 *The Journal of the Rev. John Wesley* (4 vols, London: J. Kershaw, 1827), iii.87.
11 McVeagh (ed.), *Pococke's Irish Tours*, p. 38.
12 D. J. Owen, *History of Belfast* (Belfast: W. & G. Baird, 1921), pp. 176–7; *Belfast News Letter* [hereafter *BNL*], 2 January 1759, 13 May 1768; *Belfast Mercury*, 3 October 1783.
13 *BNL*, 2 January 1759.
14 Thomas Bartlett (ed.), *Theobald Wolfe Tone, Memoirs, Journals and Political Writings* (Dublin: Lilliput, 1998), p. 135.
15 *Journals and Memoirs of Thomas Russell*, ed. C. J. Woods (Dublin: Irish Academic Press, 1991), p. 50 (12 April 1791).
16 Martha McTier to William Drennan, 12 December 1797, in Agnew (ed.), *Drennan-McTier Letters*, ii.350.
17 W. A. Maguire, 'A question of arithmetic: Arthur Chichester, fourth earl of Donegall', in Brenda Collins, Philip Ollerenshaw and Trevor Parkhill (eds), *Industry, Trade and People in Ireland 1650–1950* (Belfast: Ulster Historical Foundation, 2005), pp. 31–50; Gillespie, *Early Belfast*, p. 128.
18 Samuel Lewis (1837), quoted in C. E. B. Brett, *Buildings of Belfast 1700–1914* (rev. edn, Belfast: Friar's Bush Press, 1985), p. 5.
19 Public Record Office of Northern Ireland [hereafter PRONI], T3488/1, Charles Abbot, Journal of a Tour in Ireland and North Wales, Sept.–Oct. 1792, from an original in the National Archives, London.
20 J. A. Pilson, *History of the Rise and Progress of Belfast and Annals of the County Antrim* (Belfast: no publisher named, 1846), p. 25.
21 Eoin Magennis, 'Clubs and societies in eighteenth-century Belfast', in James Kelly and Martyn J. Powell (eds), *Clubs and Societies in Eighteenth-Century Ireland* (Dublin: Four Courts Press, 2010), pp. 466–83.
22 John Killen, *A History of the Linen Hall Library 1788–1988* (Belfast: The Linen Hall Library, 1990).
23 Brenda Collins, Trevor Parkhill and Peter Roebuck, 'A White Linen Hall for Newry or Belfast', *Irish Economic and Social History*, 43 (2016), 50–61.
24 For shipbuilding see J. J. Monaghan, 'A social and economic history of Belfast, 1801–1825' (Ph.D. dissertation, Queen's University, Belfast, 1940), pp. 233–6, and for other developments Gillespie and Royle, *Belfast to 1840*, pp. 7–8.
25 H. D. Inglis, *Ireland in 1834*, 2 vols (London: Whittaker & Co., 1835), i.249–51.

26 [George Benn], *The History of the Town of Belfast, with an Accurate Account of its Former and Present State* (Belfast: A. MacKay, 1823), pp. 85, 296. A map published in 1792 had shown just seventy-five streets: George Benn, *A History of the Town of Belfast from the Earliest Times to the Close of the Eighteenth Century* (Belfast: Marcus Ward, 1877), p. 559.
27 W. A. Maguire, 'The 1822 settlement of the Donegall estates', *Irish Economic & Social History*, 3 (1976), 17–32.
28 Inglis, *Ireland in 1834*, i.251.
29 Stephen Royle and T. J. Campbell, 'East Belfast and the suburbanisation of north-west County Down in the nineteenth century', in L. J. Proudfoot and William Nolan (eds), *Down: History and Society* (Dublin: Geography Publications, 1997), pp. 629–62.
30 *BNL*, 23 November 1813.
31 For the concept of 'peripheral suburbanisation', see S. A. Royle, 'The socio-spatial structure of Belfast in 1837: evidence from the first valuation', *Irish Geography*, 24 (1991), 1–9.
32 *BNL*, 10 July 1812.
33 PRONI, D2194/61/13, William Henry Lynn to Robert Young, 10 November 1907. I owe this reference to Dr Paul Harron.
34 Inglis, *Ireland in 1834*, i.249, 252.
35 Inglis, *Ireland in 1834*, i.252; W. M. Thackeray, *The Irish Sketchbook 1842* (Dublin: Gill and Macmillan, 1990), p. 304.
36 The available statistics on Catholic numbers are conveniently brought together in Ian Budge and Cornelius O'Leary, *Belfast: Approach to Crisis* (London: Macmillan, 1973), p. 32. For butchering as 'a low status trade in which Catholics had long predominated', see A. C. Hepburn, *A Past Apart: Studies in the History of Catholic Belfast 1850–1950* (Belfast: Ulster Historical Foundation, 1996), p. 224.
37 Catherine Hirst, *Religion, Politics and Violence in Nineteenth-century Belfast: The Pound and Sandy Row* (Dublin: Four Courts Press, 2002), p. 14 notes the involvement of a leading Catholic builder in the development of the area before 1820, and the presence of three Catholic schools by 1826.
38 The fullest account is Claire Allen, 'Urban elites, civil society and governance in early nineteenth-century Belfast c.1800–32' (Ph.D. dissertation, Queen's University, Belfast, 2010).
39 The formulaic proceedings of the town council can be followed in Young (ed.), *The Town Book of the Corporation of Belfast*. For regulation of markets see *BNL*, 16 February 1759, 12 October 1759, 21 January 1791; *Belfast Mercury*, 7 October 1783; for the dead pigs, Benn, *History of Belfast* (1877), p. 604. For the political role of the corporation, below, chapter 3.
40 *BNL*, 1 April, 19 August 1791.
41 Martha McTier to William Drennan, nd [1795], in Agnew (ed.), *Drennan-McTier Letters*, ii.138.
42 Hannah Barker, '"Smoke cities": northern industrial towns in late Georgian England', *Urban History*, 31 (2004), 175–90.
43 For a fuller account see below, pp. 43–4.

44 E.g. PRONI, LA7/10AB/1/1, Minutes of the Police Committee of Belfast Corporation, 24 April 1844.
45 PRONI, LA7/2BA/2/1, pp. 258–9, Minutes of Police Commissioners, 21 November 1808.
46 PRONI, LA7/2BA/2/1, pp. 258–9, 99, Minutes of Police Commissioners, 21 November 1808, 7 December 1814.
47 PRONI, LA7/2BA/2/1, p. 10, Minutes of Police Commissioners, 2 December 1812.
48 PRONI, D46/1a, Report Book of the Special Constables, pp. 59, 88, 174.
49 PRONI, D46/1a, pp. 38, 83, 89, 174.
50 *BNL*, 29 September 1812; Report Book of the Special Constables, p. 556.
51 See below, p. 48.
52 PRONI, LA7/2BA/2/2, p. 67, Minutes of the Police Commissioners, 9 February 1820.
53 *BNL*, 29 August 1820.
54 *BNL*, 15 January 1828, 7 August 1829.
55 *BNL*, 12 August, 7 October 1828.
56 *BNL*, 7 June 1833.
57 *Northern Whig* [hereafter *NW*], 13, 20 January 1825.
58 Narcissus Batt, 'Belfast sixty years ago: recollections of a septuagenarian', *Ulster Journal of Archaeology*, 2:2 (1896), 95. The Church of Ireland parish church was still St Anne's on Donegall St. The elegant Grecian St George's on High Street had been erected in 1816 to provide additional accommodation.
59 Brian Griffin, *The Bulkies: Police and Crime in Belfast 1800–1865* (Dublin: Irish Academic Press, 1997), chap. 4.
60 PRONI, D3856/1, Diary and account book, apparently by Mary Cunningham.

2

Lord Donegall's town

The public life of towns has always been more intense than that of the countryside. The density of population, and a more complex social structure, encourage a higher level of political mobilisation. There is also scope for a more elaborate body of civic ritual, expressing central values and allegiances, strengthening the bonds of community and confirming patterns of authority and deference. From the late eighteenth century, however, population growth and industrialisation gave new depth both to civic ritual and to urban political life. In the case of Belfast these changes were given a particular character both by the wider Irish context and by the town's changing relationship with what had been its patrons, the Chichester earls and marquises of Donegall.

Proprietorship under pressure

Eighteenth-century Belfast was universally acknowledged to belong to the Donegalls. Their proprietorship extended not just to the land on which the town stood but to its institutions. Each year, under the procedures laid down in the original charter of 1613, the thirteen burgesses of the Corporation elected the Sovereign from among three names formally presented to them by the earl or marquis in his capacity as lord of what was by this time a non-existent castle. In practice, a parliamentary enquiry of 1835 reported, 'the same person is constantly re-elected, or holds over, for a long series of years, until "the patron", the marquis of Donegall, expresses his desire that another person should succeed to the office'.[1] The burgesses themselves held office for life, with vacancies on death or resignation being filled by co-option; in practice all were Donegall's nominees, chosen from among relatives, dependents and friends. When the Lord Lieutenant of Ireland, Lord Cornwallis, toured the north in 1799 to solicit public declarations of support for the forthcoming Act of Union, he decided that it would be pointless to follow the usual course of obtaining a resolution in favour from the Sovereign and burgesses, 'for as the Corporation of that great and opulent town is entirely in the hands of Lord Donegall, it is necessary in some manner to obtain a public mark of approbation from the inhabitants at large'. Instead local supporters of the union organised a public dinner at which toasts could be drunk to the proposed constitutional change.[2] The thirteen members of the Corporation also comprised the total electorate for the parliamentary borough of Belfast, which in practice meant that both of the men who represented Belfast in the Irish Parliament owed their seats entirely and exclusively to Lord Donegall.

Throughout the eighteenth century this proprietorial status, despite the non-resident status of the family concerned, continued to find expression in the civic life of the town. In 1739 the citizens enthusiastically celebrated the birth of a son to John Chichester, who as brother to the childless fourth earl of Donegall was heir presumptive to the estate. One hundred and twenty men and 100 ladies attended a dinner in the town hall, followed by a ball. Nor was this an occasion for the elite only. Instead an apparently casual act of largesse, combined with what were in fact carefully maintained social boundaries, dramatised the ideal of a hierarchical community united in celebratory deference.

> After the bonfire at the town hall was kindled each gentleman went to it from thence with his bottle and glass in his hand and after drinking a few loyal healths threw the bottle and glass to the populace, and then returned to said hall and were served with new ones. ... Barrels of ale and a hogshead of punch were given to the populace, and the bells continued ringing all the time.[3]

Later in the century the object of these celebrations, by now fifth earl, participated in similar carefully orchestrated displays of patronage and deference. In 1788, during one of his periodic visits, he hosted a supper and ball for 360 leading inhabitants. Five years earlier the members of first Presbyterian congregation delayed the opening of their newly completed showpiece meeting house in Rosemary Street until Donegall was available to preside over the formalities.[4]

Alongside such displays of deference to the Donegalls there were public affirmations of allegiance to the ruling Hanoverian dynasty. Events such as the birthdays or marriages of members of the royal family, anniversaries such as the birthday of King William III and news of British military victories were all marked by a range of observances. On 8 June 1759, for example, Belfast marked the birthday of the Prince of Wales. Householders lit up their windows with lamps and candles, the gentry gathered round a bonfire in the market place to drink loyal toasts, while 'the ladies were entertained with an elegant ball at the market house'. Just over two weeks later there were fresh illuminations, bonfires and toasts to celebrate news of the capture from the French of the Caribbean island of Guadeloupe. A ship lately arrived from Barbados made its contribution, firing off several large cannon taken from privateers off the captured island. Eighteen months later, the Sovereign and the 'principal gentlemen' again made a circuit of the town on horseback, accompanied by a party of soldiers, pausing at points along the route to proclaim that the prince whose birthday they had celebrated was now King George III.[5]

Official accounts of these celebrations emphasised the splendour of the occasion and the enthusiastic loyalty on display. But a realistic appraisal must also take account of the modest setting provided by this medium-sized provincial town with its crumbling market hall. The party proclaiming the accession of George III, for example, must have made a circuit of no more than three or four streets. The limited scope for display can be more clearly seen in accounts of a somewhat later event. In 1791 the town's Volunteers, consisting of 'two very full companies, a troop of light dragoons, and two artillery corps with four brass six pounders', accompanied by 'a multitude of our unarmed inhabitants', marched in procession to mark the second anniversary of the storming of the Bastille. By this time Belfast's population had risen to 18,000, more than twice what it had been at the king's accession. But the progress through its streets of this substantial assemblage of men, horses and artillery was nevertheless a distinctly cramped affair. In the newer western district of the town the Volunteers were able to make a satisfying circuit through Castle Street, Mill Street and then Mill Field behind Smithfield market. Before this, however, they had had to march along one side of High Street and return by the other. Following their return through North Street they were forced once again to double back on themselves in Donegall Street, before a zig-zag progress through Ann Street, High Street and the side streets linking them took them at last to the Linen Hall.[6]

Enthusiastic contemporary accounts of the pageantry associated with civic events must thus be read with a critical eye. The same is true of the sentiments of deference and communal harmony to which these events gave expression. The Donegalls had achieved their control over the Corporation at the end of a contest with leading mercantile interests, and their victory had been secured only by invoking the much-resented sacramental test, which excluded Presbyterians from local office. In 1739 the fourth earl found himself in dispute with some of his tenants who 'have unreasonably flown in my face and disturbed the tranquillity of the town'.[7] Yet the hold of the Donegalls on Belfast, resting as it did on a combination of economic power, institutional authority and social prestige, was nevertheless considerable. This became evident during the political upheavals inspired by the revolt in 1776 of the American colonists. In 1783, against the background of a nationwide campaign for parliamentary reform, a petition called on the earl to return the wealthy merchant Waddell Cunningham for one of the town's two seats, while reserving the other for his own candidate. When Donegall refused, Cunningham turned instead to neighbouring Carrickfergus, also Donegall's borough but with a larger electorate, where he was returned, but unseated following a petition. But when some disgruntled inhabitants of Belfast took the revolt against proprietorial authority a stage further, by burning one of the two new MPs for the town in effigy, respectable citizens rushed to condemn the insult.[8]

A similar display of dissent, partly concealed behind continued respect for decorum, occurred in 1787 when Donegall and the neighbouring earl of Hillsborough had the Corporation present the Lord Lieutenant, the earl of Rutland, with the freedom of the town. The town's leading reformers refused to attend a dinner to mark the occasion. Rutland was disliked both for his heavy drinking and for his association with a set of Commercial Propositions believed to impinge on Ireland's recently achieved commercial liberty. In addition, as Dr Alexander Haliday, a leader of the more moderate wing of the reform party, explained, 'we like not this paltry oligarchy the Corporation should take the lead'. The reformers did not openly oppose the grant to Rutland. Instead they concentrated on insisting that the address presented to him should be 'nothing more than a simple civility'. But there was also a warning: 'should anything very adverse to the old and avowed principles of this town drop from them, we might think ourselves called on to assert and vindicate our better opinion; which could be a disagreeable and awkward sort of business'.[9]

Within a few years these residual restraints on the expression of political disagreement had ceased to operate. The fall of the French monarchy, and the outbreak of war between Britain and the revolutionary regime, placed radicals and conservatives in open conflict. The change was particularly evident in the institution of the town meeting. At the beginning of the 1790s the idea still held that the political issues of the day could be debated at a general meeting of the town's inhabitants. In 1792, after another Volunteer parade to mark the anniversary of the fall of the Bastille, the whole body assembled in the courtyard of the Linen Hall to consider a set of resolutions on reform. The main issue was a declaration that any new system of political representation should include Catholics on equal terms. In a lengthy but restrained exchange a moderate minority, led by the Revd William Bruce, argued doggedly that full equality for Catholics, while in principle highly desirable, was best introduced in gradual stages.[10] Over the next few years, as political tensions mounted, this sort of open exchange of views became less common. But traditional political practice was abandoned only reluctantly. In 1795 Martha McTier reported disapprovingly that Bruce and his supporters no longer attended public meetings where they knew they would be in a minority. By later standards their decision was hardly surprising. To McTier, on the other hand, such behaviour was evidence that Bruce 'has avowedly divided the town of Belfast'.[11] In September 1797 Haliday and others went as far as to present a signed requisition, in traditional form, to the Sovereign for a public meeting that would protest at a recent incident in which troops had arrested some United Irishmen and destroyed the printing press of their newspaper, the *Northern Star*, but would combine this protest with a declaration of loyalty to the constitution. In the end, however, 'it was deemed prudent not to hazard such a measure, in the present divided state of people's minds, and the irritated situation of many of them'.[12]

To appreciate the basis of Martha McTier's disapproving comment it is important to recognise that political life in Belfast, despite the more than doubling of the town's population that had taken place over the past forty years, retained the personal tone characteristic of a closely knit urban community. The public debate on the Catholic question at the Volunteer review of July 1792 had been foreshadowed in the heated discussions that took place the previous October when Wolfe Tone, the author of the offending resolutions, had attended a private dinner at which Bruce and others set out, in rather less diplomatic terms than they would later use in public, their arguments against the enfranchisement of the Catholic population. 'Broke up rather ill disposed towards each other,' Tone noted in his diary. 'More and more convinced of the absurdity of arguing over wine.'[13] The same face-to-face quality of relationships in a compact urban community gave an added twist to the outrage felt as the government stepped up its campaign against radicalism, flooding the town with soldiers and arresting leading citizens. Martha McTier described how military officers had acquired a copy of a pamphlet detailing the public debates that had taken place in the more relaxed atmosphere of earlier periods. They

> sit with it in their hands, commenting and applying its paragraphs in the coffee house and the hearing of the chief actors, in matters now dangerous to avow. The tea room is occupied by an officers' guard, over one held of soldiers below. The merchants and townsmen are jostled from the Exchange coffee house and ladies frightened from the remaining public places. ...

The tone is as much of the invasion of a private space as it is of the occupation of an urban centre. Later, in 1797, McTier offered another glimpse of town life when she commented derisively on the inappropriateness of the latest security measures 'in a town where I can walk from one end to the other without a servant at nine o'clock'.[14]

As the crisis of the 1790s deepened, the face-to-face character of Belfast civic life continued to add to the trauma experienced by the inhabitants. There was shock when Henry Joy McCracken, a well-liked member of two of the town's leading commercial families, was publicly hanged, along with six other United Irishmen, in the fashionable square of Castle Place, and the heads of all but McCracken were left to rot on spikes above the market house. In the longer term, however, the compact intimacy of the town helped to speed the return to normality. The immediate aftermath of the rebellion of 1798 saw instances of petty victimisation, as when McTier complained that she and her mother were singled out, as known radical sympathisers, to have soldiers repeatedly billeted in their houses. But it was undesirable, in so close knit a community, to perpetuate political feuds once the immediate crisis had passed. Instead the majority of inhabitants seem to have been determined to put the whole episode behind them as quickly as possible. When Thomas Russell, the popular former librarian of the Linen Hall Library, became a fugitive in 1803, following his failed attempt to raise the east Ulster countryside in support of another rising, there was considerable sympathy for his predicament, and one of his former friends, the doctor and antiquarian James McDonnell, found himself widely condemned, and in some quarters ostracised, for having contributed to the reward for his capture.[15] Meanwhile William Tennent, imprisoned for almost four years for his treasonable activities, had returned to the town on his release in 1802 and resumed his mercantile career, going on to become a leading merchant and banker. In 1807 McTier's brother William Drennan, a founder of the United Irish movement, likewise returned from Dublin, to become a central figure in the town's literary and cultural life until his death in 1820.

Proprietorship restored

To appreciate the speed with which the public life of Belfast returned to normal after the upheavals of the 1790s, it is only necessary to look at the first major civic event of the years immediately following, the visit in August 1804 of the Lord Lieutenant, the earl of Hardwicke. In 1797–98 Belfast had been the capital of Irish radicalism, singled out for a decisive exercise in political repression. Only six years later, however, Hardwicke, replying to a loyal address from the Corporation, expressed his regard for 'this opulent and flourishing town' and praised 'the enlightened inhabitants of this important and interesting part of his Majesty's dominions' for their determination to resist the efforts 'of our foreign and domestic enemies' to overthrow the British constitution.

The second notable feature of Hardwicke's visit was the prominence throughout of the Donegall family. Hardwicke and his wife spent the six days of their visit as guests of the second marquis at his town house near the White Linen Hall. Their first three full days in Belfast were taken up with a round of exclusive social gatherings: a ball and a dinner at Donegall House, a visit to Mountstewart, the family home of Hardwicke's colleague in government Lord Castlereagh, and a ball at the Assembly Rooms. The only public events were reviews of the garrison and yeomanry at Carrickfergus and Belfast. It was not until the fourth full day of the visit that the Sovereign and burgesses of the

Corporation were able to present their address to the distinguished visitor. In this sense the visit cannot really be described as a civic event. Instead it had taken the form of a round of aristocratic sociability, with Donegall in the role of proprietor and host.¹⁶ This exclusive character may account for the ambivalent attitude displayed by the town's leading inhabitants. An opportunistic local painter, Thomas Robinson, proposed to complete a large-scale painting of Hardwicke reviewing the town's yeomanry, inviting patrons to subscribe a guinea each to have their individual portraits incorporated into the work. The Revd William Bruce, in another significant display of anxiety to put past political differences aside, tried to persuade his former friend Drennan to allow himself to be included. The wealthy linen bleacher William Sinclaire, who in 1791 had been president of the first Society of United Irishmen, was also a prominent backer. In the end, however, not enough citizens were willing to pay the required guinea, and Robinson was reduced to retouching the painting by adding a statue of Nelson and seeking to dispose of it elsewhere as a Dublin street scene.¹⁷

The central position accorded to Donegall is all the more striking, given the marquis's seriously reduced circumstances. In 1795 he had outraged his father by marrying the illegitimate daughter of Edward May, a disreputable member of the lesser Irish gentry who had helped to secure his release from a debtors' prison in 1795. The first marquis had responded by stripping his heir of everything not covered by the legal settlement governing the estate. The lands and mansion in Staffordshire, his London house and the lands of Ballymacarrett had all gone to a younger son. The family estates in Antrim and Donegal, covered by an entail, had come to the second marquis, but were promptly put into the hands of trustees responsible for satisfying his creditors. Since then he had run up further debts, and in 1802 had been forced to retreat to Belfast to evade the bailiffs and to search for new sources of credit or ready money. None of this, however, prevented Donegall and his wife from becoming for a time the centre of the town's social life. The town's wealthier inhabitants responded eagerly to invitations to balls and dinners in the house which the couple had taken in Donegall Place. Martha McTier, while herself perfectly willing to accept their hospitality, commented sardonically on the deference shown to the aristocratic spendthrifts: the marchioness charmed everyone with her affability and willingness to accept invitations, and any criticism of her 'would be treason in the ears of our merchants' wives'.¹⁸ However, the idyll could not last. Already in June 1803, more than a year before Hardwicke's visit, a debt collector from London had attempted to seize the contents of Donegall's house, only to be forestalled by the marquis's father-in-law, who had already secured a judgment, in what was clearly a collusive lawsuit, assigning the contents to him on the basis of moneys supposedly owed. By the end of 1806 the town house had been shut up and the entire contents auctioned. The couple moved briefly to Scotland and the relative security of a different legal jurisdiction, before returning to Belfast to set up home, more modestly than before, in a villa at Ormeau on the other side of the River Lagan. There the marquis continued to dodge creditors as best he could: one, in 1817, did in fact manage to have the contents of the house seized by the sheriff.

After a few glittering years, the second marquis's financial difficulties thus forced him to adopt a lower profile within Belfast fashionable society. By 1822 they had also forced him to surrender his remaining power as landlord and become a mere receiver of ground rents. His political grip on the town's affairs, by contrast, remained intact, and if anything became even tighter as his circumstances drove him to extract from it what profit he could. At the core of his dominance was his control of the Corporation, where Sovereigns continued to be elected, and vacancies filled by new members, on his nomination. Donegall used the privilege primarily to benefit his wife's family, who had accompanied him to Belfast. Between 1802 and 1822 the post of Sovereign passed back and forth between the marquis's father-in-law Edward May (from 1811 Sir Edward), his son (and hence Donegall's brother-in-law) Edward junior and Thomas Verner, who was married to another of May senior's daughters. In 1809 Edward May junior took orders, with what contemporaries regarded as indecent haste, and without renouncing his claims to municipal office, in order to be able to become Church of Ireland vicar of Belfast, another position in Donegall's gift.[19] There were also more discreditable transactions. An inquiry into Irish municipal corporations in 1835 noted a range of unlawful fees extorted by the borough's legal offices, and concluded its report with a catalogue of sums, amounting in all to over £3,000, appropriated by Donegall, the Mays and others, from Corporation funds intended for poor relief.[20]

In theory Donegall's control of Belfast's affairs should have been weakened by the passage in 1800 of an Act providing the town with an elected Police Board. The Bill concerned, however, was in fact introduced by Edward May. This circumstance, along with the provisions of the Act, strongly suggest a pre-emptive move by the Donegall interest, ostensibly meeting the demand for effective and accountable administration, but in a manner that in fact allowed it to retain substantial control. The Board was to consist of twenty-five Police Commissioners, who were to be assisted in their work by a Police Committee. Members of this Committee, elected annually by householders paying not less than £1 per annum in municipal rates, were required to have a personal estate worth at least £1,000. Commissioners were required to own property worth at least £100 a year, or to have a personal estate of £2,000. They held office for life, the first cohort being named in the 1800 Act and their successors being elected by those paying £1 in church cess. A letter to the *Belfast Commercial Chronicle* in 1811 alleged that this voting qualification was so high as to render the office 'almost a place of patronage'.[21] But in any case the Sovereign and all twelve burgesses were *ex officio* members of the Commission, giving the old Corporation an automatic majority within the new body.

In addition to granting Donegall and his associates access to some valuable perquisites, and giving them a firm foothold within the new Police Board, control of the Corporation gave the marquis the power to determine Belfast's parliamentary representation, reduced to one seat following the Act of Union but still based on an electorate confined to the thirteen burgesses. Between 1800 and 1814 Belfast was represented by Donegall's father-in-law, Edward May senior; from 1814 to 1816 by his brother-in-law, Stephen May; between 1818 and 1820 by his cousin Arthur Chichester; during 1820–30 by his son the earl of Belfast; then by Arthur Chichester again from 1830 until the Reform Act of 1832.[22] The one break in the possession of the seat by members of Donegall's or his wife's family was in 1816–18, when he was tricked by the English peer Lord Westmorland into returning the English army officer John Michel, a cousin of Westmorland's wife, in the mistaken belief that this would win him the favour of the government.

Control of this seat, along with his influence in Carrickfergus and his own vote in the House of Lords, allowed Donegall to lobby successive governments shamelessly for patronage and honours. During 1802–3, citing his status as a resident proprietor and his support for the recent Act of Union, he sought to have relatives nominated to the posts of Land Waiter, Port Surveyor, Gauging Surveyor and Collector of Customs, as well as requesting a seat on the Linen Board for himself.[23] In 1816 his demands were more ambitious. His brother-in-law Stephen May, debarred by his illegitimate birth from inheriting his father's title, was to get a baronetage of his own, while for himself Donegall now wanted the post of Collector of Customs for Belfast, valued at £2,000 a year, as well as a promise that he would be appointed to the next vacant place in the ceremonial order of St Patrick and eventual promotion to a dukedom. In private the Lord Lieutenant, the earl of Whitworth, and his Chief Secretary, Robert Peel, fumed at Donegall's 'vulgar and impudent' demands. When the marquis tried to insist that the Collectorship was his by right, Peel brought him sharply to heel, reducing him almost to tears in a tense interview. Whitworth congratulated his subordinate 'on having brought the Belfast savage to a proper sense of himself and of what he owes us'. But parliamentary votes were parliamentary votes. In the end, having made a humiliating retraction of his claim of right, Donegall got his Collectorship, and the promise of a ribbon of St Patrick, while May was knighted a few weeks later.[24]

Belfast, then, despite the much reduced financial position of the family, was still in a very real sense Lord Donegall's town. The marquis, despite his frequent failure actually to pay promised contributions to local charities, continued to serve on the governing bodies of a wide range of local institutions, such as the fever hospital and the Academical Institution, and to appear in a place of honour at public functions. In 1818 the town's Sovereign headed a committee chosen to organise elaborate celebrations for the coming of age of the marquis's eldest son, the earl of Belfast. The streets were illuminated in what one newspaper described as 'a blaze of light', while bonfires flared in the surrounding countryside. Specially commissioned transparencies in front of the Exchange depicted the young earl alongside emblems representing agriculture and commerce. Other projected images, at the theatre and elsewhere, showed Sir Arthur Chichester, founder of the dynasty, engaged in combat, but balanced this celebration of the colonial warrior who had subdued the native Irish of the region with patriotic images of St Patrick and Hibernia. A motto displayed at the White Linen Hall proclaimed, with no hint of irony, that 'one resident landlord is worth a hundred parliamentary representatives'.[25] Later, in 1825, the death of the couple's third son, at the age of twenty, was the occasion for another major civic event. Shops throughout Belfast closed and business was suspended while a long train of carriages followed by horsemen 'and an immense assemblage of persons on foot' accompanied the hearse through the town centre.[26]

The celebration of hierarchy

As well as controlling the town's administration through the Corporation and through its influence on the Police Board, the circle of relatives and clients surrounding Donegall also sought to define its political identity through a range of public events. The most striking feature of their activities in this area is the absence, in the aftermath of the rebellion of 1798, of anything smacking of Loyalist triumphalism. Irish loyalism in these years was split between proponents of an inclusive allegiance to king and constitution and those who preferred to focus on the enemy within, in the form of Catholics and domestic radicalism.[27] Belfast's civic elite was firmly in the former group. Some individuals, like the marquis's brother-in-law Thomas Verner, were members of the Orange Order. But Orange marches and insignia, of the kind that elsewhere kept alive the vicious animosities of the 1790s, played no part in municipal culture. Instead the Corporation conformed to the wider public mood of seeking to leave the memory of recent divisions firmly behind. When Robert Emmet's botched Dublin rising in July 1803 created a brief alarm, Edward May, as Sovereign, clashed publicly with the military authorities over the curfew they had imposed on the town. Belfast, he complained in a later statement, had been 'severely calumniated' by those who had imposed these measures on a quiet town. He concluded his address with a call for harmony between Catholic and Protestant: 'The bigot is at all times a disgrace to society, but at this moment he must be a dangerous pest.'[28]

In place of sectarian loyalism, what the civic culture of Belfast sought to represent was a broadly based British patriotism. Royal events such as the king's birthday were marked by a parade of the garrison and local yeomanry, the firing of a royal salute and a ceremonial dinner by leading citizens.[29] George III's jubilee in October 1809 was the occasion of particularly elaborate displays, with the Exchange and Assembly Rooms brightly illuminated, while Donegall decorated his house with transparencies of the King and a figure of Hibernia. There were also regular celebrations for victories in the continuing war against Napoleon's France. As elsewhere in the United Kingdom, Nelson became a particular focus for patriotic enthusiasm. His victory at Trafalgar was marked by an elaborate dinner, four weeks later, at Donegall's house, where the marquis and leading citizens dined beneath triumphal arches of green branches supporting transparencies depicting the fleet in action. When the Donegalls' third son was born a month later, they christened him Horatio Nelson. A Nelson Club established shortly afterwards became the venue for many subsequent events. Although membership was confined to those paying a substantial subscription, the proceedings also had a public face. At a dinner in honour of Wellington in 1812, for example, the club house in Donegall Place was brightly lit up, with a large bonfire blazing in front of it, and two barrels of ale were provided for 'the numerous spectators, who cheered the celebration of the Irish hero'.[30]

Two events in particular illustrate the public political culture of early nineteenth-century Belfast. The first was the elaborate ceremonial with which, in November 1812, the town marked the return from service in Spain of a local military hero, Major General Charles Stewart, second son of the marquis of Londonderry and half-brother to the Foreign Secretary, Viscount Castlereagh. The proceedings once again blended the public and the private. The event began in Donegall's town house, where Stewart received the freedom of the borough, an honour normally reserved for lords lieutenant. From there he and others made their way to the more public venue of the Assembly Rooms, where a party of 220 awaited them. The venue was elaborately decorated. The approach to the dining room

> was ornamented with laurel, and brilliantly lighted with coloured lamps. On the first landing place was a transparency representing military trophies. The stair case was terminated by a triumphal arch, tastefully wreathed with branches of laurel and coloured lamps.

The dining room itself was lit by more than 300 wax lights. The walls were decorated with military flags and busts of the King and the Prince of Wales, while the Stewart coat of arms hung over the entrance. As on other occasions, the organisers made full use of recent technical advances, imported from France, in the projection of images.[31] In addition to the trophies depicted on the landing, further designs depicted Stewart in full uniform, as well as the duke of Wellington 'with a distant view of an action, and over it the words "Wellington and victory"'. Another transparency, positioned in the windows of the dining room, where it would have been visible to those outside, depicted a figure of Hibernia, thus incorporating an acknowledgement of Irish national pride into this display of pan-British loyalism.[32]

A second, even more eloquent expression of political values was on display in the observances that marked the accession of a new king, George IV, in February 1820. Watched by large crowds lining the streets, or gathered at convenient windows, an elaborate procession made its way through the centre of the town, stopping at four points – the Donegall Arms in High Street, the White Linen Hall, the Exchange and the Parade – while the town clerk read the proclamation of George IV's accession. The composition of the processing body had been formally set out in a printed document published by the Sovereign. At its head came the superintendent of the recently established town police, followed by the constables. Behind them, accompanied by a band from the local garrison, came the holders of various civic offices, now for the most part ceremonial: the Town Crier, the Serjeant at Mace, the Town Clerk and Town Major. Next came Donegall, mounted on horseback as befitted the 'lord of the castle', followed by the Sovereign and burgesses, the magistrates and the clergy of different denominations. The Police Commissioners walked behind Donegall. The Police Committee, on the other hand, was further back, behind the managers of the Academical Institute and some 200 students from this and other educational establishments, and just ahead of the Revenue Officers. At the rear came other inhabitants of the town, subdivided into 'professional and other gentlemen', 'merchants' and then 'tradesmen etc. etc.'. The placing of the Police Committee may well have been a deliberate slight, hinting at current tensions. But in other respects the whole document reads as a late, almost consciously archaic, expression of the traditional ideal of the urban population as a stratified but harmonious corporate community.[33]

Hierarchy contested

Public performances of this kind, orchestrated from above, cannot of course be taken wholly at face value.[34] The public response to a succession of events, up to and including the funeral of the second marquis in 1844, indicates that there was a genuine degree of respect, and possibly even affection, for the town's traditional proprietor and his family. Yet there is also clear evidence of discontent at the continued domination of public affairs by a narrow clique. The issue came into the open in 1811 when the Police Commissioners, led by Edward May senior, proposed a reform of the system of local taxation, whereby individuals would be assessed only on that part of their property that lay within the town, rather than, as had been the practice since 1800, on the value of their total estate. The Police Committee, elected as it was on a broader basis, registered its opposition. Hostile correspondents in the local press identified the scheme as an attempt by a wealthy elite to benefit themselves at the expense of the majority. One, who identified the proposal as emanating from the Corporation rather than the Commissioners, warned them of the danger of calling down on themselves the condemnation of 'an enlightened and intelligent community'. Another, appealing even more specifically to the vocabulary of class, warned Donegall that his interests as the town's proprietor were tied up with the fortunes of its merchants and manufacturers, not with those of the gentleman, who is 'a mere drone in society'.[35]

In the face of this opposition, the Police Commissioners dropped their proposal. In 1816, however, they once again proposed an amending Act, supported by counsel's opinion that the existing method of assessing liability for taxation was illegal. This time critics of the Commissioners countered by proposing that any amending Act should be broadened to strengthen the representative element within the Police Board. Corporation members not resident in the town should be ineligible to serve as Police Commissioners, the elected Commissioners should serve for a fixed term rather than for life and members of the Police Committee should be elected for a term of three years. The Commissioners rejected all these proposals. Instead they got their way by linking the amending Bill to current fears over urban crime, announcing that they could support plans for the establishment of a nightly watch only if the taxation system that supported it was reformed.[36] The new Police Act specified that rates were to be calculated on a sliding scale according to house value. It also reduced the property qualification for both Commissioners and committee members, but at the same time narrowed the franchise: Commissioners were now to be elected by those paying £4 or more in rates, and members of the Police Committee by those paying at least £2. In other respects the system of municipal government continued to be based on an institutionalised division between an oligarchic and a representative element, with the former always having the final say. The *Northern Whig*, in 1825, expressed the continued dissatisfaction of the town's liberals:

> There are here two estates, without a third to reconcile their differences; and these two not on the best terms – the one often doing and the other undoing the same measures. ... The two bodies do not pull together; whilst the majority of the one hold their places from being burgesses &c. and those of the other are men who are hourly employed in the most active pursuits of life.[37]

The municipal inquiry of 1835 heard further complaints that the narrower franchise introduced from 1816 had excluded 'a large portion of the rate payers' from any influence over the management of the town, so that both the Police Committee and the Police Commissioners had become 'the representatives rather of a party than of the body of tax payers'.[38]

Alongside these local disputes, there were also deeper-rooted ideological divisions. The bloodshed and repression of 1798 had discredited extreme radicalism, while the Act of Union had swept away the Dublin Parliament that had been the immediate focus of discontent. But the division between liberal and radical reformers on the one hand, and upholders of the established order on the other, had not gone away. Moreover, the union had also opened up the possibility of a closer alliance between Irish and British reformers. If the Donegall clique now promoted a pan-British patriotism, their local opponents showed equal enthusiasm for a pan-British radicalism. An early indication of the new terms in which long-standing divisions had been cast was in 1809 when the younger Edward May, in his capacity as deputy sovereign, received a requisition for a meeting to present an address to Colonel Gwyllym Wardle. Wardle had taken a leading part in exposing the scandal surrounding the duke of York, commander-in-chief of the army and the second son of King George III, whose mistress had been taking bribes to promote the cause of candidates for military promotion, a stand that had made him a political hero in reform-minded circles throughout Great Britain and Ireland. May duly summoned the requested meeting, but then sought to use his power as chairman to prevent any discussion of the wider political issues behind the proposed address. The main advocate of the address was J. S. Ferguson, a linen merchant who had supported Catholic emancipation and reform in the 1790s and who was to be a leading figure in the emerging Liberal party of the 1820s. Thomas Verner, on the other hand, spoke against the proposal. Donegall also spoke from the floor, condemning the assembly for taking up 'the party politics of the nation'. He also accused another of Wardle's supporters, the banker Narcissus Batt, of betraying his trust as an officer in the yeomanry by associating himself with such subversive proceedings. In the end, the assembly approved the proposed address, but May refused to discharge the chairman's usual duty of forwarding it to Wardle, leaving the task instead to Ferguson.[39]

The debate on the address to Wardle reveals the political antagonisms that persisted below the surface in post-union Belfast. But perhaps the most striking feature of the episode is that May junior had accepted the requisition for a meeting on such a contentious subject. The revival of the town meeting, with its underlying assumption of a single urban community united by shared values and allegiances, was a further indication of the desire of Belfast's ruling elite to promote their vision of an orderly, hierarchical society. Many of the issues discussed were politically uncontentious. A meeting in April 1812, for example, denounced proposals to continue the trading monopoly of the East India Company, calling on Donegall and Sir Edward May to present petitions in the Lords and Commons, respectively. Another, a month later, instituted a subscription to provide food at below market rates during a period of acute scarcity.[40] On the other hand, a requisition in February 1813 for a meeting to petition for the county gaol and the seat of the assizes to be moved from Carrickfergus to Belfast was highly unwelcome to Donegall, who aspired to control the borough of Carrickfergus but had to deal there with a larger and more independent electorate than at Belfast. Nevertheless, the meeting went ahead and agreed to petition, ignoring speeches in opposition from Revd Edward May and from Arthur Chichester, the marquis's cousin and MP for Carrickfergus. Thomas Verner, who had presided as Sovereign, declined to join the petition committee. However, his refusal was carefully worded:

> He felt it his duty, as chairman, to sign the resolution adopted by the majority of the meeting, as he did to call the meeting itself, when presented with a requisition so respectably signed, but further than that it had not his concurrence.[41]

Verner's diplomatic language makes clear that the impulse to preserve the appearance of civic harmony was genuinely felt. Just a few months later, however, another contentious town meeting made clear that the attempt to maintain this reminder of a simpler urban past was no longer sustainable. Following a riot on 12 July 1813,[42] leading reformers, headed by Dr Robert Tennent, brother of the formerly imprisoned United Irishman William Tennent, signed a requisition for a town meeting to inquire into the causes of the violence. Compromised, according to his own account, by his membership of the Orange Order, the Sovereign, Thomas Verner, agreed to summon the meeting, but then immediately adjourned the proceedings on the grounds that the trials of some of the participants was imminent. Three weeks later supporters of the requisition reconvened on the date named in the adjournment, only to be told that, with the trials now completed, an inquiry was no longer needed. In the angry confrontation that followed Dr Robert Tennent, one of the town's leading reformers, laid a hand on Revd Edward May, who had him immediately arrested and subsequently imprisoned for six months on a charge of assault. Meanwhile, in what may or may not have been a deliberate act of retaliation, some of Tennent's supporters launched what proved to be an unsuccessful prosecution of Verner for the alleged rape of a female pedlar in the grounds of his house outside Belfast.[43]

The contested outcome of the abortive town meeting provides an insight into a municipal culture in transition. From one point of view the immediate circumstances of the dispute – Tennent's supposed assault and the counter charge against Verner – highlight the extent to which politics at the upper levels of society was still a matter of face-to-face interaction between individuals personally known to one another. Not all that much had changed since Tone's fraught dinner party two decades earlier with the Revd William Bruce. From another perspective, however, what was evident was that the political sphere had expanded to a point where the informal, personalised procedures of the traditional town meeting could no longer serve a useful purpose. That institution had always depended on a web of implicit understandings of status rather than the formalities of representation. At one point during Tennent's trial, for example, it was suggested that the usual procedure was for 'persons of respectability' to enter the upper floor of the Exchange and Assembly Rooms, where the meeting was held, while 'the lower rank' remained below as partial spectators. By 1813, however, those labels were themselves being contested. One of the reasons May and Verner gave for refusing to allow the second meeting to proceed was that those involved had not followed the recognised procedure of seeking the Sovereign's authority by requisition. Instead, 'improper means had been taken to collect a rabble', by means of a handbill that had been 'circulated among the lowest class' and that was addressed to 'the inhabitants' rather than – as in meetings called by the Sovereign – to 'the principal inhabitants'.[44] The defence on the other side was partly that, since what was involved was the previously agreed resumption of an adjourned meeting, they were not obliged to go through the Sovereign. However, one of their number also took issue with the traditional phrasing: 'a number of peaceable inhabitants were not a mob, though they were not the principal inhabitants'.[45]

The same sense of a political system in transition, in which traditional forms were still invoked, but only to demonstrate their inadequacy, was evident in a second controversial episode some seven years later. In August 1820 Verner, as Sovereign, received a requisition for a town meeting to prepare an address of support for Queen Caroline, the long-estranged wife of George IV, who had returned from Italy to claim her place as his queen, forcing him to initiate parliamentary proceedings for a divorce. Radicals throughout the United Kingdom seized on the opportunity to embarrass the establishment by the unimpeachably loyal device of a campaign to uphold the rights of a supposedly injured queen. The Belfast reformers who joined in the campaign can hardly have expected their requisition to succeed. Already three years earlier one of them had dismissed as 'a useless formality' a similar requisition for a meeting on parliamentary reform, presented only to be rejected before the organisers went ahead with a meeting explicitly for their own supporters.[46] On this occasion, however, Verner chose to escalate the dispute. Having justified his refusal by arguing uncontentiously that the issue was now before Parliament, and that other parts of Ireland had so far not involved themselves in the controversy, he went on to deliver a jibe at what he now clearly regarded as political opponents rather than fellow citizens.

> I cannot, in justice to the town of Belfast, avoid observing, that the requisition, however numerous the signatures to it may appear, does not (with great

deference to them) convey the sentiments of that portion of the inhabitants always to be regarded by me upon matters of importance to the community.[47]

In response, the petitioners went on to organise their own address to the queen, pointedly condemning those who sought to exclude her as 'that same faction [that] would carry discord into the palace as well as the cabin, to multiply its powers of corruption and perpetuate its monopoly'.[48]

The Queen Caroline affair reached its crisis two months later, when the House of Lords voted to reject the Bill for a divorce. This time the queen's Belfast supporters gave Verner no chance to rebuff them. Instead they called on their own account for the town to be illuminated in celebration, ignoring Verner's protest at this invasion of one of the Sovereign's traditional functions. The general response was enthusiastic. Houses throughout the town blazed with light, as did ships in the harbour, while crowds paraded the streets dragging flaming tar barrels and firing rockets, squibs and pistols. At the town's theatre a transparency showed the queen 'laying her hand on a book called the "constitution" and looking straight at her worthy spouse who seemed very glum on the occasion'. As the evening progressed, however, the atmosphere became increasingly rowdy, and the crowd turned to smashing the windows of houses that had not placed lights in their windows. One bystander, broadly sympathetic to the queen's cause, wrote of 'standing among and around thirty policemen with their pikes [as] that unprincipled mob made the glass shower down about our heads'. Among the buildings attacked were Verner's house and the premises of the Nelson Club, where members were struck by stones as they sat at table. One of Donegall's sons, who rushed out to confront the attackers, was knocked to the ground.[49]

Belfast's Queen Caroline riot, coming just eight months after Verner's elaborate celebration of the accession of George IV, demonstrated beyond a doubt the obsolescence of the conservative, hierarchical vision that had inspired that earlier pageant. Verner's unwillingness to convene a public meeting in support of the queen was predictable. But the offensive terms of his refusal, so different to his comments seven years earlier when he had declined to join in the petition regarding Carrickfergus, confirmed the collapse of the delicate web of implicit understandings on which the institution of the town meeting was based. The organisers, for their part, seized the opportunity openly to mock the loyal festivals of the establishment, appropriating its symbols for their own elaborate piece of counter theatre. The breakdown of political consensus was also evident in the geography of the disturbances, mirroring the new partitioning of residential space that had taken place over the past few decades. Newspapers reported that most parts of the town were 'pretty generally' illuminated, 'not excepting the most insignificant lanes and courts, which were, in general, well lighted up'. On the other hand, the elite Donegall Place, where only two houses were illuminated, 'had a very sombre appearance', ensuring that the street became the target of the mob's particular attentions.[50] Yet, if the town's reformers were able to use the occasion to promote their cause, and to humble the local establishment, they were all too clearly unable to control the forces they unleashed. The later stages of the evening, when both the conservative *Belfast News Letter* and the more neutral *Belfast Commercial Chronicle* agreed that the crowd became increasingly indiscriminate, smashing the windows of both illuminated and unlit houses and in some cases demanding money in order to leave properties untouched, were clearly an embarrassment to the town's liberal bourgeoisie. A new political world was taking shape, in which the procedures of a small urban community, characterised by face-to-face interaction and vertical ties of clientship and deference, were to be superseded by the movement of anonymous crowds.

The birth of party politics

The changes that had taken place in the form of political debate remained evident during the 1820s. The traditional institution of the town meeting still had a function, as a forum for the discussion of matters of general concern. In 1828, for example, the Sovereign, now Sir Stephen May, organised a meeting in the Exchange Rooms, 'pursuant to requisition', to discuss proposals for improvements to the port and harbour, opening the proceedings by reading the requisition and announcing that 'he was ready to hear what any persons should have to say on the subject of the meeting'.[51] But the town meeting could no longer be used to address major political issues. Instead debate now took place in other venues as opposing groups organised their own meetings, petitions and political dinners. Once this happened a major point of contention became the conflicting claims of rival gatherings to represent the true weight of intelligent or respectable public opinion. In 1823, for example, the *Belfast News Letter* used the modest numbers attending a dinner in support of parliamentary reform as grounds to dismiss those involved as a factional minority: 'the people of this town ought not be to confounded, as a body, with any party whatever, much less with those of a few individuals assembled at a dinner party'. Two years later it was the turn of the liberal *Northern Whig* to denounce roundly the signatories to a petition against Catholic emancipation:

> It was got up by a Custom House official, and a workman in a cotton ware room: it is signed by coal porters, quay carmen, fruit hawkers, the meanest pedlars, and runners about steam boats and stage coaches.

The *News Letter*, in reply, defended the right of 'the humblest operative' to have his say, but insisted that in this case the signatories were in fact 'men of honourable and lucrative mercantile pursuits'.[52]

All this made clear that the rear-guard attempt of the municipal elite to preserve the public appearance of a harmonious urban community conducting its affairs under the patronage of its landed proprietor had failed. At the same time it would be wrong to assume that Belfast immediately became the theatre of a system of full-blown party politics. The whole point of the claim and counter claim surrounding the meetings and dinners of the 1820s, after all, was for each side to present itself as the true voice of the town, while branding its opponents as a mere faction. And subsequent events were to show that the traditional idea of a single urban community retained both rhetorical force and a genuine political appeal.

The extent of that appeal became clear in the agitation that preceded the Reform Act of 1832. In retrospect, the Act, replacing the single seat controlled by Lord Donegall with two seats elected on a £10 franchise, began the dismantling of the Chichester family's long domination of the town. But this outcome was not by any means immediately clear. Instead what took place was a striking, and possibly deliberate, reversion to an older manner of proceeding. In December 1830 a substantial body of inhabitants attended a town meeting summoned by the Sovereign, in response to a requisition, to discuss the question of parliamentary reform. May opened the meeting by explaining that he doubted whether it was necessary, at a time when the government was known to be already planning a Reform Bill. But he had nevertheless felt obliged to respond to the requisition 'when he considered the respectability of the persons whose names were attached to it'. In the debate that followed supporters of a Reform Bill went out of their way to insist that they intended no disrespect to Donegall personally; their campaign was against the system of which he was the involuntary beneficiary. For their part, both Donegall and his son, Lord Belfast, declared their willingness to accept any reform agreed by Parliament. May subsequently presided over two further town meetings, in March and September 1831.[53]

Not everyone was willing to join in this ostentatious display of harmony and consensus. At the September 1831 town meeting an anti-reform spokesman came forward, accompanied by a noisy crowd of supporters; the *Belfast News Letter*, earlier the defender of the right of the 'humblest operative', dismissed those involved as 'mere boys, whose appearance in general showed that they belonged to a very humble class of the community'. A more serious incident followed on 18 May 1832, after Liberal ministers had announced that they had the king's backing to proceed with a Reform Bill. When the news reached Belfast a large crowd went from the offices of the *Northern Whig* to those of the anti-reform *Guardian* newspaper, where they broke windows and burnt a tar barrel. They then attacked a public house frequented by Orangemen, where two shots fired from inside the building killed one of the crowd. Meanwhile a rival anti-reform crowd of three to four hundred was also on the street, mingling cries of 'No popery' and 'no reform'.[54] The episode made clear that, even at this relatively early stage, an ominous conjunction had occurred of what in principle should have been the wholly separate issues of constitutional reform and Catholic rights. But this merely adds to the significance of the choice that the Donegall interest appears to have made. Faced with reforms that threatened to wipe out their political control of the town their ancestor had founded two centuries earlier, they could have responded by placing themselves at the head of the forces of Protestant reaction. Instead they sought an accommodation with the town's reformers.

Why did the Donegalls and their supporters choose this path? Lord Belfast was later to be a Liberal parliamentary candidate and junior minister; his support for moderate reform can thus probably be taken as genuine. Other members of the connection may simply have recognised that a graceful surrender held out the best hope of surviving what had become an unstoppable movement for change. From a different perspective there was a body of opinion, represented in Belfast by the *News Letter*, that took up the call for electoral reform in response to the passage of the Catholic Emancipation Bill, on the grounds that a Parliament more responsive to majority opinion in the United Kingdom would be less quick to make further concessions to Catholics.[55] But, whatever the precise reason, the graceful surrender of the Donegalls made it sensible for supporters of reform to avoid sowing dissension by a direct attack on the family or its associates. In the short term the tone of ostentatious good will expressed on all sides meant that Belfast had only a minor taste of the violent confrontations that took place in other cities as monarchy and aristocracy threatened to block reform. In the longer term it had important consequences for the next stage in the development of a new political system.

The first election under the provisions of the Reform Act took place in December 1832, when 1,400 newly enfranchised voters went to the poll to choose the two MPs who would now represent Belfast. The reformers, in triumphalist mood, put forward two men of strong radical convictions. Robert James Tennent was the son of Dr Robert Tennent and a nephew of William Tennent, making him a member of the town's most prominent radical family. William Sharman Crawford was a County Down landlord known for his commitment to a far-reaching restructuring of the land system. Their platform was an ambitious programme of further reform, including the secret ballot, triennial elections and the partial disendowment of the established church. The Conservatives, by contrast, chose as their candidates two symbols of conspicuous moderation. James Emerson Tennent was a firm supporter of the recent Reform Bill, who had accepted the Conservative nomination only after the Liberals had passed him over in favour of his cousin Robert James. His running mate, Arthur Chichester, was a younger son of the marquis of Donegall, thus offering a reassuring symbol of continuity rendered acceptable by his family's gracious surrender to reform. When the votes were cast it was this studied appeal to the centre ground that proved successful. Emerson Tennent and Chichester between them collected 1,557 votes, compared to 1,241 for Tennent and Crawford. The *Northern Whig* commented angrily on the 'old professed reformers' and even 'liberals of [17]98' who had given their votes to one or even both of the Conservative candidates.[56]

Over the next few years this claim to represent the voice of moderate consensus remained an explicit part of the rhetoric of the Conservative party. Emerson Tennent, speaking in 1836 at a meeting of the Belfast Conservative Society, insisted that its members were not 'a mere faction in the state'. Instead it represented a broad cross section of opinion: 'men of as tolerant views in religion, and as liberal opinions in politics ... as any in the community – men who, some years ago, would have been found, in all probability on different sides, or, more likely still, connected with no party whatsoever'. John Bates, the society's secretary, likewise insisted that its principles were indeed Conservative, 'but at the same time of such a moderate character as not to exclude any but the Whig-Radicals of the borough'. Instead, he alleged, it was their Liberal opponents who had sought to seize control of public institutions in the name of an unrepresentative faction.[57] When elections to fill five vacancies on the Police Commission took place the following year, both Liberal and Conservative managers came forward on behalf of their respective parties, but promptly launched into a debate 'as to when and by which of them the struggle for ascendancy in the management of the different public institutions in the town commenced'.[58]

In assessing these charges and counter charges of a discreditable factionalism it is important to remember that acceptance of the legitimacy of political parties as something more than self-interested cliques was everywhere in the United Kingdom a slow process. Moreover it was genuinely difficult, during a period of transition, to draw a clear line between a civic sphere open to all and the new world of party politics. The scope for genuine ambiguity, as well as mendacious posturing, became clear when the town's Liberals, in October 1835, solicited a formal visit by the Lord Lieutenant, Lord Mulgrave. Mulgrave was a Whig, committed to extensive reforms in policing, education and other areas, and the purpose of the invitation, as one of those involved admitted in a private letter, was 'to establish and consolidate a Liberal and ministerial interest in this part of Ireland'.[59] In public, however, the organisers sought to present the event as a non-partisan civic ceremony paying due respect to the king's representative. The Sovereign responded by pointing out that the proper procedure in that case would have been to ask him to summon a town meeting. As things stood he could not, as chief magistrate, attend an event 'supported by any mere section or party of the inhabitants whatever'. Emerson Tennent appears to have made a genuine attempt to establish whether a proposed dinner would be of a non-party character, before deciding that he could not take part.[60] The eventual outcome was a compromise. The Sovereign, Emerson Tennent and the town's other Conservative MP attended a meal provided for the Lord Lieutenant during a visit to the local garrison, but not the later public dinner. The main sticking point with regard to the latter was whether the inclusion among other loyal toasts of one to the king's ministers was mere politeness or a political gesture. R. J. Tennent, proposing the disputed toast, adopted an ingenious formula that represented one approach to the ambiguities of this transitional period: he and others drank from the bottom of their hearts, but 'others have perfect freedom to drink it only from the lips outward'.[61]

This being said, it remains the case that the rhetoric of non-partisanship adopted by both parties was seriously out of line with their actual practice. From 1832 onwards parliamentary elections were contested by rival party organisation, each using both legal and illegal methods to maximise its vote and whittle away that of its opponents. A parliamentary inquiry into charges of corruption in the return of two Conservative candidates in 1841 cast an unflattering light on the practices of both sides. Witnesses agreed in putting the number of properly qualified electors at around 1,800 or 1,900, as compared to between 4,000 and 5,000 names on the electoral register. A Liberal activist estimated that the votes of between 500 and 600 could be bought. Car drivers were won over by hiring their services for the six days of the elections, and publicans by renting their premises. 'Everybody who is not actually a temperance or a tee-total man is drunk', a Conservative supporter complained, while 'each party has 100 or 150 vehicles'. More seriously, there were reports that the Conservatives had brought in four men from County Monaghan whom they sent out repeatedly to vote in the names of different individuals on the register. One of the four testified to having been set to work on a printed list of voters, picking out those marked as having moved house, died or emigrated to America and copying their names onto slips of paper. The Conservative witness, who spoke most frankly of organising personation, insisted that he had held back until 'bad votes' had begun to appear on the other side. But their eventual victory, and the general run of election successes they enjoyed throughout the 1830s and 1840s, suggests that in this dubious contest the Conservatives were the more adept.[62]

The mastermind behind the Conservative political machine was John Bates, a solicitor who had come to prominence as an activist during the 1832 election and went on to become secretary of the Belfast Conservative Society, established immediately after to give the party a permanent organisation. His success lay not just in his willingness to engage in the sort of malpractice exposed by the 1841 inquiry, but also in his mastery of the complex system of electoral registration established by the Reform Act and in the attention to detail that allowed him to ensure that Conservative voters were properly registered while potential Liberal supporters were excluded on a range of technicalities. Under his management the Conservatives won one of two seats in 1835, captured the second in a by-election when the Liberal candidate died just a few months later, then took both seats following a successful petition against the return of two Liberals in 1837. The return of two Conservatives in 1841 was a step too far, leading to the annulling of the result and a fresh election, in which the two parties agreed to split the representation. Only the following year, however, Bates achieved his greatest political triumph. The Irish Municipal Reform Act of 1840, passed five years after its British counterpart, had at last abolished Belfast's archaic Corporation, replacing it with an elected mayor and Council. When elections to the new Council took place in October 1842 large numbers of potential Liberal voters, possibly with the collusion of officials in the tax office, were found to be ineligible, while attempted objections to Conservative electors failed on a technicality. Conservatives took all forty seats on the new Council.

As well as confirming the dominance of the town by the Conservative party, the first elections to the Town Council marked the final end of the Donegall interest as a force in Belfast public life. The second marquis had surrendered what remained of his economic power with the mass granting of perpetual leases from 1822. He had lost his automatic control of the town's parliamentary representation with the Reform Act of 1832. The return of his son Arthur in Belfast's first open election may have seemed to suggest that the family had capitalised on their graceful surrender to Reform by making a transition to the new world of electoral politics. But Arthur was in fact the town's last Chichester Member of Parliament. Donegall's heir, the earl of Belfast, ran twice as a Liberal, in 1837 and again in 1841, but in each case without success, and another son also failed to gain election, as a Conservative, in 1841.[63] Control of local government – of the Corporation and, through it, of a majority of the Police Commissioners – lasted longer. But the creation of the new Council removed the marquis's last source of influence and profit. The new Conservative councillors included two former members of the Donegall circle. However, Thomas Verner junior, the last Sovereign and Donegall's nephew, was refused a place on the party's list of candidates, ostensibly on the grounds that he was ineligible due to unpaid rates.

To Donegall this rejection by what had been his family's town was a bitter blow. 'He had lived among them', he complained, 'and had been as one of them, and he did not know what he had done calculated to offend any person.'[64] To some extent he may have brought his troubles on himself. Over the preceding years his continuing financial difficulties had led him to become less discriminating in his search for money. In particular he and the earl of Belfast had held up improvements to the harbour and to the town's water supply as they attempted to extract compensation for their residual proprietorial rights. Yet Donegall had not entirely forfeited the respect and affection of the Belfast public. His funeral, just two years later, was to be a major civic event. Shops and businesses throughout the town closed by order of the Council, while 200 carriages joined the procession to the family vault at Carrickfergus. Instead, it seems clear, the main reason for the marquis's humiliation was simply that the Conservatives no longer needed him. The long transition from acceptance of the paternalistic authority of an aristocratic proprietor was over, and the time had come for a very different type of conservatism to take control.

Notes

1 *First Report of the Commissioners on Municipal Corporations, Ireland* (Parliamentary Papers [hereafter PP] 1835 (23–28) 28), p. 698.
2 Cornwallis to Portland, 22 October 1799, in Charles Ross (ed.), *Correspondence of Charles, First Marquis Cornwallis* (3 vols, London: John Murray, 1859), iii.139.
3 George Benn, *A History of the Town of Belfast from the Earliest Times to the Close of the Eighteenth Century* (Belfast: Marcus Ward, 1877), p. 590.
4 Jean Agnew (ed.), *The Drennan-McTier Letters* (3 vols, Dublin: Irish Manuscripts Commission, 1998–99), i.99, 301; Haliday to Charlemont, 21 June 1788, in Historical Manuscripts Commission, *The Manuscripts and Correspondence of James, First Earl of Charlemont* (2 vols, London, 1891–94), ii.75.
5 *BNL*, 8, 26 June 1759, 4 November 1760. For other examples see *BNL*, 26 October 1759 (the taking of Quebec), 5 June 1761 (the king's birthday), 8 November 1768 (birthday of King William III). See also 21 August, 18 September, 26 October, 11 December 1759; 4 November 1760; 5, 23 June 1761; 8 November 1768.
6 Benn, *History of the Town of Belfast* (1877), pp. 647–8.
7 D. W. Hayton, 'Exclusion, conformity and parliamentary representation: the impact of the sacramental Test on Irish Dissenting politics', in Kevin Herlihy (ed.), *The Politics of Irish Dissent 1650–1800* (Dublin: Four Courts Press, 1996), pp. 52–73, at pp. 63–6; PRONI, D562/701, Donegall to –, 28 February 1739.
8 Martha McTier to William Drennan, nd, in Agnew (ed.), *Drennan-McTier Letters*, i.125.
9 Haliday to Charlemont, 24 July 1787, in Historical Manuscripts Commission (ed.), *Manuscripts of the Earl of Charlemont*, ii.58.
10 [William Bruce and Henry Joy], *Belfast Politics, Or a Collection of the Debates, Resolutions and Other Proceedings of that Town in the Years 1792 and 1793* (Belfast: Joy & Co., 1794), pp. 52–72.
11 Martha McTier to William Drennan, in Agnew (ed.), *Drennan-McTier Letters*, ii.138.
12 Haliday to Charlemont, 21 September 1796, in Historical Manuscripts Commission (ed.), *Manuscripts of the Earl of Charlemont*, ii.284.
13 Thomas Bartlett (ed.), *Theobald Wolfe Tone, Memoirs, Journals and Political Writings* (Dublin: Lilliput,1998), pp. 124, 126.
14 Martha McTier to William Drennan, 22 March 1794, 29 March 1797, in Agnew (ed.), *Drennan-McTier Letters*, ii.33–4, 306.
15 Agnew (ed.), *Drennan-McTier Letters*, iii.139, 144–5, 156, 15–61, 165.

16 *BNL*, 28, 31 August 1804; British Library [hereafter BL], Add MS 35752, ff. 41, 43, Corporation address and a draft of Hardwicke's reply.
17 Eileen Black, *Art in Belfast 1760–1888: Art Lovers or Philistines* (Dublin: Irish Academic Press, 2006), pp. 8–10.
18 Martha McTier to William Drennan, 10 April, 3 June 1802, in Agnew (ed.), *Drennan-McTier Letters*, iii.35, 48.
19 For a general account of Donegall's dealings with the Mays and Verner see W. A. Maguire, *Living like a Lord: The Second Marquis of Donegall 1769–1744* (Belfast: Ulster Historical Foundation, 1984).
20 *First Report … Municipal Corporations, Ireland*, pp. 701–5, 728–31.
21 *Belfast Commercial Chronicle* [hereafter *BCC*], 14 January 1811.
22 R. G. Thorne (ed.), *The House of Commons 1790–1820* (5 vols, London: Secker and Warburg, 1986), ii.625.
23 BL, Add MS 35,739, ff. 19, 113, 180, Donegall to Hardwicke, 5 May 1803, 25 May 1803, 3 June 1803; BL, Add MS 35,734, ff. 309, 326, same to same, 2 June 1802, 6 June 1802.
24 BL, Add MS 40191, ff. 133, 150, 184, Whitworth to Peel, 5 or 6 March 1816, 12 March 1816, 21 March 1816; BL, Add MS 40192, f. 15, same to same, 22 April 1816; BL, Add MS. 40290, ff. 134–5, Peel to Whitworth, 9 March 1816.
25 *BNL*, 10 February 1818.
26 *BNL*, 17 June 1825.
27 Allan Blackstock, *Loyalism in Ireland 1789–1829* (Woodbridge: Boydell Press, 2007), pp. 144–53.
28 *BNL*, 5 August, 18 November 1803; PRONI, T1565, Diary of Anna Walker, 16 August 1803.
29 *BNL*, 5 June 1804; *BCC*, 7, 10 June 1809, 5 June 1811.
30 *BNL*, 28 August 1812.
31 For the role of advances in lighting effects in transforming the character of popular spectacle during this period see Paul Johnson, *The Birth of the Modern: World Society 1815–1830* (London: Weidenfeld and Nicolson, 1991), pp. 152–7.
32 *BNL*, 24 November 1812.
33 *BNL*, 15 February 1820. For the role of processions in representing social hierarchy see Robert Darnton, 'A bourgeois puts his world in order', in *The Great Cat Massacre and Other Episodes in French Cultural History* (New York: Vintage Books, 1984).
34 For political life in Belfast in the period up to the Reform Act see Jonathan Jeffrey Wright, *The 'Natural Leaders' and their World: Politics, Culture and Society in Belfast c.1801–32* (Liverpool: Liverpool University Press, 2012).
35 *BCC*, 16 January 1811. For May's role in initiating the proposed change see PRONI, LA7/2BA/2/1, pp. 334–5, Minutes of Police Commissioners, 31 December 1810.
36 PRONI, LA7/2BA/2/1, pp. 153–8, 165–6, 171–5, Minutes of Police Commissioners, 3 February, 6 March, 20 April 1816. See above, pp. 29–30.
37 *NW*, 3 February 1825.
38 *First Report … Municipal Corporations*, p. 706.

39 *BCC*, 3 May 1809; *Belfast Monthly Magazine*, 2:10 (May 1809), 394–5.
40 *BNL*, 7 April, 15 May 1812.
41 *BNL*, 2 March 1813.
42 See below, pp. 74–5.
43 W. A. Maguire, 'The Verner rape trial, 1813: Jane Barnes v. The Belfast Establishment', *Ulster Local Studies*, 15:1 (1993), 47–57.
44 For the meeting see *BNL*, 20 August 1813. The events of the day were subsequently picked over in detail at the trial of Dr Robert Tennent: *BNL*, 12 October 1813; *Belfast Monthly Magazine*, 11:63 (1813), 312–30.
45 *Belfast Monthly Magazine*, 11:63 (1813), 319.
46 John Hancock to O'Connell, 5 February 1817, in Maurice O'Connell (ed.), *The Correspondence of Daniel O'Connell* (8 vols, Dublin: Irish Manuscripts Commission, 1972–80), ii.130–1.
47 *BNL*, 18 August 1820. Verner's comments were probably aimed at John Lawless, the militantly radical journalist who was one of the three delegates who laid the requisition before him. But applied to others among the eighty signatories, such as the millowners Robert Grimshaw and John and Andrew Mulholland, or the country gentleman Edward Charley, it was clearly a partisan slur.
48 *BCC*, 6 September 1820.
49 PRONI, D1748/G/457/8, William Mitchell to Robert Tennent, 24 November 1820. See also *BNL*, 21 November 1820; *BCC*, 15, 18 November 1820.
50 *BCC*, 18 November 1820.
51 *BNL*, 21 October 1828.
52 *BNL*, 3 March 1825, 6 May 1823; *NW*, 25 February, 3 March 1825.
53 *BNL*, 3, 7 December 1830, 1 March, 27 September 1831.
54 *BNL*, 22, 25 May, 8 June, 20 July 1832.
55 *BNL*, 17 April 1829, 8 June 1832.
56 *NW*, 24 December 1832.
57 *BNL*, 19 January 1836, 23 December 1836; *The Times*, 27 December 1836.
58 *BNL*, 7, 10 November 1837.
59 PRONI, D1748/G/314/6, J. E. Kidley to R. J. Tennent, 10 October 1835.
60 See Emerson Tennent's letter to one of the organisers asking 'candidly, as a friend', how the proceedings were to be managed: *BNL*, 23 October 1835.
61 *BNL*, 29 September, 23 October 1835.
62 *Report from the Select Committee on the Belfast Election Compromise* (PP 1842 (431) 5), pp. 10–11, 43–4, 67–9, 110.
63 The earl of Belfast had sat as a Liberal for County Antrim during 1835–37. In Belfast he was declared elected in 1837 but unseated on petition. In 1841 he was defeated, but the result was overturned on petition and he was not chosen to contest the by-election, when the two parties agreed to take one seat each. Lord Hamilton Francis Chichester ran as a Conservative in 1841, challenging this party agreement, but was defeated.
64 *BNL*, 25 October 1842.

3

The making of a municipal culture

Municipal reform and urban improvement

The Whig government that introduced municipal reform Acts for Great Britain in 1835 and Ireland in 1840 was not primarily concerned with the quality of urban government; instead it envisaged the Acts as a logical extension to local politics of the same principle of equal representation on a limited franchise that had applied in the reform of parliamentary elections in 1832. In the event, municipal reform was a landmark in the history of the British city. Control passed from the hands of landed patrons and oligarchic corporations into those of a new urban elite, drawn from the industrial, commercial and professional middle classes. The new 'urban squirearchy' used these powers to embark on an unprecedented programme of development. Huge new construction schemes provided for the disposal of waste and the provision of clean water. Massive rebuilding projects cleared away slum areas and remodelled congested centres through the construction of broad avenues and central squares. Large-scale improvement schemes were initially a response to increasingly alarming problems of pollution, disease and the threat of social disorder. Later, as the worst of these problems were brought under control, what emerged was a positive sense of civic pride, reflected in ambitious building projects. Town halls, art galleries, concert rooms and libraries created a new landscape of commanding public buildings, visible symbols of a new sense of collective achievement in self-governing urban communities. The prominence of Gothic and Renaissance Italian architectural styles asserted a kinship with the last great age of urban civilisation. At a more practical level the Victorian city also became an economic powerhouse, as municipalities became direct providers of transport, gas and water, between them raising and spending money on a scale comparable with central government, or with the whole of manufacturing industry.[1]

In the case of Belfast the response to municipal reform followed very much the same pattern.[2] As elsewhere there was some initial uncertainty as to how far the Act had superseded earlier provisions for the government of the town. The Police Board, headed by the recently snubbed Verner, tried for a time to assert its continued responsibility for raising rates and maintaining urban amenities, and the issue was finally settled only by a court action. There were further difficulties about the tolls at Smithfield market, which Donegall had leased to Verner two months before the new Council met for the first time, as well as wrangles over the charter of the town and a set of standard weights, both now in the possession of a son of the former town clerk.[3] Once the extent of its powers had been clarified, however, the Council embarked on a major programme of public works. As with progressive urban government elsewhere in the United Kingdom, the key to its achievements was the confidence and vision required to borrow against future income for large-scale capital projects. Between 1845 and 1850 Belfast Council secured the passage of four separate Improvement Acts authorising it to raise money on the security of future rate income. By 1857 it had raised and spent a total of over £270,000, as compared to rate receipts in 1852 of just over £21,000.[4]

The work of the new Council was in two main areas. The first was the clearance of a run-down area close to the river, to make way for a new, broad thoroughfare, Victoria Street. Expectations that the street would become the heart of a new central commercial district were not fulfilled. Early purchasers of sites found that the low-lying location created serious problems of subsidence, while it quickly emerged that changing established patterns of movement within an urban centre was less easy than these novice planners had assumed.[5] By the 1860s, however, Victoria Street had become the location for some of the most impressive contributions to a new phase of ostentatious commercial building (Figure 3). In addition, and providing the main rationale for its construction, it fulfilled a vital function in enabling the greatly increased volume of traffic crossing the new Queen's Bridge – completed in 1843 to replace the crumbling Long Bridge – to pass around the town centre rather than creating impossible congestion along its main streets.

The Council's second major area of expenditure was in buying up existing market rights and carrying out a large-scale programme of building and relocation. The construction of Smithfield in 1788, removing the noisy and dirty business of trading in livestock and other produce from the town centre, had been one of the first marquis of Donegall's central projects. Since then, however, the continued growth of Belfast's provisions trade, and the expansion of the town, had overtaken this early improvement. By 1837 slaughtered pigs from six Ulster counties were regularly coming by road into Belfast. 'A single dealer frequently brings, at once, ten of the long country carts with a full load (nearly a ton) on each.' Their destination was Waring Street, which on market days became wholly blockaded, as on occasion was the neighbouring

3 Victoria Street in the 1880s. The street, Belfast's first major exercise in urban improvement, was laid out in 1843 through what had been a run-down waterfront district. The large building in the centre was built in 1867–68 as a pair of warehouses for the rival seed merchants Samuel McCausland and John Lyttle and Sons, and is decorated with emblems of the five continents with which both traded. The town's memorial to Prince Albert, a clock tower, is visible at the far end of the street.

Donegall Street. Another fair, for horses, regularly closed off York Street and an adjoining street. Smithfield, meanwhile, was by now at the centre of a residential district, approached by narrow streets and unable to expand to match the scale of the business carried on there. The Council's response, following fact-finding visits by the clerk of the markets to Birmingham and Liverpool, was to relocate the town's main markets to new sites, at easily accessible points on the periphery of the town centre. Smithfield, equipped with new buildings, continued as a city centre market dealing primarily in clothes and household goods. However, the sale of most agricultural produce was now concentrated on a spit of land that projected into the Lagan south of the Queen's Bridge, easily reached by the new Victoria Street. Here the Council reconstructed the former May's market and George's market, the first as a substantial brick building faced with stone, the second as a large square surrounded by sheds.

To the north of the bridge another new roadway, Corporation Street, led to a second market for pork and butter.[6]

The take-over of the markets represented Belfast's first venture into what was to be one of the great innovations of Victorian urban administration, the development of municipal enterprise. (The Council's original plans had included a second step in the same direction, the municipalisation of the gas works, but this was abandoned after the private company concerned had responded to the threat to its position with a much reduced rate for supplying the town.) Such ventures undoubtedly improved the facilities available to urban dwellers; in addition, as the Council pointed out, the creation of a centralised market prevented the abuse of forestalling, where speculators bought up available stocks and then sold them on to consumers at inflated prices.[7] But municipalisation also had a financial aspect. Although the acquisition of land and market rights and the erection of premises had cost a total of £101,000, receipts from rents and tolls by the late 1850s amounted to over £5,200 a year. In 1858 this income made it possible to reduce the borough rate by 20 per cent.[8] In the same way income from the leasing of building plots was expected eventually to recoup much of the money borrowed for the development of Victoria Street.

Alongside these largely self-financing improvements, the new Council took the first steps towards tackling the acute environmental problems created by industrialisation and urban growth. Between 1800 and 1850 the population of the town increased almost four-fold. The new working-class housing on the periphery was often hastily built, with two-storey, four-roomed dwellings standing back to back, leaving no space for any sort of sanitary provision and severely curtailing the possibility of ventilation. The numbers crammed into the courts and alleyways behind the main streets had also increased. A survey in 1852 counted 1,800 dwellings that could be reached only by a covered archway, in most cases with only a single entrance, again making the free circulation of air impossible. Out of 379 such streets, lanes and courts, 331 were less than twenty feet wide.[9] Here the first Improvement Act broke new ground in laying down minimum standards for building. No houses were to be built in courts or alleys less than twenty feet wide, or where there was not an open passage at each end. Ceilings were to be of a minimum height, there were to be no thatched roofs and no dwelling spaces below ground level, and all newly built houses were to have a yard and a 'suitable necessary house'. Hotels, pubs and eating houses were likewise required to provide privies and urinals for the use of their customers.[10] These provisions, governing new houses, did not eliminate existing poor conditions: the last of the inner-city courts and alleyways were cleared only in the early twentieth century. But their impact on further construction, as the city expanded more than three-fold over the next sixty years, was enormous. A geographical survey published in 1960 noted that most of what were known as the 'by-law houses' constructed following the Improvement Acts, 'built to conform with the law and sturdy enough to serve several generations ... are still standing and occupied'.[11]

Against these achievements must be set other areas in which the Council's record was less impressive. Andrew Mulholland, taking over as the town's third mayor in 1845, promised to use his period in office to promote the welfare of Belfast's much-expanded working class. Mulholland himself was as good as his word. A few weeks later he chaired the public meeting that agreed to establish a Society for the Amelioration of the Condition of the Working Classes, whose main aim was to provide public baths and wash-houses on a site at Townsend Street, adjacent to the new working-class suburb spreading westwards along the lines of the Falls and Shankill Roads. A year later Mulholland was again one of the organisers behind a second body, the Belfast Working Classes' Association, set up to promote popular education through a newsroom, library and courses of lectures. In 1853, however, the Council rejected a proposal to take over the running of the baths and wash-houses, now in financial difficulties, and the premises closed by 1860. These were early days in the development of municipal services, and Mulholland himself had made clear in his inaugural speech that the improvements he described were 'not the business of the Town Council'; its role was rather to encourage 'benevolent individuals' to make the necessary provision.[12] But the refusal to contribute to such a basic amenity, at a time when only 3,000 out of 10,000 houses had a piped water supply, nevertheless indicates that the Council's conception of what constituted worthwhile improvement projects remained a fairly narrow one.

A second important area in which the Council notably failed to take action concerned drainage. The long-term problems here were acute. Much of the town centre was below sea level, with the result that at high tide sea water surged up the main sewers beneath High Street and other main thoroughfares and 'a large portion of the solid refuse ... has time to deposit in all the main lines of conduits'. In the suburbs beyond the municipal boundary, accommodating around 10,000 of the inhabitants, no sewers of any kind existed, so that 'the rain from the clouds and the sewage from the dwellings are at liberty to make their own intersections and channels'.[13] The most immediate problem, however, was the River Blackstaff, flowing through the industrial district to the west, then across the area immediately south of the Linen Hall, before entering the Lagan upriver from the Queen's Bridge. A combination of effluent from factories and waste from private houses had turned the waterway into an open sewer. The river was also prone to flooding: one report, in December 1849, counted twenty-three streets, containing 300 houses, all flooded to a depth of between eleven and thirty-nine inches.[14] The Improvement Acts did in fact empower the Council to borrow up to

£15,000 to culvert the river, but it was unable to reach agreement with the owners of the land concerned. How far their failure to act was due to genuinely insurmountable difficulties, and how far to a reluctance to interfere with leading industrialists who preferred to be able to use the existing polluted waterway, remains unclear.[15] But in either case the long-term consequences were grave. The London *Times* in 1865 picked up the highly critical assessment of Ireland's leading architectural journal: 'While Belfast has been widening its chief thoroughfares, and laying out spacious markets, it has been systematically neglecting some of its most disgraceful and gigantic nuisances.' Prominent among these was still the Blackstaff, where 'the outpouring of half a hundred factories, and the sewage of a vast quarter of the town, have made it a filthy, reeking open sewer'.[16]

The culture of civic pride

The new elected Council created for Belfast by the Municipal Reform Act clearly had a selective vision of what constituted social improvement, and was quite possibly unduly attentive to vested interests. At the same time its vigour contrasts favourably with the performance of many other provincial urban centres. In Birmingham, for example, it was only in the 1870s that control of municipal affairs passed from an 'Economist' party of small traders and shopkeepers to a more dynamic elite drawn from leaders of the city's commercial life.[17] By contrast, the Belfast Council was from the start recruited from among the leaders of the town's commercial life, and embarked immediately on major schemes of urban development, including an ambitious programme of borrowing.[18] Its willingness to do so is all the more striking because there had been no enthusiasm in Belfast Conservative circles for the Act that brought the Council into being. When the Commons had debated Irish municipal reform in 1836 the town's two MPs, George Dunbar and Emerson Tennent, both Conservatives, spoke against it, arguing that the existing Police Board provided a satisfactory system of local government, to which the creation of municipal corporations would simply add a greater level of religious and political partisanship. Even in November 1842, as he took office as the town's first mayor, Dunbar recalled his opposition to the Bill, and announced that he had not changed his mind on the subject.[19]

This conversion of an apparently reluctant new class of urban governors to large-scale improvement projects is less surprising than it might appear. The initial hostility of Dunbar, Emerson Tennent and others to municipal reform reflected the fear of Irish Conservatives that elected councils, as indeed happened in most towns outside Ulster, would be dominated by Catholics and Repealers. In the case of Belfast, Bates's triumph in the municipal elections of 1842 quickly put such fears to rest. The dynamism shown by the new Council, meanwhile, can in part be attributed to the town's continuing economic growth. Elsewhere in Ireland municipal government, throughout the century, was to be hampered by lack of resources as commerce and manufacturing faltered and urban population stagnated. Urban improvement in Belfast, by contrast, drew on the expanding tax base of a thriving and rapidly expanding industrial and commercial centre, and on the confidence that came with continued economic success.

Of equal importance, however, was the changing character of public expectations. The expansion of the built-up area during the 1820s and 1830s had been impressive, but the comments of Inglis and Thackeray make clear that the profits of rapid construction had taken precedence over architectural sophistication.[20] By the 1840s a growing number of the town's inhabitants had also come to feel that its appearance fell short of what might have been expected. The architect Robert Young, who travelled to Glasgow to attend university in 1839, recalled much later 'what a feeling took hold of me at the sight of the grand cutstone buildings in Argyle Street, Buchanan Street and George's Square. It was one of pain and humiliation thinking of the poor, shabby, mean brick and plaster of my native town.' Returning to Belfast a year or so later, his first thought was once again 'what an awfully shabby, second rate place compared to Glasgow'.[21] Lord John Chichester, addressing an electoral crowd in August 1847, did not mince his words: 'Gentlemen, till within these few years your town was certainly more remarkable for industry than elegance.' Since then, 'a new spirit' had inspired the erection of some private dwellings and commercial premises of better quality. However, its public buildings – the Excise Office, the Post Office and the Custom House – remained 'an eyesore, a disgrace to your town'. The *Belfast News Letter*, a few months later, agreed that the town's public buildings 'have been of an ordinary and mean appearance, totally unworthy of the rank which the borough has attained'.[22]

The programme of improvements undertaken by the new Council was thus part of a wider drive, commencing in the mid-1840s, to give Belfast an urban landscape appropriate to its wealth and economic status. Already by 1847 the *News Letter*, having acknowledged the scale of the problem, could go on to talk approvingly of new projects that 'will, in a few years, render Belfast one of the most commodious, healthful and handsome towns in the British empire'. It singled out the new railway terminus at York Street, currently being upgraded by the addition of a new façade in Tuscan style, the Queen's College, being erected in the new suburb growing up on the Malone Ridge south of the town centre, and the new market buildings erected by the Council. The paper could have added a second railway terminus, at Great Victoria Street, completed in 1848, and the substantial School for the Deaf and Dumb, erected in 1845 close to the Queen's College and designed in the same Elizabethan Gothic. There was also the new court-house and county jail erected between 1846 and 1850 by the Grand Jury of County Antrim. The transfer of both prison and assizes from Carrickfergus belatedly recognised what was now Belfast's unquestionable precedence over the senior town, while the location of the new buildings, on the Crumlin Road, provided a visible symbol of retributive authority in the heart of the town's main working-class district. Meanwhile the Belfast Bank in 1845 gave a new lease of life to a survivor from an earlier age of urban renewal when it had the town's premier architect, Charles Lanyon – also responsible for the Queen's College, the gaol and the court-house – refurbish the Exchange and Assembly Rooms in Waring Street for use as a branch office.[23]

The sequence of major building projects continued into the 1850s and beyond. The completion in 1854 of a new suite of offices for the Harbour Commissioners, and three years later of a new Custom House (see Figure 9), the latter again by Lanyon, confirmed the continued centrality of the port to Belfast's commercial status, and at the same time responded to the complaint that the town lacked public buildings of style and elegance. Both buildings were in the style of an Italian palazzo, echoing the assertion of kinship with the great city republics of an earlier era that had also become fashionable throughout Great Britain. The completion in 1862 of the Ulster Hall gave Belfast what was at the time one of the largest musical venues in the United Kingdom, capable of accommodating up to 2,000 followers of the preferred public art form of the Victorian bourgeoisie. Meanwhile commercial firms also begun to make their contribution to a new, more impressive urban landscape. By this time Donegall Square had lost its status as an elite residential area, as the commercial centre spread remorselessly outwards. But the offices and warehouses that by the 1860s had begun to replace the original Georgian terraces were designed with a subdued elegance, again often Italianate in style, that belied their functional purpose. The Jaffe Brothers' linen warehouse, completed in 1863, was decorated with busts showing Shakespeare and Schiller alongside Stephenson and Watt, the heroes of steam power – a clear assertion of the harmony of culture and commerce. Elsewhere the warehouse of the seed merchants McCausland, erected on Victoria Street in 1867–68, proudly advertised its global connections with elaborate carvings representing the five continents from which its produce came.[24]

The Belfast that gained control of its own affairs through municipal reform was thus a town well on the way to developing the same lively spirit of self-confidence and energy that was emerging among the provincial industrial centres of mid-nineteenth-century Britain. A member of the Board of Customs, writing in 1850, summed up the impressions formed during regular visits on official business:

> I am quite surprised at what I see going on here. In a few years there will be finished one of the noblest harbours in the Empire (and that is a large phrase) for

the reception and accommodation of all kinds of vessels. It is entirely the work of man's hand, struggling against the obstacles of nature, and overcoming them in a most masterly manner. ... Within the last three years four noble public buildings which would be an ornament to any city have been executed, the New College, a lunatic asylum, a new County Court House and a County Gaol. They give this town a very handsome appearance, which together with the new docks or quays, and the lines of a very noble street, partly built upon, instead of three or four wretched cross streets containing above a thousand houses now pulled down, give one a high idea of the taste and spirit of the people of Belfast.

He was particularly impressed by Bates, 'a most clever man, the first in his profession in Belfast, and the chief person who has been instrumental in carrying on all the improvements in that rising town'.[25] The *Belfast News Letter*, in 1851, admitted cheerfully that a visitor to the town would not discover 'a single trace of architectural antiquity; everything would impress him with the idea of a new city'. It went on to praise 'the beautiful lines of streets, no sooner laid out than built upon, and the miles of quayage, occupied by the keels of commerce almost before they are completed', and to look forward to the time when further building in the fashionable southern outskirts of the town would replace the remaining villas and demesnes 'by tasteful streets, terraces, squares and crescents'. Even the smoke and soot hanging over the town was evidence 'of ceaseless activity and profitable perseverance'.[26] Four years earlier, the paper had commented approvingly on the first suggestions that Belfast, 'the acknowledged metropolis of Ulster', was more deserving of the title of a city than declining southern centres such as Cashel or Kilkenny.[27] City status would have to wait for another four decades. In 1854, however, Parliament acknowledged Belfast's extraordinary growth by a Boundary Extension Act that increased the municipal area three-fold, taking in Ballymacarrett across the river, as well as new districts to the north, west and south.

Two other events confirmed Belfast's rising status, in the eyes both of its own inhabitants and of a wider world. The first was the visit in August 1849 of Queen Victoria. The town's inclusion on the itinerary was not quite the compliment it appeared: the main focus of the royal visit was Cork and Dublin, and the Lord Lieutenant, the earl of Clarendon, had to intervene to ensure that Belfast, 'the Liverpool and Manchester of Ireland', should not be slighted. Once the visit was confirmed, however, the town rose eagerly to the occasion. The Mayor and Council, asserting their status as the embodiment of the town's civic dignity, commissioned an elaborate corporate uniform, scarlet gowns trimmed with ermine, worn over blue dress coats with velvet collars and buttons bearing the town's crest, in which to receive the queen. A carefully planned itinerary took in the showpieces of the growing town: from High Street, still the town's centre and decorated for the occasion with a huge triumphal arch, the royal party proceeded to the Linen Hall, where the queen paused to inspect a display of local produce, before driving past one of the town's two new railway stations to the Botanic Gardens and Queen's College, then doubling back to view the jewel in Belfast's industrial crown, the giant linen-spinning mill of Mulholland Brothers off York Street (Figure 4). Exhilarated by the success of the visit, the Council gave its recently completed new route from the Queen's Bridge the name Victoria Street. Two newly created squares were named Queen's Square and Albert Square, while the island created out of waste from the recent cutting of a new harbour channel became the Queen's Island, and for several years was the site of a commemorative fete.[28]

Three years later Belfast received its second mark of outside approval. In a society that saw useful knowledge as the key to social progress, the conferences of the British Association for the Advancement of Science, held each year in a different provincial centre, had become a major event. The Association had come to Dublin in 1835 and to Cork in 1843. Belfast's successful application to host the 1852 meeting, accepted in preference to Hull, Leeds and Brighton, was thus taken as an important triumph. During the week-long event the town proudly opened its public buildings to visitors and entertained guests with a round of soirées and banquets, as well as excursions to surrounding sights such as the Giant's Causeway and a display of antiquities in the museum of the Belfast Natural History and Philosophical Society. There was some disquiet when the crusading local doctor, Andrew Malcolm, used the occasion to present his hard-hitting paper demonstrating the link between poor sanitary conditions in the town and major outbreaks of disease.[29] For the most part, however, the town congratulated itself on having played host to the scientific elite of the United Kingdom, and basked in the positive coverage it received in the national press. The *Northern Whig*, with a mixture of diffidence and pride characteristic of this phase in the development of the Victorian industrial town, wrote of the opportunity such occasions gave to 'the Glasgows, the Belfasts, the Manchesters of Great Britain', towns of 'less polish and more rude strength', to lose their 'roughness and angularity' through friendly intercourse with distinguished visitors.[30]

A divided civic

To all appearances, then, mid-nineteenth-century Belfast was a thriving industrial centre in which political reform had placed power in the hands of an active, forward-looking middle class. But this was at best only part of the picture. Belfast was also a town in which political power was the monopoly of a single party. The ruling Conservatives themselves continued to appeal to the same rhetoric of non-partisanship, and the same claims to represent a

Civic identity and public space

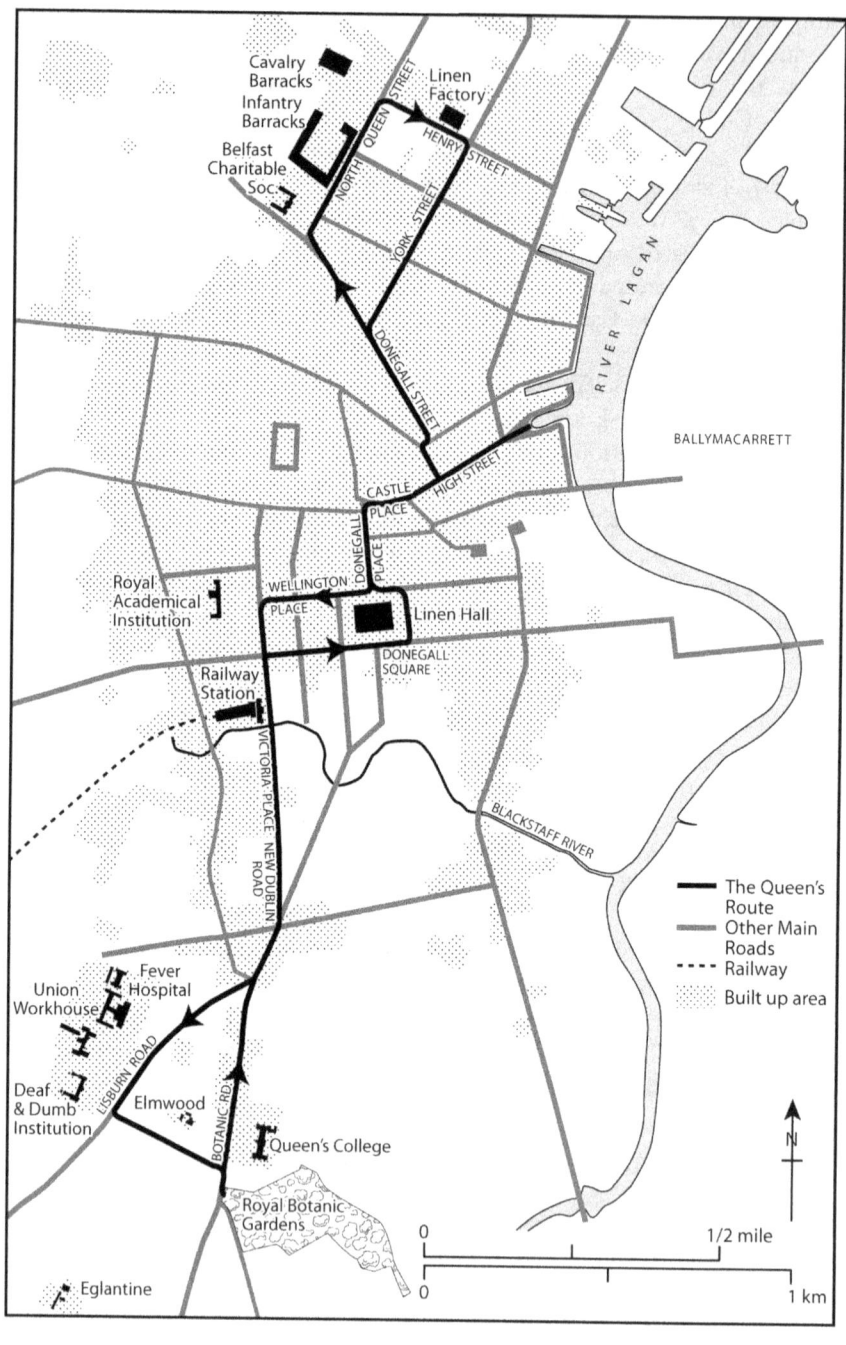

community rather than a sectional interest, that they had developed in the 1830s. The *Belfast News Letter*, in 1847, while conceding that all forty members of the Council were Conservatives, insisted that it was nevertheless 'a non-political body'. Its members 'put off their politics before they seat themselves at the board, and if they put them on again after they retire from it, it is nobody's business but their own'.[31] The town's Liberals, on the other hand, complained that its affairs were in the hands of a 'monopolizing clique' that maintained its dominance through systematic malpractice.[32] Catholics too protested, when given the opportunity, at what they presented as their total exclusion from employment and influence, and at the partisan character of law enforcement.

Charges that Conservative dominance rested solely on electoral chicanery need not be uncritically accepted. In private correspondence, Liberal party leaders complained of the lack of activists willing to undertake the tedious and time-consuming labour of compiling and checking lists of householders and voters.[33] Cries of foul play may thus have been an alibi for a failure to match Bates's machine in skill and diligence. There is also the possibility that the Conservative party, offering a combination of support for the established political order, a careful appeal to the political middle ground and efficient, progressive local administration, was genuinely more attractive to the majority of Protestant voters. The Liberals, by contrast, relied for support on a sometimes difficult alliance between a minority of reform-minded Presbyterians and the town's Catholic electors.[34] At the same time there seems little doubt that the Conservatives did in fact abuse their control of the Council to ensure that their dominance continued. The appointment of Bates to the twin posts of Town Clerk and Town Solicitor was of particular importance here. One major complaint was that Corporation tax collectors deliberately allowed potential Liberal voters to fall behind in the payment of lesser borough taxes, thus losing their right to vote, while Conservative supporters received the certificates required to allow them to register as electors.[35]

4 The route taken by Queen Victoria during her visit to Belfast on 11 August 1849 illustrates the high points of the emerging industrial city. From the quay at the end of High Street the royal party passed through High Street, Castle Place and Donegall Place to the White Linen Hall, where the queen paused to inspect samples of fabric on display. The party then proceeded up what later became Great Victoria Street, past the town Workhouse and a large school for the deaf and dumb, before briefly visiting the newly opened Queen's College. The last stage of the journey took the queen back to the centre, then on a brief circuit through the area immediately to the north. There she passed by the Charitable Society's Poor House and the jewel in Belfast's industrial crown, the extensive Mulholland's Mills, where the introduction in 1830 of the machine spinning of linen had secured the town's future as a manufacturing centre.

Partisanship and the determined exclusion of perceived enemies also had a strong religious dimension. In the late eighteenth century both the Belfast Volunteers and the United Irishmen had linked political radicalism to religious toleration, supporting the removal of remaining legal restrictions on Catholics. Even at that point, however, as events at the Volunteer review of 1792 made clear, not all Protestants, even among the town's reformers, were convinced that Catholic political power would not constitute a serious threat to their religion, liberty and property.[36] The United Irishmen's appeal for Protestants to abandon traditional hostility and distrust, moreover, came at a time when Catholics made up less than one tenth of Belfast's inhabitants. Even then the sight of a Christmas Eve religious procession in 1802 was enough to alarm the staunchly radical Martha McTier to write with alarm of 'the R. Catholics here, now a large though poor and unknown body ... I begin to fear these people and think like the Jews they will regain their native land.'[37] Over the next three decades, as immigration from a religiously mixed countryside brought the Catholic share of total population up to just under one third, such fears intensified. By the second half of the century higher rates of overseas emigration among Catholics, both in rural Ulster and in Belfast itself, were to lead to a relative (though not an absolute) fall in numbers. In 1861 their share of the population of Belfast, 34 per cent, was only marginally higher than the 32 per cent recorded in 1834, and by 1901 it had fallen to 24 per cent. Long before that, however, the idea of the Catholics as menacing intruders was well established in many Protestant minds.

Protestant fears were also a response to political developments elsewhere in Ireland. The tradition of religious liberalism was still strong enough to ensure substantial Protestant support for Catholic emancipation right up to the final victory for O'Connell's campaign in 1829. Over the next two decades, however, O'Connell and his associates organised further campaigns of mass agitation, against the financial claims of the Church of Ireland and for repeal of the Act of Union. These renewed assaults on the established order, with bishops and priests playing a central role in directing the Catholic masses, gave ever greater credibility to the claim that emancipation, far from removing the divisive issue of religion from Irish public life, had placed Ireland's Protestant minority in deadly peril. In the second half of the century the rise of first the Fenians and then a powerful movement for Home Rule confirmed to Belfast Protestants that, even if they remained a solid majority in their own city and its immediate hinterland, they were nevertheless menaced by a formidable Catholic nationalism, making the city's Catholic minority a potentially dangerous enemy within.[38]

At the same time that many middle-class Protestants were rethinking their religious liberalism, relations between plebeian Protestants and Catholics were also deteriorating rapidly. An incident in 1813, when Orangemen returning

The making of a municipal culture 75

from a Twelfth of July parade in Lisburn were attacked as they entered the town and fired on their attackers, is often cited as Belfast's first sectarian riot. In fact both of the men killed by Orange gunfire were themselves Protestants, raising the possibility that this was as much a brawl between conflicting political allegiances inherited from the 1790s as a sectarian affray.[39] From the early 1820s, however, reports began of regular violent clashes between Catholic and Protestant, often associated with the annual Orange processions on the Twelfth of July. Most of the fighting took place in the working-class districts of the town, between residents of the Pound and of the adjacent, predominantly Protestant Sandy Row, or in the streets off York Street to the north. But as early as 1825 clashes between Orangemen returning from a Twelfth of July meeting at Carrickfergus and their Catholic opponents spread into the town centre, forcing shopkeepers in High Street to close their premises as the two parties fought outside.[40] Thereafter sectarian clashes were to recur with depressing regularity: during the parliamentary elections of 1835 and 1841, following the Twelfth of July processions in 1843, and during the parliamentary election of 1852, until the two great explosions of violence in 1857 and 1864 that alerted the outside world to the scale of Belfast's divisions.[41]

In this environment of rising sectarianism, the Belfast Conservatives openly associated themselves with an exclusive ultra-Protestantism. In the aftermath of Emerson Tennent's victory in 1832, one of his supporters appeared at the window of his campaign headquarters to announce 'that the Protestants had gained this victory, and that they would continue to maintain their ascendancy: they had trodden down their enemies and they would keep them down'. Soon after, a band playing Protestant tunes forced its way into Hercules Street, starting a riot that ended with four men being shot dead by police.[42] In 1848 the *Northern Whig* indignantly reported that a Conservative circular relating to elections to the town's Water Board had called on voters to return the 'Protestant candidates'.[43]

The same spirit of sectarian exclusiveness permeated the Council's management of the town. Two incidents, in particular, illustrated the level of partisanship. The first concerned John Clarke, who at the end of 1843 took office as Belfast's second mayor. His acceptance speech continued the rhetoric of neutrality, promising 'to be guided in the discharge of my official duties by a principle of entire freedom from partiality towards the one or the other of the different sects and parties of this great town'. Soon afterwards, Clarke matched his words with action by attending the opening of a new Catholic church, St Malachy's, and making the ceremonial gesture of assisting in taking up the collection. In this he did no more than follow a precedent set in 1815, when the marquis of Donegall, his son Lord Belfast and the Sovereign had all attended the opening of Belfast's second Catholic church, St Patrick's on Donegall Street, and had similarly assisted in the taking up of a collection. By

1844, however, times had changed. Clarke was denied the customary vote of thanks at the end of his period of office and was not selected as a candidate at the next election to the Council.[44] The second revealing episode was in 1849, when a group of prominent Catholics, including the bishop, Cornelius Denvir, wrote to the Lord Lieutenant to protest at the way in which 'newspapers, magistrates and other parties holding respectable rank' had joined in attempts to present a recent spate of arson attacks in the surrounding countryside as part of an organised Catholic conspiracy. In particular they complained of an incident where the Catholic witnesses against two Protestant women who had fabricated an attack on their father's farm, using animal blood that one of them had been seen buying in Smithfield market, had been abused and accused of perjury. A neighbouring landlord, Lord Castlereagh, confirmed that a panel of local magistrates – what he scathingly called 'no less than eleven metropolitan Solons' – had supported the two women 'in the teeth of sworn evidence of the strongest nature'.[45]

Partisanship was also evident in the policing of the town. Witnesses at the inquiry into the riots of 1857 agreed that there were no more than five or six Catholic constables in a force of some 100 men. The municipal authorities indignantly rejected allegations of sectarian bias brought forward by Catholic spokesmen, and four Catholic policemen produced to the 1857 inquiry loyally insisted that they had encountered no religious discrimination. But the verdict of outside observers was damning. The government-appointed stipendiary magistrate reported in 1857 that the local force were of little use in cases of disturbance: 'with the exception of a very few of them, their sympathies are strongly with the Orange party, and, for very sufficient reasons, they fear to enter the Roman Catholic quarter of the town'.[46] The constabulary sub-inspector charged with dealing with the riots of 1864 likewise reported that the force had 'exhibited partisanship to a high degree'. Constables themselves living in Sandy Row had failed to identify a single Protestant rioter from the district; several had themselves been seen taking part in the violence; and an inspector was in jail after handing over a man who had sought shelter in his house to be beaten by a hostile crowd.[47]

At the heart of the civic culture of nineteenth-century Belfast there thus lay a central contradiction. The rhetoric of the dominant political grouping was forward looking and progressive. Where the Donegall group had looked back to an older world of hierarchy and deference, the leaders of the new Town Council identified themselves as followers of the modernising Conservatism of Sir Robert Peel. Thus Emerson Tennent, addressing the Belfast Conservative Association in January 1836, recalled how Peel had stressed the need to come to terms with the consequences of the Reform Act, warning the merchants of London that they could no longer rely on hereditary privilege, as represented by the Crown and the House of Lords, to protect their interests. Instead 'it was henceforth at the registries and the hustings that the battle for the constitution must be fought'.[48] In practice, however, the dominance of the Belfast Conservatives also involved a highly developed system of electoral malpractice, while the progressive rhetoric of their spokesmen concealed a narrow spirit of sectarian exclusion and discrimination. The poisonous consequences of corrupt and oppressive one-party rule became evident in 1855 when the radical solicitor John Rea initiated a successful legal action against the Council for misuse of public funds. The offence was technical: the Council had exceeded the borrowing limits set by the Improvement Acts, and had used some of the money for purposes other than those it had been raised for. But the town's Liberals and Catholics pursued the issue with a determination inspired by over a decade of helpless fury at the sharp practice of their opponents, and the town's public life remained paralysed for several years. Just as the affair was at last brought to a conclusion, Belfast suffered a second humiliation when the government responded to the riots of 1864, and the damning evidence which they presented of a partisan and ineffective force, by abolishing the Belfast Town Police and putting the policing of the town in the hands of the Irish constabulary.

How is the dysfunctional civic culture of Belfast to be explained? Bates, who resigned following Rea's successful legal action and died soon after, provided a convenient scapegoat. But more was involved here than mere political chicanery on the part of one individual. The programme of urban improvement initiated by the Belfast Conservatives in the years after 1842 makes clear that they were in fact a dynamic and forward-looking urban elite, similar in many ways to their mainly Liberal counterparts in the great provincial cities of early Victorian Britain. If in other respects they failed to live up in practice to their Peelite language, the reason lies in the very different political context within which they operated. In Great Britain the threats to the established order, from political radicalism, economic discontent and the disruption of traditional social ties, were real enough. In this context Peel's achievement was to move his party from a stance of self-destructive reaction to a pragmatic, flexible Conservatism that accepted the necessity for rational reform. The threats faced by Irish Protestants, however, were, in their eyes at least, of a wholly different order. O'Connell's demand for repeal of the Act of Union, put forward as soon as he had achieved Catholic emancipation, created the grim prospect that Protestants would become an endangered minority in a self-governing Ireland. The violent assault on the tithe system during the 1830s seemed to confirm the threat to their survival. Most alarming of all, the political alliance between O'Connell and the British Liberal party, concluded in 1834, meant that the Irish Protestants, heavily outnumbered in their own country, could no longer be confident of enjoying the protection of the United Kingdom government.

Against this background, the other side of the repeated claim of the Belfast

Conservatives to be above party politics was the argument that such indulgence was no longer permissible. 'The time was gone', Emerson Tennent told the Belfast Conservative Society in 1836, 'when men would be content to play at politics as at a game of chess. ... The stakes had become serious of late and the public were beginning to discover that they had something to lose in the matter.' The Presbyterian leader Henry Cooke, addressing a later meeting, took the same line: the contest was now between two opposing forces – improving Conservatism and destructive Whig-Radicalism – and 'these are not the times when any man should, or dare, be neutral'.[49] Seen in this context, the combination of Peelite rhetoric and the politics of no surrender is evidence less of double-think than of the limitations of liberalism when confronted with a conflict on fundamental values and markers of identity.

A provincial capital

The chancery suit initiated by John Rea was a sharp check to the mood of confident expansionism that had characterised the Town Council in its first decade and a half. The court's finding that a total of £273,000 had been illegally raised or applied to an unauthorised purpose cast a shadow of apparent impropriety over the achievements of the past few years. Individual councillors, held to be personally liable for the whole of these sums, faced financial ruin, and the general uncertainty depressed the town's trade. The electoral damage to the dominant Conservative party was short term. The eventual settlement of the Chancery suit, whereby the disputed money became a charge on the rates, involved a humiliating electoral bargain. Twenty Liberals were allowed to stand unopposed for seats on the Council, and went on to elect the town's first Liberal mayor. The Liberals, however, were divided among themselves over how far to pursue a vendetta that was seen to be damaging the town's economic life, and were in any case a declining electoral force.[50] By 1864, Conservatives once again held all but five of the forty council seats. The psychological effects, however, lasted longer. A full ten years later the town's mayor, Philip Johnston, speaking at the opening of a new Town Hall on Victoria Street, dutifully praised the building, and declared his confidence that in time the town's continued growth would require the construction of something even larger. But he went on to offer an astonishingly misleading account of the Council's financial past, maintaining that it had merely taken over a debt of £284,000 borrowed by the Police Board for the construction of the market and other improvements, part of which it had since paid off. 'The town, he was glad to state, had progressed to a degree far beyond its liabilities, so that the Belfast Corporation was not in a hopeless state of insolvency as had been said in some quarters.'[51]

Already by the time of this brazen rewriting of a still clearly embarrassing past, however, urban government was beginning to regain some of its vigour. The completion of a new, purpose-built Town Hall was itself evidence of a revived self-confidence. In 1874 the mayor acquired a new chain of office. From about the same time, in a further expression of corporate self-awareness, the Council began to commission portraits of each holder of the office, eventually extending the series back to the 1860s.[52] By the end of the decade urban improvement too was back on the agenda. A new Improvement Act, in 1878, authorised the Council to embark on two major schemes: a remodelling of the town centre, focussed on the construction of a new thoroughfare, Royal Avenue (Figure 5), and a solution to one of the town's long-standing environmental problems through the culverting of the heavily polluted and flood-prone River Blackstaff.

The construction of Royal Avenue was the single most important work of urban redevelopment prior to the giant motorway schemes of the 1960s and after. As with the development forty years earlier of Victoria Street and

5 Royal Avenue, the showpiece of the late nineteenth-century city, laid out in 1880–81 and photographed here c.1906. On the near left, the Provincial Bank branch (1864–69) was the only building on the former Hercules Street to be left intact. Next door to it, dating from 1883–85, is the Reform Club, built as the social centre of the Liberal party, although from 1886 open only to 'Liberal Unionists'.

Corporation Street, the scheme was presented as combining slum clearance and more efficient traffic management. Hercules Street, continuing the line of Donegall Place but thanks to projecting buildings connected to it only by a narrow passage, was reputed to be congested and insanitary, particularly due to the concentration there of butchers' shops. The main impetus for the scheme, however, appears to have been the urgent need to relieve traffic congestion by creating a major artery linking Donegall Square and the south end of the town centre to the railway terminus and tramway depot at York Street to the north.[53] (Hercules Street's other reputation, as a street inhabited by periodically unruly Catholics, did not figure explicitly in the discussion.) The new thoroughfare was planned on a grand scale, with buildings individually designed but required to maintain a uniform height. Among the buildings constructed along its length and testifying to its status were a new General Post Office, a public library and a luxury hotel. Both roadway traffic and shoppers appear to have taken a little time to adjust to so radical a reorganisation of the centre. But by September 1883 the *Belfast Newsletter* could point to the rising volume of vehicles and to the Saturday-night crowds attracted there by shops 'which would do credit to Regent Street or Broadway in New York'.[54] In the longer term, as noted by the veteran journalist Frankfort Moore, the new artery produced a dramatic reshaping of urban geography. Where previously the town centre had run in an east–west direction, from Castle Place down High Street, the main axis was now from north to south.[55]

Other major infrastructural projects followed. The culverting of the Blackstaff involved the laying out of a new street, Ormeau Avenue, less grand than Royal Avenue, but lined with solid brick warehouses as a further extension of the commercial district. By the early 1890s North Street, conveniently adjacent both to working-class west Belfast and to the elite retail and business district of Donegall Place and Royal Avenue, had become a heavily congested shopping street, and was the focus of a major street widening scheme. In 1890 the Albert Bridge, replacing an older structure that had collapsed, provided an improved passage between Ballymacarrett and the rest of the city. In the same year, in what was to be its most ambitious undertaking of all, the Council purchased the White Linen Hall as a site for a new City Hall (Figure 6). Construction began in 1898 and the new building, a municipal palace in Portland stone with elaborate marble interiors, opened in 1906. By this time too there had at last been serious action to tackle one of the largest blots on Belfast's municipal record, its woefully inadequate system of sanitation. A main drainage system in 1893 provided for the first time an adequate network of sewers. In 1901 a major scheme to bring adequate supplies of clean water from the Mourne Mountains (the responsibility of a separate body, the Water Commissioners) provided the second essential element for a proper waste disposal system, allowing households to move from the ash-pit and privy to

The making of a municipal culture 81

6 Belfast City Hall, c.1905–7. The building, completed in 1906, dominates Donegall Square and provides a monumental showpiece at one end of the new artery created by the laying out of Royal Avenue. The first statue of a civic worthy, Edward Harland (1903), is just visible on the left, while that of Queen Victoria stands in front of the main entrance.

the water closet. Even then, however, pollution of Belfast Lough remained a problem until the installation in 1913 of an improved outlet pipe.[56]

The last decades of the nineteenth century also saw the Town Council embark on large-scale municipal trading. In 1872 it authorised a new tramway system, with horse-drawn vehicles running on an integrated network of rails on main routes throughout the town and suburbs. Although some members pointed to the potential profits of the enterprise, the Council was not yet ready to take direct responsibility, and instead entrusted the running of the scheme to a private company. In 1874, on the other hand, the Council took charge of the town's gasworks. The municipal take-over of the tramways followed in 1904, and the following year the system was converted to electricity. Belfast had already acquired an electricity generating station in 1897–98. But it was the increased demand from the trams that boosted generating capacity and reduced unit costs sufficiently to bring domestic electricity within the reach of ordinary householders.

These were substantial undertakings. The municipalisation of the gasworks cost £386,000, with a further £300,000 invested over the next seventeen years in increasing capacity, as compared to a total municipal revenue in 1892 of £575,000.⁵⁷ But cost could be offset against future income. There was also investment in amenities that could not be expected to pay for themselves, although here the pace of improvement was rather slower. Appeals for the creation of public parks to provide the town's working classes with access to sunlight and fresh air, for example, dated back to the 1850s. But it was not until 1871 that the Council acquired the demesne attached to the marquis of Donegall's abandoned mansion at Ormeau and converted it into a public park, partly paid for by letting some of the land for grazing and for building. By 1906, however, there were five more public parks, and the Council had also in 1895 taken over what had been the subscriber-owned Botanic Gardens.⁵⁸ A municipal public library opened in 1888, again rather late by the standards of the most progressive municipalities, but housed in an impressive building on Royal Avenue that also provided premises for an art gallery and museum

7 Belfast Public Library, c.1910. The library, completed in 1888, in many ways typifies the history of civic Belfast. The provision of this important amenity came late in comparison to what was done in many other provincial towns and cities but, when eventually provided, it was on a grand scale, providing space not just for a library but for an art gallery and museum.

(Figure 7). A Technical College, opened in 1901 partly in response to pressure and inducements from the newly established Department of Agriculture and Technical Instruction in Dublin, addressed long-standing concerns about the absence of the facilities for training in science and technology required by an industrial town.[59]

The essential background to these different improvements was the continued growth of Belfast's economy. Linen remained one of its two signature industries. Production had soared during the American Civil War, then suffered a temporary slump as cotton supplies resumed. The spinning side of the industry also faced competition, by the late nineteenth century, from low-cost producers in eastern Europe. But the high quality of the Ulster product sustained its place in international markets. Meanwhile shipbuilding, a minor industry in the first half of the century, expanded rapidly following the establishment in 1858 of the firm of Harland and Wolff, joined from 1880 by the firm of Workman Clark and Company. Proximity to the great shipbuilding centres of the Clyde and Mersey compensated for the lack of local raw materials that elsewhere crippled Irish heavy industry, while high wages and good-quality housing facilitated the recruitment of skilled workers from England and Scotland. Other manufacturing enterprises were also attracted to the growing city. In 1863 Thomas Gallaher moved his tobacco business from Londonderry to Belfast, where it expanded into one of the largest producers in the United Kingdom. A rope-works established in 1873 as a spin-off from the shipyard became reputedly the largest single producer in the world. There were also significant export-based producers of whiskey and aerated waters, as well as large engineering plants, initially developed to meet the equipment needs of local manufacturing but now expanded into major producers in their own right. Against this background of broadly based industrial growth, providing work for skilled and unskilled, male and female, immigrants continued in decade after decade to pour into the city. In 1901, 60 per cent of Belfast residents, and almost four in every five heads of household, had been born outside the city.[60] Population rose from 87,000 in 1851 to 208,000 by 1881 and 387,000 by 1911, making Belfast the United Kingdom's eighth-largest centre. In 1888 the Privy Council recognised its exceptional status when it agreed to make Belfast a city, the first time the title had been granted to an urban centre that did not have an Anglican cathedral. Four years later, Belfast's mayor became a lord mayor, a title previously held only by the mayors of London, York and Dublin. Here too Belfast established a precedent. Lords mayor followed in Liverpool and Manchester in 1893, and in Birmingham in 1896. Applications by Cork, Waterford and Limerick, on the other hand, all failed to win approval.[61]

Religious divisions in an urban landscape

Against this background of economic expansion and population growth, the physical landscape of Belfast assumed the classical features of a mature industrial city. By the beginning of the twentieth century the town centre had long ceased to be a place of residence. Instead it was a site for commerce by day and by night, with its bright lights and glittering displays of plate glass, for sociability and consumption. Its character as a public space was further marked out by the monumental character of much of the most recent building: along Royal Avenue and Donegall Place, and around the four sides of Donegall Square, imposing new office blocks and department stores overshadowed the elegant, medium-sized warehouses that survived from the 1860s and 1870s, while at the centre of the square stood the baroque bulk of the new City Hall. Beyond the centre, lay the working-class districts, their long rows of small terraced houses overshadowed by the chimneys of linen mills to the north and west, and by the cranes of the shipyard to the east. Further out, removed from the congestion and smells of the industrial city but now easily accessible by tram and railway, were the middle-class suburbs. The continued expansion of the city's commercial centre and working-class population, along with improved public transport, meant that some of the earliest out-of-town districts had by now lost their middle-class character. Ballymacarrett, just across the Lagan, had for a time provided those fleeing the town centre with a convenient suburban retreat. By the late nineteenth century, however, it was wholly devoted to housing the labour force of the shipyards and engineering works of east Belfast, while beyond it villas, followed by groups of semi-detached and terraced houses, spread along the east shore of Belfast Lough. The large houses erected on the lower reaches of the Antrim Road had likewise been abandoned to lodging-house keepers. Further from the town, on the other hand, the road had become the spine of a dense network of neat residential avenues. Only to the south, where Queen's College and the Botanic Gardens preserved the social status of the first suburbs, did middle-class Belfast begin where the city centre ended.[62]

Alongside these typical characteristics, however, the urban landscape of late nineteenth- and early twentieth-century Belfast displayed one feature that set it apart from its British counterparts: the residential segregation of its population by religion. In 1901, 59 per cent of Belfast households lived on streets where over 90 per cent of the residents were either Catholic or Protestant. Middle-class Belfast was mixed, though only in the sense that affluent Catholic households, too few in number to permit the development of a separate enclave, were distributed across predominantly Protestant districts. Working-class Belfast, by contrast, was rigorously partitioned. The districts east of the River Lagan were overwhelmingly Protestant, with the exception of one small

Catholic district, the Short Strand. Across the river there were further small Catholic enclaves in the markets area, close to the docks and in two sections of the mill district of north Belfast, Ardoyne and New Lodge. But the largest Catholic district, housing 41 per cent of the total Catholic population of the city, was in the south-west, in a district stretching from the original Catholic heartland of Smithfield and the Pound along the line of the Falls Road.[63]

The pattern of religious segregation was maintained by recurrent violence. The initial development of largely, though not exclusively, Catholic and Protestant districts in the Pound and Sandy Row may have arisen primarily from the immigrant's instinct to seek out one's own kind. However, a new feature of the riots of 1857, the most extensive so far experienced by the town, was a campaign of house-wrecking and intimidation, designed to drive Protestants out of the Pound and Catholics out of Sandy Row. Subsequent outbreaks of communal fighting, in 1864, 1872 and 1886, brought a further tightening of the pattern of sectarian exclusivity. One particularly important incident was in 1872, when the success of Catholic street-fighters in asserting their dominance over Leeson Street prevented Protestant encirclement of the Pound, and instead guaranteed the ability of the Catholic district of the Falls to expand along a south-western corridor bounded on the south by the Blackstaff River and the surrounding marshy ground of the Bog Meadows, and on the north by the aggressively Protestant Shankill Road.[64]

If violence helped to shape the urban landscape, it was in turn shaped by a changing physical environment. The riots of July 1857 were a conflict between the inhabitants of two densely packed working-class districts. Much of the actual fighting, however, took the form of confrontations across the large areas of open space that still, at this relatively early stage in the westward expansion of the town, lay within easy reach – on waste ground adjoining the half-completed streets running off Durham Street, and also in one of the fields belonging to Betty Donahue, a dairy woman and possibly an illicit dealer in spirits, who still grazed her cattle on the western fringe of the Pound. In the late 1870s, similarly, rival groups on the east side of the Lagan, close to the Catholic enclave known as the Short Strand, assembled on Sunday afternoons to stone one another on the slob lands of the tidal river and on open ground adjoining the railway line. Over time, however, unregulated open spaces of this kind disappeared beneath the expanding tide of brick and paving. Fighting now took place in streets lined with small terraced houses. Already by 1864 the undersecretary at Dublin Castle complained of the impossibility of dispersing rioters in such an environment:

> This part of the town consists of small houses and narrow lanes (like the Wynds of Glasgow) in which it is very difficult to follow people; driven from one street they turn down the cross lanes and courts, and come out into the street again in

the rear of the party who dispersed them. They rush into each other's quarters, break windows and smash doors, and are off again. The other party retaliate and from their yards and windows they fire shot or blank as may be, often more for noise than work. The whole is more like an *émeute* [tumult] of the Arabs I remember seeing at Tangier many years ago than a disturbance in a Christian town.[65]

At the same time that it made sectarian clashes even harder to police, the transfer of fighting from open ground to residential streets also helped to make violence less discriminating and potentially more lethal. Instead of the ritualised, to some extent recreational, clashes of self-selected combatants, attacks now threatened residents of both sexes and all ages, with fewer opportunities for withdrawal or retreat.[66]

Who took part in these increasingly destructive clashes? Contemporary observers used a highly charged vocabulary of respectable and rough. A report on the attacks directed against a Catholic demonstration in 1896, for example, went out of its way to exonerate the 'Islandmen', the skilled workers of the shipyard, instead blaming 'a few irresponsible rowdies from their place who took part in the attack, and they were joined by all the idle rowdies on their side in town'.[67] And it is indeed the case that much of the fighting that took place involved the unskilled and semi-skilled workers crowded into poorer districts like the Pound and Sandy Row. However, the 'Islandmen' were also more than ready to play their part, particularly when violence had a more explicit political aim. In September 1857, for example, it was shipyard workers who assembled in force to defend Protestant controversialists preaching in Custom House Square from protesting Catholics. The riots of 1864, similarly, taking place against the background of the rise of Fenianism and frustration at the denial of Protestant marching rights, pitted Protestant shipyard workers against Catholic navvies engaged in works on the harbour.[68]

The response of the Protestant middle classes to sectarian violence was complex. Many had little enthusiasm for the noisy rituals, and recurrent outbreaks of disorder, that were associated with plebeian Protestantism. That much was evident from the initial acquiescence of the Belfast municipal elite in the succession of Acts of Parliament that between 1832 and 1872 restricted Orange parades. In the long run, the rising threat of Home Rule from the 1870s onwards was to promote a new cross-class solidarity in defence of the Act of Union. But even before this occurred there was evidence of a degree of ambivalence in the face of sectarian violence. Frank Wright has shown how even liberal Protestants, initially disposed to deplore what they saw as Orange aggression, became less certain in their condemnations as the town's Catholics, in 1857 and on subsequent occasions, relinquished the role of passive victim, instead mobilising in their own defence.[69] In a revealing episode later in the century, Protestant leaders, including the Orange Grand Master of the Belfast district, the Revd R. R. Kane, were vocal in calling on their followers to simply ignore a major Nationalist commemoration of the rebellion of 1798. In the event there was serious rioting, leading to the death of a policeman and extensive violent evictions. The *Belfast News Letter*, however, insisted that the blame lay not with the rioters but with the Nationalist marchers, who had allegedly taunted their antagonists from the safety of a police cordon. It even went so far as to suggest that the police were likewise responsible for the violence they had encountered, because of their unnecessary harassment of Orange bandsmen. Meanwhile Kane, who had earlier condemned plans to attack the procession, now argued that those arrested should not be subjected to 'punishment of a vindictive nature' that took no account of the provocation they had endured.[70]

At the beginning of the twentieth century Belfast thus continued to present a contradictory face to the outside world. The imposing bulk of the new City Hall testified both to the solid prosperity and confidence of a great manufacturing centre and to the culture of civic pride characteristic of the major cities of Victorian and Edwardian Britain. All around it, however, stretched an urban landscape shaped by sectarian hostility and aggression. Civic life, too, remained fractured. The virtual exclusion of Catholics from all levels of municipal government, already documented in the official inquiries that followed the riots of 1857 and 1864, continued. In the fifty years following the implementation of municipal reform in 1844, just three Catholics were elected to serve on the Town Council. When the Council, in 1892, sought legislation to give it more control of the city's asylum for the mentally ill, and of delinquent children committed to industrial schools, Catholics presented a petition arguing that a body guilty of such blatant religious discrimination should not be entrusted, without safeguards, with control of vulnerable Catholics. The evidence they presented was damning. In 1886 an official inquiry into the violence resulting from the Home Rule Bill had already received a list of ninety officials of the Council, with a total in salaries of £14,000 a year. Of these just five were Catholics, earning between them £397. Further statistics, produced for the 1892 proceedings, found just one Catholic among the fifteen Commissioners on the Water Board, three among the Board's ninety-one employees, and none at all among the thirty-seven employees of the Harbour Board, or among the eleven officials employed by the Petty Sessions.[71]

The campaign against the Mental Hospital Bill was an indication that Belfast's Catholic population had begun to recover from the general collapse of morale that had followed the Parnell divorce case and the consequent split within the Irish Nationalist party. Three years later this revived Catholic opposition was able to score a minor political victory. The Council now sought a further Act of Parliament to extend the city's municipal boundaries to include outlying suburbs. The extension made necessary a redrawing of the boundaries for municipal elections. The Council's initial proposal was for fifteen new wards radiating outwards from the city centre, an arrangement that would have distributed the one in four Catholic voters within the enlarged city across the maximum number of districts, in none of which they could be sure of constituting a majority. A vigorous campaign of opposition, backed in Parliament by the whole body of Irish Nationalist MPs, ensured that instead two of the fifteen new wards, the Falls and Smithfield, were defined in such a way as to ensure solid Catholic majorities. The smaller and more homogenous constituencies thus created permitted the return in 1897 of eight Catholic councillors and six Labour representatives.[72] Control of the new sixty-strong Council, however, remained firmly in the hands of stridently Protestant Conservatives, made if anything more uncompromising by the token representation now given to their opponents. Within a few years, from 1910, the return to the centre of political life of the issue of Home Rule was to add further to the tension. It was against this fraught background that long-standing debates relating to control of public space were to move towards a conclusion.

Notes

1 See above, pp. 3–4.
2 The progressive character of Belfast Town Council in the first years after municipal reform was first noted in a pioneering article by Cornelius O'Leary, 'Belfast urban government in the age of reform', in David Harkness and Mary O'Dowd (eds), *The Town in Ireland* (Belfast: Appletree Press, 1981), pp. 187–202. See also S. J. Connolly, 'Belfast: the rise and fall of a civic culture?', in Olwen Purdue (ed.), *Belfast: The Emerging City 1850–1914* (Dublin: Irish Academic Press, 2013), pp. 25–48.
3 PRONI, LA/7/2EA/1, Corporation Minute Book, 22 December 1842, 10, 25 January 1843; Ian Budge and Cornelius O'Leary, *Belfast: Approach to Crisis* (London: Macmillan, 1973), p. 54.
4 *Report of the Commissioners Appointed to Enquire into the State of the Municipal Affairs of the Borough of Belfast* [hereafter *Municipal Affairs*] (PP 1859 (2470) 10), p. 13; *Captain Gilbert's Report upon the Proposed Extension of the Boundaries of the Borough of Belfast* (PP 1852–3 (958) 94), p. 13; *BNL*, 2 December 1857.
5 *Municipal Affairs*, pp. 161, 187, 215.
6 *Municipal Affairs*, pp. 63–4; *BNL*, 17 December 1847. For the cartloads of pork see *Second Report of the Commissioners Appointed to Consider and Recommend a General System of Railways for Ireland* (PP 1837–8 (145) 35), p. 26. For the visits to English markets see PRONI, LA/7/2EA/2, Council Minutes, 2 August 1847.
7 PRONI, LA/7/2EA/2, Council Minutes, 2 August 1847.

8 *Municipal Affairs*, p. 13; *BNL*, 2 December 1857.
9 A. G. Malcolm, *The Sanitary State of Belfast, with Suggestions for its Improvement* (Belfast: Belfast Social Enquiry Society, 1852), pp. 5–6.
10 Statutes 8 & 9 Victoria, c. cxlii, sections 124, 170.
11 Emrys Jones, *A Social Geography of Belfast* (London: Oxford University Press, 1960), p. 52.
12 *BNL*, 3 January 1845. For the two societies see H. G. Calwell, *Andrew Malcolm of Belfast 1818–56: Physician and Historian* (Belfast, 1977), pp. 63–70, 79–92.
13 Malcolm, *Sanitary State of Belfast*, p. 10.
14 *BNL*, 20 July, 28 August 1849; *NW*, 20 November, 11 December 1849.
15 A later enquiry attributed the Council's failure to tackle the Blackstaff problem to an issue of timing: the powers of compulsory purchase conferred by the Improvement Act of 1847 had lapsed before the power to borrow the necessary funds was granted in the Act of 1850. See *Municipal Affairs*, p. 19. For the suggestion that objections by industrialists played a part, see Budge and O'Leary, *Belfast*, p. 55.
16 *Dublin Builder*, reprinted in *The Times* (London), 6 September 1865.
17 Tristram Hunt, *Building Jerusalem: The Rise and Fall of the Victorian City* (London: Weidenfeld and Nicolson, 2004), pp. 321–38.
18 The social composition of the Council is analysed in G. J. Slater, 'Belfast politics 1798–1868' (D. Phil. dissertation, New University of Ulster, 1982), p. 341.
19 *Hansard*, vol. 31, cols 1301–8, 7 March 1836; *BNL*, 4 November 1842.
20 Above, chap. 3.
21 PRONI, D2930, R. M. Young, 'Recollections of a nonagenarian 1906–8' (typescript), pp. 86, 95.
22 *BNL*, 6 August, 17 December 1847.
23 The best overview of Belfast's architectural history remains C. E. B. Brett, *Buildings of Belfast 1700–1914* (2nd edn, Belfast: Friar's Bush Press, 1985). See also Paul Harron, 'Big vision city: the physical transformation of Belfast by provincial architects, 1870–1910', in Olwen Purdue (ed.), *Belfast: The Emerging City 1850–1914* (Dublin: Irish Academic Press, 2013), pp. 49–76.
24 Today both buildings are hotels, 10 Square on Donegall Square South and Malmaison on Victoria Street (see Figure 3).
25 PRONI, T2603/10, 15, George Dawson to Sir William Freemantle, 10 May 1850, 10 November 1851.
26 *BNL*, 18 April 1851.
27 *BNL*, 30 March 1847.
28 S. J. Connolly, 'Like an old cathedral city: Belfast welcomes Queen Victoria, August 1849', *Urban History*, 39 (2012), 571–89.
29 Malcolm, *The Sanitary State of Belfast*.
30 *NW*, 14 September 1852. For this quotation and other details I am indebted to Alice Johnson's study of the Belfast Victorian middle class, forthcoming from Liverpool University Press, which she kindly allowed me to read in draft.
31 *BNL*, 29 October 1847.
32 *NW*, 3 February 1848.
33 PRONI, D1748/G/314/24, J. E. Kidley to R. J. Tennent, 16 October 1838;

PRONI, D1748/G/242/12, Robert Grimshaw to Tennent, 12 October [1845].
34 See, for example, the explicit threat of revolt by Catholic electors, reported with glee in *BNL*, 15 March 1852.
35 *Report of the Commission of Enquiry into the Origin and Character of the Riots in Belfast in July and September 1857* [hereafter *Riots Enquiry 1857*] (PP 1857–8 (2309) 26), pp. 146–7. See Budge and O'Leary, *Belfast*, p. 57.
36 Above, pp. 39–40.
37 Jean Agnew (ed.), *The Drennan-McTier Letters* (3 vols, Dublin: Irish Manuscripts Commission, 1998–99, iii.92.
38 The best overview of the interaction of politics and sectarianism is Frank Wright, *Two Lands on One Soil: Ulster Politics before Home Rule* (Dublin: Gill and Macmillan, 1996).
39 Blackstock, though with no direct evidence, suggests a plot by Belfast liberals to discredit the Orangemen by provoking them to violence: Allan Blackstock, *Loyalism in Ireland 1789–1829* (Woodbridge: Boydell Press, 2007), p. 166.
40 *NW*, 14 July 1825.
41 Sybil Baker, 'Orange and green: Belfast 1832–1912', in H. J. Dyos and Michael Wolff (eds), *The Victorian City: Images and Realities* (2 vols, London: Routledge and Kegan Paul, 1973), ii.789–814; Catherine Hirst, *Religion, Politics and Violence in Nineteenth-century Belfast: The Pound and Sandy Row* (Dublin: Four Courts Press, 2002), chaps 2, 3; Mark Doyle, *Fighting Like the Devil for the Sake of God: Protestants, Catholics and the Origins of Violence in Victorian Belfast* (Manchester: Manchester University Press, 2009).
42 *NW*, 24 December 1832.
43 *NW*, 3 February 1848.
44 *BNL*, 5 December 1843, 29 October 1847; *Riots Enquiry 1857*, p. 243.
45 National Archives of Ireland [hereafter NAI], Outrage Papers, Co. Antrim (1849), 1/28, Memorial from Belfast Catholics, 5 February 1849; Bodleian Library Oxford, Clarendon Papers, Irish Box 18, Castlereagh to Clarendon, 29 January 1849.
46 NAI, Chief Secretary's Office, Registered Papers [hereafter CSORP], 6270 on 1858/16743, William Tracy to Thomas Larcom, 23 July 1857. For the Catholic policemen see *Riots Enquiry 1857*, pp. 81, 152, 153, 165.
47 The National Archives, Kew, HO45/7649, pp. 79–80, 91, 101, Report of Sub Inspector Rudolphus Harvey, 1 October 1864.
48 *BNL*, 19 January 1836.
49 *BNL*, 19 January, 23 December 1836.
50 For the decline of Liberalism see Gerald R. Hall, *Ulster Liberalism 1778–1876* (Dublin: Four Courts Press, 2011); John Bew, *The Glory of Being Britons: Civic Unionism in Nineteenth-century Belfast* (Dublin: Irish Academic Press, 2009).
51 *BNL*, 3 October 1871.
52 Gillian McIntosh, 'Symbolizing the civic ideal: the civic portraits in Belfast Town Hall', *Urban History*, 35:3 (2008), 363–81.
53 Lesley Donaldson, '"A street of butchers": an economic and social profile of

Hercules Place and Hercules Street, Belfast 1860–90', *Irish Economic & Social History*, 44 (2017), 102–21.
54 *BNL*, 18 September 1883.
55 Frank Frankfort Moore, *In Belfast by the Sea*, ed. Patrick Maume (Dublin: UCD Press, 2007), p. 86.
56 W. A. Maguire, *Belfast, a History* (Lancaster: Carnegie Press, 2009) provides the best overview of late nineteenth- and early twentieth-century infrastructural development.
57 *BNL*, 28 January 1891.
58 Robert Scott, *A Breath of Fresh Air: The Story of Belfast's Parks* (Belfast: Blackstaff Press, 2000).
59 Eileen Black, *Art in Belfast 1760–1888: Art Lovers or Philistines* (Dublin: Irish Academic Press, 2006), chap. 10; Don McCloy, *Creating Belfast: Technical Education and the Formation of a Great Industrial City 1801–1921* (Dublin: Nonsuch, 2009).
60 A. C. Hepburn, *Catholic Belfast and Nationalist Ireland in the Era of Joe Devlin 1871–1934* (Oxford: Oxford University Press, 2008), pp. 9–10.
61 J. V. Beckett, *City Status in the British Isles 1830–2002* (London: Routledge, 2005), pp. 43–52, 67–9.
62 For a general overview of Belfast's suburbs see Jones, *Social Geography of Belfast*, chap. 15. For Ballymacarrett see R. T. Campbell and S. A. Royle, 'East Belfast and the suburbanization of North-West County Down in the nineteenth century', in L. J. Proudfoot (ed.), *Down: History and Society, Interdisciplinary Essays on the History of an Irish County* (Dublin: Geography Publications, 1997), pp. 629–62.
63 A. C. Hepburn, *A Past Apart: Studies in the History of Catholic Belfast 1850–1950* (Belfast: Ulster Historical Foundation, 1996), p. 118; Hepburn, *Catholic Belfast and Nationalist Ireland*, p. 24.
64 Hepburn, *Catholic Belfast and Nationalist Ireland*, p. 24.
65 The National Archives, Kew, HO45/7649, Larcom to Sir George Grey, 26 August 1864.
66 Doyle, *Fighting Like the Devil for the Sake of God*, pp. 162–9.
67 NAI, CSORP, 14273 on 1912/11935, District Inspector E. Seddall, 18 August 1896.
68 For details of these conflicts, see below, pp. 96–102.
69 Wright, *Two Lands on One Soil*, p. 373.
70 *BNL*, 9 June 1898.
71 *Report of the Select Committee on the Belfast Corporation (Lunatic Asylums etc) Bill* (PP 1892 (228) 11), pp. 61–3, 125.
72 Hepburn, *Catholic Belfast and Nationalist Ireland*, pp. 43–9.

4

Freedom and order

In January 1841 the Irish nationalist leader Daniel O'Connell travelled to Belfast to hold a political rally. The visit was from the start expected to be problematic. Indeed O'Connell took the precaution of booking a coach under his own name, but then making his journey two days earlier using an assumed identity. In Belfast he was able to preside over a dinner in the adapted premises of one of the town's theatres, but then abandoned plans to hold a meeting in the same venue. Instead he attempted to address supporters from the balcony of his hotel, but was drowned out by hostile shouting as police struggled to keep Catholic Repealers and their Protestant opponents apart. Later, as he attended a soirée hosted by a charity for Catholic orphans, Protestant crowds smashed the windows, as well as attacking his hotel and the houses of known Repealers in the town. The next morning he retreated under a heavy police guard.

At first sight this episode might seem to suggest a simple continuity: the same monopoly of public space enjoyed throughout most of the twentieth century by Protestant supporters of the union with Great Britain was already being enforced in the 1840s. But appearances, in this case, are deceptive. The fifty years or so that followed O'Connell's retreat from Belfast saw major changes both to the actual contours of the urban landscape and to the rules that governed behaviour within it. It is only against this background, as well as that of a changing political environment, that Belfast's progress towards the establishment of a sectional monopoly of public space can be properly understood.

Contesting the streets

The municipal council that took power in 1842 inherited a town in which behaviour in public space was still lightly regulated. Its predecessors on the Police Committee had introduced an impressive set of by-laws, and in 1816 had created a police establishment to enforce them. But the order they maintained was by later standards minimal. Thomas Gaffikin, looking back from 1875, recalled the noisy, jostling streets and pavements of his youth, fifty years earlier:

> We had abundance of ballad-singers and musicians, who, with the old watchmen calling the hours, striking their pikes on the pavement, or springing their rattles on the slightest disturbance or report of a fire, and sweeps, oystermen, piemen, tapesellers, cries of 'Ballinderry onions' and 'Cromac water', kept up the noise from morning till night … The narrow footways were not only irregular but greatly obstructed by water and milk carriers, bakers' and butchers' baskets, bagmen with coals on their backs, sedan chairs and wheelbarrows.

Popular amusements, too, retained their often rowdy and violent character. Dog fights, cock fights, bare-knuckle boxing all took place on the traditional space provided by the Points Fields north of the city centre, as well as in the new working-class districts to the west. In 1836 there were complaints that a bear was being baited regularly in a court off May Street. Another report in the same year referred to small boys in the town centre amusing themselves by firing pistols in the streets, in one case sending a brass button through the window of a house.[1]

It was not solely plebeian indiscipline, however, that gave the streets their rumbustious character. In the first half of the nineteenth century the violence of the state was also meted out in the streets and squares of British and Irish towns. Belfast had only limited experience of public hangings. The assizes, and with them the gallows, were located in the county town of Carrickfergus. By the time they moved to Belfast in 1850 major reforms in the criminal code had sharply reduced the number of capital offences, and there were only two executions, in 1854 and 1863, before the whole procedure was transferred to the privacy of the prison yard. However, the special circumstances of the insurrection of 1798 dictated that the execution of six United Irishmen should take place in Castle Place, and that the severed heads of five of them should be displayed on the market house nearby. A similar logic inspired the hanging on the same spot of two men convicted in 1816 of attacking the house of a cotton manufacturer during an industrial dispute, while two of their confederates endured an equally public flogging, receiving 584 lashes between them, the following week.[2]

The public application of the whip and the hangman's rope reflected an official acknowledgement of the noisy and disorderly character of public space. So too did the traditional routines of electoral politics. In a ritual inherited from the days when small communities chose a representative in a face-to-face process, elections began with the hustings, where candidates addressed the crowd and the returning officer called for a show of hands. The vote was irrelevant, in that the losing side invariably called for a formal poll. But the hustings were nevertheless an important test of each side's support and morale, demonstrated by cheering, hissing and heckling, accompanied at times by attempts by one side or the other to take over the premises by force. Later the casting of votes, a public act until the coming of the secret ballot in 1872, encouraged a further gathering of supporters and the same noisy expression of support and opposition. The official ritual did not, of course, sanction serious violence. Episodes like the post-election riot of 1832, when the provocative chairing of the victorious Conservative candidates led to fighting and four deaths, put Belfast clearly outside the sphere of acceptable political behaviour. But traditional electoral practice did carry with it the message that the right to be heard in public depended in part on the capacity to assert oneself against noisy and boisterous opposition.

Seen against this background of an institutionalised jostling for control of the public stage, O'Connell's unsuccessful visit to Belfast becomes easier to understand. Opponents were to mock his unsuccessful visit as arrogant overreach. But in fact he appears to have been all too aware of the risk of humiliation presented by this foray into hostile territory. A letter to his Belfast supporters in advance of the visit warned them against ostentation, and he later, it appears, criticised them for not taking his advice.[3] His opponents, it is important to note, did not deny his right to appear in the town. The *Belfast News Letter*, responding to the first news of the impending visit, acknowledged that the town's Repealers 'are entitled to have their dinner and their after dinner manifestations', adding only that, at a time when the Orange order was not allowed to hold public processions, the same restrictions should apply to the Repeal movement.[4] The Presbyterian leader Henry Cooke issued a public challenge to O'Connell to debate the Repeal issue with him in front of an audience to be equally divided between supporters of the two men. But when, instead, noisy crowds prevented O'Connell from speaking at all, Conservative leaders displayed no discomfort or embarrassment. On the contrary, Cooke and others immediately afterwards organised a triumphant counter demonstration, bringing together an assembly of peers, landowners, MPs, clergymen and other leading citizens to celebrate O'Connell's retreat in the face of the licensed disorder of their plebeian supporters.[5]

In 1848, as political tensions mounted following the death of O'Connell and the secession from the Repeal movement of the radical Young Ireland faction, there were further illustrations of the ambiguous balance between a commitment to free speech and an acceptance of politics as a form of competitive public theatre. In April the mayor, in response to a requisition, convened a meeting in the court-house to draw up a declaration of loyalty. The reversion to the traditional language of the town meeting was possibly deliberate, on an occasion where leading Liberals joined with Conservatives in repudiating Chartist and Young Ireland radicalism. But when Repeal supporters tried to take the idea of a meeting of inhabitants at face value by asserting their right to speak, they were told that the occasion was only for those friendly to the declared object. One of their number, the bumptious solicitor John Rea, later to be the instrument of John Bates's downfall, was physically ejected when he tried to claim a space on the platform. A week earlier the Young Irelanders had tried to hold a meeting in the town's theatre, only to be excluded by police and a magistrate after the building's owner had withdrawn his permission. They adjourned to a yard used to keep horses and lumber, where Rea was drenched with a fire hose as he made an inflammatory speech about the right to bear arms. The Conservative *Belfast News Letter* celebrated 'the happy idea' of 'extinguishing the ardour of their eloquence' with 'a thorough ducking'. The town's main Liberal paper, on the other hand, expressed concern 'upon public grounds' about this use of municipal equipment, pointing out that if men in office were allowed to disperse even foolish people contrary to law, they could do the same to others assembled for a proper purpose.[6]

All these were cases where the Protestant majority used force of numbers to stifle the expression of Catholic and nationalist views. But the most dramatic illustration of the rough-and-tumble character of Belfast's street politics involved a quite different conflict. In November 1847 some of the Dublin leaders of Young Ireland had sought to hold a meeting in Belfast. On this occasion, however, the vocal and physical opposition did not come from Belfast Protestants, who seemed willing to give these southern (and in some cases Protestant) visitors a more polite reception than their own local (and almost invariably Catholic) nationalists. Instead it was plebeian Catholics, with the butchers of Hercules Street allegedly at the forefront, who turned out to demonstrate their loyalty to the recently deceased O'Connell, and their hostility to a party whose attacks on him they blamed for having helped to bring about his death. The visitors' first assembly, in the music hall on May Street, ended in chaos as constables with fixed bayonets intervened to clear the hall of hostile interlopers. Three days later, attempting to get to a second meeting at the Theatre Royal in Arthur Square, the platform party was forced off the pavement, driven back into Castle Place, and forced to retreat to its hotel in Donegall Place. A third meeting the next day, in the same venue, got under way but had to be abandoned when speakers found themselves drowned out by a barrage of noise from heckling, exploding firecrackers, bird-calls and watchmen's rattles.[7]

This background is also relevant to an understanding of Belfast's distinctive pattern of sectarian violence.[8] Discussion has tended to be dominated by the murderous armed conflicts that were to take place in the early 1920s, and again from 1969. Seen without the benefit of hindsight, however, the clashes that took place in the 1840s and 1850s can be recognised as largely an extension of the generally rough and unregulated character of interaction in public space. Violence was casual, random and unstructured. A typical incident in 1849 involved some carters who decorated their horses with orange lilies and then came under attack, as they drove through Ballymacarrett, from Catholic navvies working on the harbour improvements nearby.[9] Even the more serious disturbances of 1857, in their first phase at least, were a curious mixture of real violence and aimless rowdiness. Their location was the working-class district west of the town centre, where Durham Street linked the Protestant Sandy Row and the Catholic Pound. Here, on a succession of evenings following the local Orange society's Twelfth of July gathering, the inhabitants engaged in running battles with one another and with the police. There were distinctly ugly incidents. Catholics and Protestants crossing hostile territory on their way to work were beaten and abused, and householders living in areas dominated by the other religion were forced to leave or had their houses wrecked. But there was also much theatrical display. Both sides, in particular, used firearms. They did so, however, by trading shots back and forth along almost the whole length of Durham Street, minimising the risk to themselves or their opponents. The resident magistrate, William Tracy, dismissed the gunplay as mere 'bravado', with guns being loaded with ball as well as powder only because this was believed to result in a louder report. His assessment seems to be borne out by the almost complete absence of reported casualties. (The only exception was two children wounded by a Protestant gunman who, for whatever reason, stalked and shot them – a malicious act, but an isolated one.)[10]

The lack of serious purpose was also evident in other respects. Both sides made occasional incursions into each other's territory. But there were also ritualistic confrontations on the waste ground and open fields that adjoined the newly constructed streets. Here too shots could safely be traded at long range. 'I do not think they wanted to get near each other,' Tracy commented in his report of one such episode. 'I think they were glad of our arrival, for they scampered off ...'. Another witness described the ritual exchange of insults on waste ground adjoining Quadrant Street, where Protestants calling out 'Down with pope and popery', 'To hell with the pope', and 'To hell with the pope's grandfather', were taunted in their turn:

> There were twenty girls of the Catholic party formed themselves into a ring, and they reeled round up and down the road ... and they were singing some song. ... The chorus was
>
> Hurrah for Mullan's corner
> And to hell with Sandy-row
> And the devil build Sandy-Row up.[11]

If sectarian violence was often vicious and destructive, there was clearly also a recreational element that reflected its place as part of a plebeian culture not yet domesticated by urban by-laws and police enforcement and surveillance.

Regulating public space

In Belfast, as in other British cities, the middle decades of the nineteenth century saw major changes in the management of public space. The new Council elected in 1842 quickly took up the work of regulating everyday behaviour that had been commenced by its predecessors on the Police Board. The first Improvement Act, in 1845, reiterated and gave statutory force to many of the Board's regulations. Householders were still expected on pain of a fine to sweep the path in front of their doors. Drivers of carts were still to go no faster than 'a common walk'. There were also new restrictions. Householders, for example, could be fined for placing a flower pot or box at an upper window without sufficient precautions against it being dislodged. It also became an offence to fly a kite, 'trundle any hoop' or play other games to the annoyance of others, or to make or use a slide on ice or snow 'to the common danger of the passengers'.[12] Much of this activity represented the common-sense rules of behaviour required to allow life to go on in an increasingly crowded urban space. But there were also regulations designed to impose a particular standard of decorum. In Belfast as elsewhere the opening up of new types of public space, in which people of all classes mingled, inspired a fresh drive to define what sorts of behaviour were and were not acceptable in these shared venues.

The change in attitude was particularly clear in the case of drunkenness. Here the shift in policy had already begun before municipal reform. A report in 1836 noted 201 convictions for drunkenness between the end of August and the middle of October.[13] Police court reports from the 1840s and after reveal a continuing stream of offenders detained overnight and fined for the same reason. In August 1846, for example, 'about twenty unfortunate topers' were fined for having been drunk at a fair in the town.[14] Incomplete official statistics confirm the scale of prosecutions. Between 1841 and 1851 convictions for drunkenness or disorderly conduct averaged 2,426 per year. This was substantially less than Cork, where there were 5,035 arrests per year in roughly the same population. But arrests on this scale were in sharp contrast to thirty years earlier, when the voluntary watch had escorted inebriated citizens to their homes. Statistics after 1851 relate to the different category of persons arrested for drunkenness combined with disorderly conduct. But these indicate a further decline in tolerance, with committals rising from 3.5 per 1,000 inhabitants in 1851 to 5.4 in 1861 and 11.5 in 1871. In the twelve months between May 1885 and April 1886 the number arrested for drunkenness alone was 382.[15]

Publicans too felt the effects of the new spirit of regulation. In 1853 magistrates agreed to tighten up the procedure for granting licences, reducing the number of public houses in the town from over 800 to 550. About the same time a group based in the Church of Ireland parish vestry, using dormant legislation from the 1830s, revived the practice of appointing overseers to visit public houses and ensure that they observed licensing hours. Some of the publicans responded by hiring the radical lawyer John Rea to challenge what they claimed was a campaign of harassment. They also petitioned the Lord Lieutenant, alleging that the 'moral reformers' behind the campaign were in fact driven by the rewards paid for convictions and the subscriptions extorted, under threat of prosecution, from publicans themselves. The resident magistrate, William Tracy, asked to report on the petition, wholeheartedly backed the reformers. Prior to the reduction in licences, he claimed, the great majority of public houses had been 'nothing better than licensed brothels, and meeting places for thieves and vagabonds', while even now no more than fifty of the reduced number could be considered 'in the ordinary sense of the term, as being respectable'. One obvious point, discreetly left unmentioned on all sides, was that the campaign pitted mainly Catholic publicans against Protestant temperance advocates, and it is possibly for this reason that the overseer scheme was discontinued after 1855, despite the continued evident concern with drunkenness.[16]

A second regular feature of police court business was prosecutions for playing games in the street. In line with the provisions of the 1845 Improvement Act, children were prosecuted for throwing snowballs or making slides, and more frequently for playing ball games on the street. The most common offence, however, was playing pitch and toss. Since the offence in this case involved gambling as well as obstructing the public thoroughfare, prosecutions took place even where the accused had assembled in a field or other open place. An added dimension was that many offences had taken place on a Sunday; one prosecuting constable in 1862 noted specifically that 'people going to their places of worship were very much annoyed by the party in which the prisoners were conspicuous'.[17] Other gatherings for amusement were likewise criminalised. In 1849, for example, two men were fined for having met for a boxing match in a field adjoining the newly built Crumlin Road court-house and prison, and later jailed when they failed to pay.[18]

The instrument by which the municipal authorities imposed this strict new discipline was the police force created in 1816. The number of constables rose from 80 in 1834 to 165 in 1858. Internal discipline was poor: the minutes of the Council police committee record a steady succession of cases of drunkenness, neglect of duty and, on occasion, corruption.[19] The methods by which they kept order were correspondingly harsh. Even the loyal crowds that gathered to greet Queen Victoria in 1849 were controlled with an aggression that horrified one English newspaper reporter: 'in clearing the streets the police did their duty with something which I am strongly tempted to call brutality; ... All day long batons and switches were falling upon the shoulders and faces of sturdy struggling malcontents.'[20] The real key to the imposition of a new level of order, however, was surveillance. Both day and night components of the force patrolled constantly. From the 1830s there were also plain-clothes officers. As in other towns, the constant presence of patrolling police encouraged a culture of counter surveillance as publicans, gamblers and others maintained their own lookouts. A witness before the commission of inquiry into the riots of 1857, speaking of juvenile troublemakers, put the matter succinctly: 'Oh, they watch the police just as well as the police watch them. They have their time for that.'[21]

Arrangements for policing changed radically in 1865, when the government intervened to disband the Belfast Town Police, widely condemned for its partisan conduct during the riots of 1857 and 1864, replacing it with an allocation from the Irish (after 1867 the Royal Irish) Constabulary. Unlike the almost entirely Protestant Town Police, the new force was to be mixed, though with a small Protestant majority to reflect the balance within the town. The style of policing, however, did not change radically. In fact a major source of contention in the decades that followed was the insistence of the Town Council that the police should continue the policy of rigorously enforcing minor by-laws and prosecuting offenders, regardless of the impact on relations with the public.[22] Surveillance also remained important, although one correspondent to the *Belfast News Letter*, in 1898, complained that the constabulary, where even plain-clothes officers were drawn from a force organised and trained along military lines, was ill suited to this role. '[A]nd as to their efficiency, why any corner boy can "spot" a straight-backed detective anywhere, and "can keep him safe".'[23]

From the 1840s onwards, then, the working-class population of Belfast found itself subject to largely new rules of behaviour. People were prevented from gathering in crowds for amusements or sporting events, adults and children were fined for playing games on the street, public houses were subjected to a new regime of inspection and their clients locked up and fined if they walked home visibly the worse for drink. The law was not wholly inflexible. In June 1857, for example, Tracy dismissed a case against two mill-workers accused of having run along the banks of the River Lagan 'in a state of nudity', after their lawyer pointed out that 'it was a great pity that there was no proper bathing place for young lads like the prisoners'.[24] Yet the zeal with which many cases were pursued suggests a concern not just for the efficient functioning of urban life but for the imposition of new standards of decorum. In some instances, indeed, the aim was unambiguously to impose by coercion the deference so easily undermined by the anonymity of a large urban centre. In 1848 a coal porter was fined five shillings for remonstrating with a gentleman who had promised to employ him but then hired another, and for telling the fickle customer 'that he might go to –'. The following year, when a cab driver was prosecuted for refusing to take a passenger a mile out of town for the standard fare, telling him to 'go to hell for a pup', the Council agreed to suspend his licence for two months, as 'we are determined to protect gentlemen from such insults'. In other cases too it was the Council that intervened to threaten cab drivers and porters with the loss of their licences following allegations of offensive language or other forms of 'insolence'.[25]

For those on the receiving end of such regulation the activities of the courts and the police represented an assault on already impoverished opportunities for leisure and amusement. With the physical expansion of the town access to open space – which did not in any case provide immunity from police attention – became more difficult, leaving the streets as the only convenient playground for children and adults alike. The prohibition of Sunday amusements ignored the reality of what remained up to the 1860s a six-day working week. The new system of regulation thus aroused real resentment. In 1854 the mother of a boy fined £1 for playing pitch-and-toss on a back street on a Sunday was expelled from court, and threatened with arrest, for protesting to the magistrate. A year earlier the arrest of two young men for the same offence in Hercules Street precipitated a minor riot, in which the police were pelted with stones and brickbats as they sought to detain the offenders.[26] In other cases too, assaults on policemen, in some cases escalating into full-scale riots, testified to the hostility which their activities created.[27]

Alongside the official narrative of 'improvement' in mid-nineteenth-century Belfast it is thus necessary to put a parallel account of the coercive reshaping of popular culture to create inhabitants better suited to the demands of the new urban environment. The harshness of the attack is all the more remarkable because by this time other influences were at work, promoting very much the same changes in behaviour and attitude. In the first place the response to middle-class educational ventures such as the Mechanics Institute, established in 1828, the Working Classes Association (1846) and the Belfast Working Men's Institute (1866) testifies to the strong impulse towards self-improvement within the culture of the working classes themselves; some of the strongest opponents of blood sports, gambling, alcohol and other 'rough' elements in popular life, as has long been recognised, came from the ranks of serious-minded trade unionists and working-class radicals.[28] Religion, strengthened by the rise of evangelicalism among Protestants and by the intensification of popular piety known as the 'devotional revolution' among Catholics, was another powerful influence working in the same direction.[29]

Social change was also important. The shortening of working hours, in particular the spread from the 1860s of the Saturday half holiday, followed by the creation of the bank holiday and eventually the concession of a paid summer holiday, radically altered the pattern of work and leisure. Instead of long periods of toil and frugal living, punctuated by short, explosive periods of release, life moved to a more even rhythm between labour and free time. Meanwhile the growing commercialisation of leisure, made possible by slowly rising living standards, imposed its own restraints. Behaviour that might be acceptable in the drinking dens denounced by Tracy became less so among the bright lights and polished mirrors of the gin palace or music hall. Commercialisation also meant a transition from the rough and tumble of participatory sports to the more regimented world of the spectator. Here the founding in 1880 of the Irish Football Association marked a turning point in Belfast's working-class culture.[30]

The transformation being wrought in public behaviour by a combination of policing, cultural change and the reshaping of the urban environment can be easily seen by following the development of Belfast's most important popular festival, Easter Monday. At the beginning of the nineteenth century large crowds gathered on the slopes of Cave Hill outside the town for what was at that stage Belfast's only regular festive event. The crowds were large, and there are clear references to the sale of drink, as well as to the traditional children's custom of rolling coloured eggs down the hill. Yet, as early as 1847 the *Belfast News Letter* wrote approvingly of the 'well dressed and orderly' crowd seen on the road to the hill, and noted that only five persons had been arrested for drunkenness. Meanwhile the Belfast Natural History and Philosophical Society began in 1845 to open its museum to working-class visitors on Easter Monday, at a reduced charge of two pence, recording 1,200 attendances the first year, and 2,000 by 1847. From 1851 much of the holiday crowd began to forsake Cave Hill for the more sophisticated entertainment available at the Queen's Island, the flat expanse of reclaimed land created by recent harbour improvements, where visitors paying a penny admission, and another penny for the ferry, could enjoy a small zoo, an amusement arcade and other facilities.[31]

The Queen's Island pleasure garden disappeared after 1879, eaten up by the expansion of Harland and Wolff's shipyard. But already by that time its clientele were reportedly country folk attracted by its former reputation. The more sophisticated city dwellers instead chose from a range of alternative entertainments: two pantomimes at the Theatre Royal, a circus in the Ulster Hall and a special programme at the Alhambra music hall. For those who preferred the open air there were the Botanic Gardens, normally open only to shareholders and subscribers, but on Easter Monday admitting visitors for a small fee, and offering races, displays of acrobatics and an exhibition of swordsmanship and boxing by soldiers from the local garrison.[32] Easter Monday in Belfast was still a day for pleasure and sociability, and for large assemblies in the open air. But instead of a jostling crowd drinking and dancing on a hillside above the town, there was now the staid enjoyment of commercialised spectacle, or an orderly strolling, probably in family groups, between lawns and flowerbeds, under the watchful eyes of park-keepers. What was on display was a discipline partly imposed by coercive regulation, partly developed in response to changing circumstances and opportunities, but in both cases a product of the requirements of large-scale urban living.

Party processions

The reshaping of codes of public behaviour that thus took place in the middle decades of the century had major implications for the culture of political parading. But the impact of that broader context is masked by a sharp, legally imposed discontinuity. In 1832, in response to the recurrent violence arising from Twelfth of July and other celebrations in different parts of Ireland, the government had introduced a Processions Act. This made it illegal to hold any assembly 'for the purpose of celebrating or commemorating any festival, anniversary or political event relating to or connected with any religious or other distinctions or differences between any classes of His Majesty's subjects'.[33] The Act lapsed in 1844, but was re-imposed in 1850 following a particularly bloody clash at Dolly's Brae near Castlewellan, County Down on 12 July 1849. A Party Emblems Act in 1860 introduced further limitations on the exhibition of flags and banners and the playing of music.

The sweeping restrictions imposed by this body of legislation set the emerging public spaces of Victorian Ireland clearly apart from those of the rest of the United Kingdom. The enforcement of the legislation, however, was in practice pragmatic. In the overwhelmingly Catholic southern counties the police generally ignored nationalist parades, even those organised by the militantly nationalist Fenians. The same tolerance extended to Protestant processions in predominantly Protestant areas. In Belfast, however, as in other religiously mixed areas where there was a real threat to public order, the law was rigorously enforced. Between 1850 and 1867 more than 500 Protestants were convicted for violations on the Twelfth of July or other occasions.[34] Resentment at what was seen as the double standards thus obtaining came violently to the surface in 1864. Belfast Catholics returning by train from the elaborate ceremonies accompanying the laying of the foundation of a monument in Dublin to Daniel O'Connell, another major nationalist event allowed to proceed unimpeded, were met by hostile demonstrations as they arrived, initiating seven days of violence in which nine people died.[35] Shortly afterwards Protestant discontent found a political voice. William Johnston, a minor County Down landlord, led a large Twelfth of July parade to the seaside town of Bangor in 1867, then steadfastly rejected the government's desperate attempt to avoid having to impose a custodial sentence. Jailed for two months, he emerged as an Orange martyr, and went on to contest the next general election in Belfast, defeating the official Conservative candidate. In 1872, following a continued campaign of protest, the government repealed the laws governing 'party processions'.[36]

The new legal dispensation had its first test in the summer of 1872. On 12 July members of 100 Belfast Orange lodges walked in procession from Great Victoria Street to Belvoir Park, carrying flags and banners and accompanied by music. The day passed without incident: evidence from other centres suggests that organisers made a concerted effort to avoid having their new-found liberty called into question by aggressive or disorderly conduct.[37] Two months later Belfast Catholics, in what was generally recognised as a bid to assert their equal rights of access to public space, organised their own parade. The occasion was a religious festival: 15 August, the Feast of the Assumption, more commonly referred to by the traditional English title of Lady Day. The content, however, was blatantly political. Marchers, estimated to number 20,000, carried banners showing the republican image of the harp without the crown, along with depictions of the nationalist heroes Robert Emmet and Patrick Sarsfield. They did not attempt to march through the town centre, but instead set out for Hannahstown, a hamlet of six or seven houses whose situation on the slopes of the Antrim plateau made it a convenient destination from west Belfast. But Protestant counter demonstrators nevertheless attacked the procession as it left, and again on its return. Later that day, and in the days that followed, Protestant crowds tried to invade Catholic areas. The fighting, involving the free use of firearms, continued for over a week. Official figures counted 247 houses wrecked or damaged, and 837 families forced from their homes in a further tightening of residential segregation.[38]

The immediate result of the repeal of the Party Processions Act was thus to throw open, in a radical and alarming manner, the whole question of the access to public space of groups parading their religious and political allegiance. To the London *Times* the behaviour of the Protestant counter demonstrators was a clear violation of basic principles.

> They cannot admit that impartial justice requires that if one party be allowed to flourish Orange flags and play 'The Protestant boys', the other party ought to be allowed to flaunt the 'Green flag of Erin' and play 'Garryowen' and 'God save Ireland'. … The broad fact … remains that on the 12th of July and 12th of August the Orange party were allowed to have their demonstrations without interruption, and on the 15th of August the Roman Catholic party were obstructed and attacked.[39]

Such comments, from an organ wholly out of sympathy with the political aspirations of Belfast nationalists, is vivid testimony to the dominance that the principle of free access to public space had attained in mid-Victorian British culture. (It can also, of course, be read as evidence of the continued failure of Orangeism to attain the political respectability it craved.) *The Times*, however, spoke from the security of liberal London. In Belfast, where disputes of this kind increasingly had lethal outcomes, what transpired was a period of uncertainty as conflicting principles of civil liberty, public order and political legitimacy jostled for primacy against a background of growing political instability.

The immediate response of the municipal authorities to the violence of

Lady Day 1872 was to impose a new set of regulations, issued on the authority of the mayor, James Henderson, prohibiting processions of any kind involving music or the display of flags within the boundaries of the borough. For the next three years Orangemen celebrating the Twelfth of July assembled in processional order on the outskirts of the municipality, at Connswater in 1873, Lower Windsor in 1874 and the Lisburn Road in 1875, unfurling their flags and striking up music only as they marched towards a 'field' outside the town. Placards calling for another march to Hannahstown in 1873 likewise insisted that there would be no flags or emblems displayed within the municipal area. In the event, the march was abandoned when only small numbers turned up, and the attempt was not repeated in the next two years.[40] By 1876, however, this self-restraint had begun to break down. The Twelfth of July processionists once again assembled on the edge of town, at York Street, to march to Carnmoney. Two months earlier, however, in an event that drew Orangemen from all over Ulster, a massive procession had made its way, with flags and music, down the Lisburn Road and into Great Victoria Street to witness the unveiling of a statue to Henry Cooke, the champion of Presbyterian rights and Protestant unity who had died in 1868. In 1877 the main Twelfth of July demonstration was in the Botanic Gardens. The *Belfast News Letter* announced proudly that the Orangemen had 'arranged to organise their procession and have their entire line of march through portions of the town and suburbs occupied chiefly by Protestants'. In practice this seems to have meant simply that they avoided the main Catholic districts, since the same report described them 'passing along the principal thoroughfares of the town, their handsome banners and fliers raised aloft'.[41]

As the mayor's restrictions on parading lost their force, the contest for processional rights resumed. In August 1876 Catholics held their first Lady Day parade in four years, proceeding from Smithfield through the central thoroughfare of Victoria Street, High Street and Castle Place before marching on to Hannahstown. Once again the parade was overtly political rather than liturgical, with green flags and banners depicting nationalist heroes, and the resolutions proposed at Hannahstown called for Home Rule and the release of Fenian prisoners. There was no repeat of the violence of 1872, but the procession came under attack at three separate points from stone throwers, causing a range of injuries.[42] The following year, ignoring the opposition of their own clergy, Catholic leaders organised a march to mark the birthday of Daniel O'Connell on 6 August. During the march itself police and soldiers largely succeeded in preventing violence, but there was one outbreak of hand-to-hand fighting between marchers and opponents from the Shankill Road, and clashes between stone-throwing crowds continued for several days.[43]

This upsurge in competitive parading, commencing in the 1870s and continuing into subsequent decades, was a direct result of the repeal of the Party

Processions legislation. Equally clearly, much of its energy, and its potential for violence, derived from the fraught political background created by Fenianism and the rise of the Home Rule movement. But some part was also played by the changes that by this time were taking place in the culture of the urban working classes. In contrast to the fast-growing but chaotic shock city of earlier decades, the mature industrial economy of the late nineteenth century supported more stable patterns of both employment and residence, allowing a richer social life to grow up around neighbourhood and workplace. Slowly rising living standards, following the hard years of the 1840s, also helped to increase the opportunities available. So too did the progressive reduction in working hours, including the spread of the Saturday half holiday. Against this background new associations spread rapidly. Football clubs, for example, took shape from the 1860s, and by 1881 the sport was organised enough to permit the establishment of an Irish cup. Friendly societies also thrived, offering both mutual insurance and a supplement to the informal sociability of the local pub and shop. The Orange lodges that took to the streets with such enthusiasm after 1872, and the Catholic and nationalist groups that set out to emulate or challenge them, were clearly part of this broader development, at the same time that they sought to advertise and defend a particular set of political and confessional values.

This link with the rise of a new associational culture was particularly evident in the clashes that arose from band parades. Bands had always been a part of Orange parades, and of the outings of their Catholic and nationalist imitators. But in the summer of 1878 there were growing complaints of a new development: individual bands that sallied forth on their own accord, accompanied by sometimes aggressive groups of supporters, to play music through the streets on Sundays and during the long, bright evenings. In doing so, they were not alone. In other Irish cities too marching bands, associated with trade associations and with the temperance movement, had been common since at least the first half of the nineteenth century. But the 1870s and 1880s seem to have seen a proliferation of new bands, generally fife and drum ensembles rather than the more expensive brass band, in cities throughout Ireland. Nor was it only in Belfast that their appearance gave rise to problems of public order. In Cork a dispute in 1879 over payment for performing at a wedding set off a cycle of confrontations between rival groups of bandsmen and their supporters, leading to the deaths of two men in violence that continued over several years. In Limerick during 1894–95 similar clashes were in part due to the fracturing of the Nationalist party into pro- and anti-Parnell factions, but also involved bands representing two distinct localities inhabited by the city's fishermen.[44] But in the case of Belfast this potential for factional rivalry, as noisy and assertive groups closely linked to particular districts took to the streets, was exacerbated by political and sectarian animosities that raised tensions to a wholly different level.

As complaints mounted the mayor, Sir John Preston, made a second attempt to return to a policy of legal suppression. On 7 August he issued a proclamation banning bands and processions from the streets of the borough. This was too late to affect the Twelfth of July parade, which had passed off peacefully. Catholics, in obedience to the proclamation, made no attempt to organise a Lady Day procession in the town. From the other side of the religious divide, however, there were immediate complaints that the ban curtailed Sunday School and church outings, and critics alleged that the mayor had exceeded his powers. Matters came to a head when the shipyard workers announced their intention to defy what they denounced as an infringement of their constitutional liberties by marching with their accustomed flags and banners when they held their annual holiday excursion on 24 August. Faced with this threat from the town's largest and most formidable body of male workers, the mayor and council backed down. A hastily arranged meeting of magistrates agreed that the ban had now served its purpose by restoring peace and should therefore be withdrawn.[45]

The victory of the shipyard workers in August 1878 marked the end of any legal restraint on Orange marching rights in Belfast. But in fact by this time the status of the annual Twelfth of July demonstration had passed well beyond mere toleration. The *Belfast Morning News*, reporting on the 1878 celebrations, noted that the sound of drumming could be heard throughout the town, and that major streets were impassable. In addition, factories, workshops and warehouses were closed for the day, and 'even those who could have no faith in the Orange articles of belief were fain to drop their employment and issue forth in crowds "to see the show"'.[46] Orange parades, in other words, had become part of the civic culture of Belfast. The Twelfth of July in subsequent years was to follow the same pattern, with parades passing freely through city centre streets, and the town's trade suspended for the day.

This acceptance of Orangeism as a recognised part of the town's civic ritual represented a remarkable recovery. The movement's reputation had reached its lowest point in the mid-1830s. Following an official inquiry that had pitilessly documented the movement's record of sectarian aggression, the Grand Lodge of Ireland dissolved itself in 1836 rather than endure the humiliation of being suppressed. Orangeism survived as a popular movement, but subdued in its public manifestations and stripped of middle- and upper-class endorsement. Even in Belfast, despite the rise in sectarian animosities evident from the 1840s if not earlier, the Protestant middle classes remained inclined to regard the disorderly plebeian rituals of the Twelfth of July as a threat or an embarrassment. The journalist Frankfort Moore, born in Belfast in 1855, later recalled that in his youth the Orangemen were regarded as the equivalent of noisy children, and their Twelfth of July parades as 'an unmitigated nuisance – a perpetual menace to the peace and comfort of people who only wanted to be left alone'.[47]

Frankfort Moore's comments do much to explain the attempts of Henderson and Preston to restore the restrictions on Orange and other processions formerly imposed by the Party Processions Act. By the late 1870s, however, Orangeism had established its right to unrestricted access to public space. The reasons for its triumph were in part political. Frankfort Moore himself dated the change in middle-class Protestant perceptions to the Home Rule crisis of 1885–86, when the noisy children became a potentially valuable defence against the forces of Catholic nationalism. Well before that, however, the appearance first of Fenianism and then of a Home Rule movement had begun to modify attitudes to unruly but vigorous displays of plebeian loyalism. In addition, and probably more important, the 1860s saw a shift in the balance of power within Belfast Conservatism. By this time continued economic progress, especially in shipbuilding and engineering, had boosted the numbers of skilled workers. This relatively prosperous and politically assertive group were the main beneficiaries of the second electoral Reform Act, in 1868, which reduced the property valuation required of voters from £8 to £4. The Belfast electorate rose from 3,415 in 1865 to 12,168 by 1868, with about 7,000 of the new voters created by franchise reform, the remainder by an extension of the constituency boundaries.[48] It was the support of this working-class elite, coordinated through a Protestant Working Men's Association created in 1868, that allowed William Johnston successfully to challenge the Conservative candidates in the general election of that year. The Mayor and Council's surrender, ten years later, to the shipyard workers was a further acknowledgement that the demands of what was now referred to as 'Orange democracy' could no longer be ignored.

Alongside this shift in political relationships, the new respectability of the Twelfth of July also reflected changes in the character of Orangeism itself. By the 1860s several decades of pressure from more intensive policing, and from temperance and other moral reformers, along with the influence on the working classes themselves of higher living standards and new social aspirations, had done much to tame a boisterous, unruly plebeian culture. Against this background the proceedings of the Orange Order began to assume a new ethos of self-conscious respectability. In 1861, for example, brethren assembled in the music hall to welcome members of the Grand Lodge, holding their annual meeting in the town. According to the *Belfast News Letter*:

> The numbers present of respectable citizens, of intelligent artisans – all stalwart men wearing their insignia of office – showed the strength of the loyal Orange Institution in this town, and the earnestness and zeal of its members and their attachment to the cause in which they are united.[49]

The same change in tone was evident in the Twelfth of July demonstrations. Where their predecessors had straggled along the road behind crude banners, frequently discharging blank pistols as they went, the Orange processionists, empowered by the repeal of the Party Processions Act, prided themselves on the smartness of their suits, while the banners they carried, and the bands that accompanied them, were now specimens of a well-developed popular art form.[50]

An essential part of this new respectability, and of the legitimacy it brought with it, was that the Twelfth of July celebrations themselves no longer led, as they had repeatedly done in earlier decades, to serious violence. The sheer scale of the mobilisation involved, along with police protection, ensured that the event passed off peacefully. The 1884 procession, which came under attack from stone throwers, was in this respect an exception.[51] Violence involving Orange processionists generally took place after the main procession had broken up, as individuals or groups made their way home. Alternatively, it arose from the separate outings of bands, of the kind that Preston had sought to curb in 1878.

In contrast to the acceptance now enjoyed by Orange parades, the status of Catholic and nationalist events remained unclear. When a second 15 August procession was announced for 1876, after the hiatus created by Henderson's ruling, the *Belfast News Letter* went so far as to suggest that it should not be permitted. A public celebration of Lady Day was 'an infringement of propriety in a thoroughly Protestant town'. On the other hand, William Johnston, who had always insisted that his campaign against the Party Processions Act was in defence of the marching rights of all parties, came forward to call for the event to proceed unimpeded. The leadership of the other main Protestant organisation in Ulster, the Apprentice Boys of Derry, took a similar stand.[52] Thereafter there seems to have been a general acceptance that Catholic and nationalist events had to be permitted. Yet they continued to be subject to both formal and informal constraints. In the case of the O'Connell anniversary demonstration in August 1877, police vetoed a planned circuit through the town centre, along Donegall Street, Victoria Street and Castle Place, instead requiring the procession to proceed directly from west Belfast to Hannahstown. When violence nevertheless followed, the Catholic-owned but moderate *Belfast Morning News* complained that the police and military were disproportionately deployed against the Catholic crowds, alleging that the constabulary themselves objected to the partisan use being made of them by magistrates.[53] In March 1879 Catholic activists, again ignoring their clergy and middle-class leaders, sought to insist that a St Patrick's Day procession should be allowed to pass through the town centre, as the Orange parade had done the previous July. Police refused permission, leading to a violent clash. On this occasion, however, the issue was not the demand for access to the centre, but an approach route that would take the processionists past the Protestant working-class district of Millfield. The following year Lady Day marchers were permitted to pass through the heart of the town, proceeding from Oxford Street through High Street and Castle Place before entering west Belfast and taking the road to Hannahstown. A massive police operation, sealing off points of entry and clearing the streets concerned of bystanders, ensured that the march went off peacefully. But elsewhere in the town there were attacks on Catholic houses, and violent clashes between rival crowds, some involving firearms, continued over several days.[54]

For over a decade thereafter wider political events pushed the issue of marching rights into the background. During 1881–82, against the background of a land agitation that for a time united Catholic and Protestant tenants, the Twelfth of July passed uncontentiously while nationalists abstained from marching on Lady Day. The 15 August observances remained in abeyance for the next three years, although in 1884 a flute band, accompanied by 200–300 supporters, proceeded along the edge of the town centre, from Cromac Street through Victoria Street, Ann Street and Oxford Street, before taking the train to Lurgan.[55] During the summer of 1886 the introduction and defeat of the first Home Rule Bill inspired three months of street fighting, leading to more than thirty deaths. The Twelfth of July parade went ahead as normal, and without incident, further confirming the extent to which the event had been lifted out of its former context of overt confrontation. Catholic civic leaders and clergymen agreed to a request that there should be no 15 August observances. On the other hand, the funeral procession of a young man killed by rampaging shipyard workers in the first days of the violence proceeded from Ballymacarrett, across the Queen's Bridge and through the centre of the town, to the cemetery in west Belfast. Its peaceful progress possibly reflected a degree of embarrassment on the Protestant side at the shocking nature of this early killing.[56]

In the years after 1886 Catholic processional activity continued at what was initially a fairly low level. Lady Day continued to be observed in other Ulster centres, but there were no further demonstrations in Belfast. By 1891, according to the *Belfast News Letter* 'the 15th August and its old associations seem of late to have gone out of favour in this city'.[57] Instead, Catholic demonstrations were more clearly political in focus. As such they received differing levels of licence, depending on the nature of the challenge they presented to official political values. In 1890 members of two bands were arrested and prosecuted when they attempted to mark the anniversary of the execution of the Manchester martyrs.[58] The bands had not attempted to enter the city centre, but had left west Belfast for Hannahstown in carriages, playing music as they went. They were prosecuted on the grounds that their performance was likely to cause a breach of the peace either on their route out of the city or at Hannahstown itself. On St Patrick's Day 1894, on the other hand, two bands from Ballymacarrett passed through the city centre to the Falls district, accompanied by a large crowd, without interference from the attending police.[59]

Notes

1. Thomas Gaffikin, *Belfast Fifty Years Ago* (2nd edn, Belfast: Belfast News Letter, 1885), pp. 17–19, 50; *BNL*, 7 June, 2 September 1836.
2. Steven Moore, *Behind the Garden Wall: A History of Capital Punishment in Belfast* (Antrim: Greystone Books, 1995).
3. Maurice O'Connell (ed.), *The Correspondence of Daniel O'Connell* (8 vols, Dublin: Irish Manuscripts Commission, 1972–80), vi.389, vii.12–13 and note 7.
4. *BNL*, 23 October 1840.
5. William McComb, *The Repealer Repulsed* (1841), ed. Patrick Maume (Dublin: UCD Press, 2003).
6. *BNL*, 11 April 1848; *NW*, 8, 18 April 1848.
7. *BNL*, 16, 19, 23 November 1847; Charles Gavan Duffy, *Four Years of Irish History* (London: Cassell, 1883), pp. 434–40; Christine Kinealy and Gerard MacAtasney, *The Hidden Famine: Hunger, Poverty and Sectarianism in Belfast* (London: Pluto, 2000), pp. 149–52.
8. For general surveys of sectarian violence see Sean Farrell, *Rituals and Riots: Sectarian Violence and Political Culture in Ulster, 1784–1886* (Lexington: University Press of Kentucky, 2000); Catherine Hirst, *Religion, Politics and Violence in Nineteenth-Century Belfast: The Pound and Sandy Row* (Dublin: Four Courts Press, 2002), chaps 2, 3; Mark Doyle, *Fighting Like the Devil for the Sake of God: Protestants, Catholics and the Origins of Violence in Victorian Belfast* (Manchester: Manchester University Press, 2009).
9. NAI, Outrage Papers, Co. Antrim, 1849, 1/89, Sub-Inspector J. B. Grant to Dublin Castle, 12 July 1849.
10. *Report of the Commission of Enquiry into the Origin and Character of the Riots in Belfast in July and September 1857* [hereafter *Riots Enquiry 1857*] (PP 1857–8 (2309) 26), p. 33.
11. *Riots Enquiry 1857*, pp. 24, 100.
12. Statutes 8 & 9 Victoria, c. cxlii.
13. *BNL*, 16 October 1836.
14. *BNL*, 14 August 1846.
15. *Return of the Number of Persons Taken into Custody for Drunkenness ... in each Year from 1841 to 1851* (PP 1852–3 (531) 81); *Return ... for the Years 1851, 1861, 1871, and 1876* (PP 1877 (437) 69); *Arrests for Drunkenness (Ireland)* (PP 1886 (53) 53).
16. Brian Griffin, *The Bulkies: Police and Crime in Belfast 1800–1865* (Dublin: Irish Academic Press, 1997), pp. 100–3; NAI, CSORP 1856/20628, Publicans' memorial and Tracy's report, 15 December 1856. The figures of 800 and 500 given above are Tracy's; Griffin, using newspaper sources, gives 889 and 726.
17. *BNL*, 17 June 1862.
18. *Banner of Ulster*, 19 June 1849.
19. Griffin, *The Bulkies*, pp. 40–58.
20. *Morning Chronicle*, 13 August 1849.
21. *Riots Enquiry 1857*, p. 87.

22 Mark Radford, *The Policing of Belfast 1870–1914* (London: Bloomsbury, 2015), pp. 16–17, 56–7.
23 *BNL*, 18 March 1898.
24 *BNL*, 18 June 1857.
25 *BNL*, 21 November 1848; *NW*, 1 September 1849; PRONI, LA7/10AB/1/1, Minute Book of the Committee on Police Affairs, 4 September 1844, 20 August 1845, 10 December 1845, 31 December 1845, 5 August 1846.
26 *BNL*, 10 May 1854, 18 April 1853.
27 Griffin, *The Bulkies*, pp. 109–15.
28 Alice Johnson, 'Some hidden purpose: class conflict and co-operation in Belfast's Working Men's Institute and Temperance Hall 1865–1900', *Social History*, 42:3 (2017), 399–419. See also H. G. Calwell, *Andrew Malcolm of Belfast 1818–56: Physician and Historian* (Belfast: Brough, Cox and Dunn Ltd, 1977), pp. 63–78; Don McCloy, *Creating Belfast: Technical Education and the Formation of a Great Industrial City 1801–1921* (Dublin: Nonsuch, 2009), chaps 3, 5. For the wider background see F. M. L. Thompson, 'Social control in Victorian Britain', *Economic History Review*, 34:2 (1981), 189–208.
29 For a fuller discussion see S. J. Connolly, 'Religion and society', in Liam Kennedy and Philip Ollerenshaw (eds), *Ulster since 1600: Politics, Economy and Society* (Oxford: Oxford University Press, 2013), pp. 74–89.
30 Neal Garnham, *Association Football and Society in Pre-Partition Ireland* (Belfast: Ulster Historical Foundation, 2004). For popular culture in general see S. J. Connolly and Andrew Holmes, 'Popular culture', in Liam Kennedy and Philip Ollerenshaw (eds), *Ulster since 1600: Politics, Economy and Society* (Oxford: Oxford University Press, 2013), pp. 106–20.
31 *BNL*, 6 April 1847, 23 April 1851; Eileen Black, *The People's Park: The Queen's Island, Belfast 1849–79* (Belfast: Linen Hall Library, 1988).
32 *BNL*, 15 April 1879.
33 Statutes 2 & 3 William IV, c. 118 (1832).
34 Farrell, *Rituals and Riots*, pp. 155–7.
35 Doyle, *Fighting Like the Devil for the Sake of God*, chap. 6.
36 Aiken McClelland, *William Johnston of Ballykilbeg* (Lurgan: Ulster Society, 1990); Frank Wright, *Two Lands on One Soil: Ulster Politics before Home Rule* (Dublin: Gill and Macmillan, 1996), pp. 315–32.
37 Farrell, *Rituals and Riots*, p. 173. No 'refreshments' were permitted in Belvoir Park: *BNL*, 13 July 1872.
38 NAI, CSORP 1872/13,518, attached to 1873/1022, Report of Major W. Percy, R.M., 22 August 1872; PRONI, LA/7/3DF/1, p. 110, Marquis of Hartingdon, Chief Secretary of Ireland, to Sir John Savage, mayor of Belfast, 6 January 1873. For Lady Day as 'a counter procession to the processions of the Orangemen', see the Chief Secretary's letter, and also *Belfast Morning News*, 16 August 1876.
39 *The Times*, 19 August 1872; 12 August was the anniversary of the lifting of the siege of Derry in 1689, celebrated by the Apprentice Boys.
40 *BNL*, 14 July 1873, 14 July 1874, 13 July 1875; *Belfast Morning News*, 10, 14, 16 July 1873, 16 August 1873, 13 July 1874, 13, 14 July 1875.

41 *BNL*, 13 July 1877.
42 *Belfast Morning News*, 15, 16 August 1876. See also *BNL*, 16 August 1876.
43 *BNL*, 13 July 1877; *Belfast Morning News*, 6, 7, 9 August 1877.
44 Fintan Lane, 'Music and violence in working class Cork: the "band nuisance", 1879–82', *Saothar*, 24 (1999), 17–31; John McGrath, 'Riots in Limerick, 1820–1900', in William Sheehan and Maura Cronin (eds), *Riotous Assemblies: Rebels, Riots and Revolts in Ireland* (Cork: Mercier Press, 2011), pp. 153–74, at pp. 170–1.
45 *NW*, 2, 12, 16, 19, 22, 24, 26 August 1878.
46 *Belfast Morning News*, 13 July 1878.
47 F. Frankfort Moore, *The Truth about Ulster* (London: Eveleigh Nash, 1914), pp. 235–6.
48 B. M. Walker, *Parliamentary Election Results in Ireland 1801–1922* (Dublin: Royal Irish Academy, 1978), pp. 101, 107; Ian Budge and Cornelius O'Leary, *Belfast: Approach to Crisis* (London: Macmillan, 1973), p. 84.
49 *BNL*, 15 May 1861.
50 Dominic Bryan, *Orange Parades: The Politics of Ritual, Tradition and Control* (London: Pluto Press, 2000), chap. 4.
51 *BNL*, 14 August 1884.
52 *BNL*, 16 August 1876, 14 August 1876; *Belfast Morning News*, 15 August 1876. For Johnston's stance see also Wright, *Two Lands on One Soil*, pp. 340–2.
53 *Belfast Morning News*, 9 August 1877.
54 *Freeman's Journal*, 18 March 1879, 17 August 1880; *Belfast Morning News*, 17 August 1880.
55 *BNL*, 16 August 1884.
56 *Report by One of the Commissioners of Inquiry, 1886, Respecting the Origin and Circumstances of the Riots in Belfast* (PP 1887 [C.5029] 18), p. 10.
57 *BNL*, 17 August 1891.
58 For this anniversary see above, p. 8.
59 *BNL*, 25 November 1890, 19 March 1894.

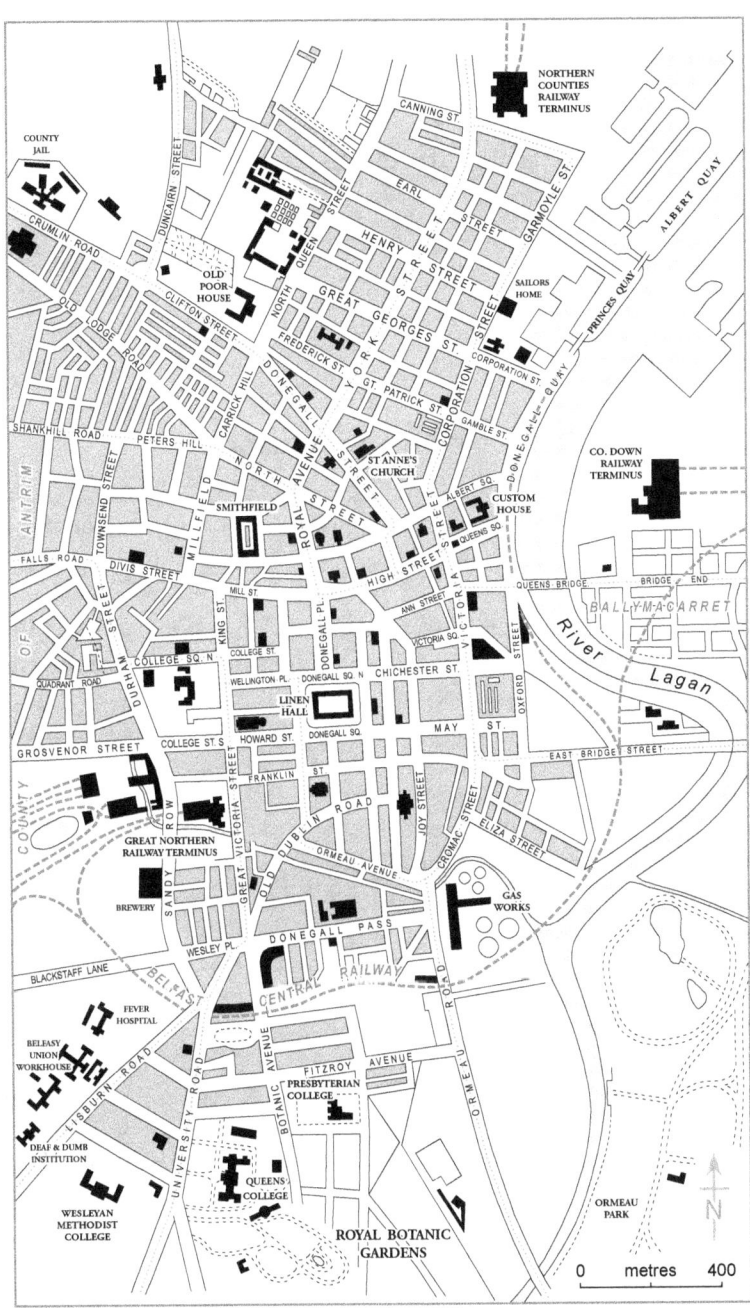

8 Plan of the city of Belfast, from *The Emerald Isle Album of Belfast and County Down* (1897). The Linen Hall was replaced soon after by the new City Hall (1906).

5

Public space and civil conflict

Partitioning an urban landscape

The conflicts over marching rights that followed the repeal of the Party Processions legislation reflected, and to some extent were shaped by, the major changes that took place, during the second half of the nineteenth century, in the physical shape of the town. Three developments in particular were important. The first was the expansion of working-class residential Belfast. The second was the emergence of certain supposedly public areas as sites of symbolic importance in the contest for legitimacy. The third was the growing prominence, as a source of particular contention, of the redeveloped city centre.

The physical expansion of the working-class residential quarters of Belfast was dramatic. In just twenty years, between 1861 and 1881, the town's population grew by 75 per cent, from 119,000 to 208,000. Pressure of numbers pushed the built-up areas outwards in all directions. To the north and south the expansion was mainly of middle-class housing, along the lines of the Antrim and Lisburn roads. To the east the large, new working-class districts erected in the vicinity of the shipyards and engineering works were overwhelmingly Protestant, with the exception of the Catholic enclave of the Short Strand. In the older working-class quarter to the west, on the other hand, what took place was the extension of an existing pattern of segregation, as Catholic Belfast continued to grow westwards along the line of the Falls Road, while Protestant Belfast kept pace along the line of the more or less parallel Shankill Road. This increase in physical scale had important implications for the nature of communal conflict. In 1857 Protestants and Catholics had fought each other across the narrow border that separated the Pound and Sandy Row, with repeated incursions into one another's territory. By the 1880s and 1890s, on the other hand, the Falls and Shankill districts represented solid blocks of denominationally defined territory. At times of exceptional stress, as during the Home Rule crisis of 1885–86, both areas were capable of erupting into violence. In normal circumstances, however, trouble tended to take place along the frontier between the two districts, or on the fringes, where the populations of the two districts intermingled.

Two names that recurred throughout the period were Carrick Hill and Peter's Hill. Both were dangerously located between the mainly Catholic Smithfield and the Protestant Shankill and Old Lodge Roads. In addition, both lay across the route from both Catholic and Protestant west Belfast to the city centre, and in particular to North Street, which by this time had emerged as the city's prime working-class shopping street.[1] North Street itself acquired a particular significance as the main route home for Protestant shipyard workers living in west Belfast. During the riots of 1886 the Queen's Island men agreed to an appeal to 'proceed homewards by two separate routes, and in small parties, instead of marching in a compact body through North Street'. In 1893, on the other hand, shipyard workers returning home at noon on the Saturday following a reading of the second Home Rule Bill formed into procession in North Street and sang the national anthem.[2]

The development of these much-enlarged residential districts had important implications for the creation of separate associational cultures. This was particularly the case for the numerically much weaker Catholic population. By the third quarter of the nineteenth century Irish Catholicism was undergoing what has been described as a 'devotional revolution', characterised by the introduction of a whole range of new ceremonial practices. In most parts of Belfast, however, any public display of Catholic ritual or religious imagery remained out of the question. Even in the absence of provocation, Catholic churches remained vulnerable to insult, as when in 1879 a Protestant band marching down Donegall Street chose to strike up the sectarian anthem 'The Protestant Boys' as they passed in front of St Patrick's church. The ornate St Malachy's fared still worse, coming under direct attack from Protestant mobs in 1857, and again in 1864.[3] In the emerging stronghold of the Falls, on the other hand, pious Catholics were already, by this time, beginning to enjoy a novel freedom of action. When the new church, St Peter's, erected to serve the expanding district opened its doors in 1866, the bishop organised a defiant display of ecclesiastical ceremonial. Paul Cullen, archbishop of Dublin and Ireland's only cardinal, was guest of honour, alighting from his coach in full robes to sing the high mass, while 'twelve bishops with mitres and copes walked processionally, full in public view, around the church'.[4] In political terms, too, Catholic west Belfast provided a safe venue for meetings, parades and cultural events. Where processions were concerned, the Falls and Smithfield provided a secure base from which marchers denied entrance to the centre could set out for what became the regular venue of Hannahstown.

Alongside this development of new and much-enlarged residential districts, certain places emerged as sites of particular significance. By the 1850s the area

9 Sunday evening at Custom House Square, c.1900–5. Charles Lanyon's Italianate building was one of the first fruits of the appetite for architectural refinement that emerged in mid-nineteenth-century Belfast. The open space in front of the entrance steps was for over a century a favourite site for public meetings and open-air orators. More recently it has become a key site both for commercial entertainment events and for cross-community festivals such as the Council-sponsored celebration of St Patrick's Day.

in front of the Custom House on Hanover Quay, facing out over the river, had become a favourite spot for open-air preachers. The location was strategic, lying within easy reach of the town centre and close to the route taken by people crossing the Queen's Bridge to and from east Belfast, while the quay and the nearby Queen's Island were a popular place of resort on Sundays. After 1857 the focus switched to the new Custom House a little further along the quay, still strategically placed in relation to the town centre and the river crossing, but now facing across an enclosed square, with a large set of front steps to provide a ready-made podium for speakers. This new space was to serve, up to the 1950s, as Belfast's speakers' corner, the prime site for public oratory (Figure 9).

Just before this change the area around the old Custom House had become the focus of the second phase of the sectarian riots of 1857, when Catholic crowds gathered to protest against a planned series of sermons by Protestant controversialists, only to be confronted by shipyard workers and others assembled to defend their preachers.[5] The new Custom House Square, by contrast, did not become the site of significant sectarian confrontations. The most likely explanation was geographical: the square, however attractive as a venue, was too far from the strongholds of the Pound and Falls, and too close to the workplace of the formidable Islandmen, to be an attractive battleground for Catholics or nationalists. In the mid-1890s, however, attempts by the small Belfast branch of the Independent Labour Party to secure a foothold on the Custom House steps met with ferocious violence, particularly from members of the militantly anti-Catholic Belfast Protestant Association. The objection was in part to anything that might interfere with the use of the space by Protestant open-air preachers; in part it was a response to the well-known support of most of the leaders of the British labour movement for Irish Home Rule. The attacks continued even when the heavily outnumbered Socialists withdrew from Custom House Square to a less prominent venue on the nearby Queen's Bridge, and in the end they were forced to abandon their attempt to secure a venue.[6] A few years later, between 1902 and about 1905, the square was again the scene of violent clashes, this time involving rival factions following a split in the Belfast Protestant Association itself.[7]

A second contested site was significant at a very different social and political level. The Ulster Hall, completed in 1862, was designed primarily as a concert hall, giving Belfast a first-class venue for the favourite cultural pursuit of the Victorian middle classes. However, it was also used for public entertainments, such as variety shows and boxing matches, as well as for public meetings. It was from there, in particular, that Lord Randolph Churchill in 1886 assured a huge Protestant audience that the Conservative party would back them in their resistance to Home Rule. In 1902 the hall, originally built by private subscription, was taken over by the city Council. Municipalisation required a local Act of Parliament, and at this point Belfast Catholics, backed by their allies in the Nationalist party in Parliament, intervened. Their complaint was that the proprietors of the hall had denied Catholics, one quarter of the population, access to 'the only great public hall of the city', and that the Unionist-dominated Council could not be trusted to be any more impartial. Nationalist MPs pressed for an amendment writing into the Act a formal requirement that use of the building should not be refused to any group on religious or political grounds. In the end they settled for a verbal assurance, given in Parliament, that the hall would be open to all.[8] Even before the change of ownership had been completed, in October 1891, the proprietors allowed the Belfast branch of the United Irish League to hire the premises for a rally; speakers addressed a capacity crowd from a platform decorated with banners relating to the recent commemoration of the United Irish rebellion of 1798. Over the next few years the Hall, now formally in public ownership, provided the venue for both nationalist and unionist meetings, assuming a particularly prominent place in the Home Rule crisis of 1912–14.[9]

The third major development that helped to shape conflicts over access to public space was the new status of the city centre. By now both much expanded and largely non-residential, this had been dramatically reshaped by the construction in 1880–81 of Royal Avenue, and given an additional grandeur by the erection at the southern end of the new artery of a set of monumental buildings, culminating in the completion in 1906 of the City Hall. Already in the 1870s the right to process through the centre had been one cause of contention. But it was only from the late 1890s that it became the central issue in a contest to redefine the boundaries of political legitimacy.

The subdued demeanour of Catholic Belfast in the late 1880s and early 1890s was understandable, given the loss of the Home Rule Bill, the frightening violence that had accompanied its defeat, and the split in Nationalist ranks that followed Parnell's involvement in a divorce scandal in 1890. For a time, leadership passed to a Catholic Association, dominated by the local bishop and concerned with the promotion of Catholic interests at local level. By the mid-1890s, however, this conservative, would-be assimilationist body was being challenged by a more assertive plebeian nationalism, organised through the Ancient Order of Hibernians and the United Irish League and led by the rising local politician Joseph Devlin.[10] Against this background members of the Hibernians organised a new 15 August procession in 1896. The aim was to support a national campaign for the release of imprisoned members of the Irish Republican Brotherhood. But the choice of Lady Day suggested an intended revival of tradition. More directly, the wording of one placard, announcing that the meeting place would be Hannahstown, 'the old hillside of '72', made clear that the event was intended as a new phase in a struggle seen as having commenced with that first attempt to assert equal marching rights following the repeal of the Party Processions Act.[11]

The intended route of the march was uncompromising. It began in Cromac Square, close to the Catholic markets district, and proceeded through Victoria Street, High Street and Castle Place before entering west Belfast and then going on to Hannahstown. The local police commanders, however, were not unduly alarmed. They recognised the potential for trouble with 'Orange rowdies', particularly at a time when several thousand shipyard workers were unemployed following a fire on the Queen's Island, but were confident that order could be maintained. In preparing for likely problems, moreover, their attention was on potential flashpoints as the procession navigated the segregated residential quarters of the city rather than on the city centre. The marchers, one senior officer reported, 'do not (it would appear) intend to traverse any particularly hostile locality, still they will go very close to several dangerous points, which will require careful supervision'. This emphasis, however, ignored a report from an informant within the Protestant camp that 'it has been decided upon never to allow a nationalist procession through Belfast'. And, in the event, a hostile Protestant crowd assembled to challenge the processionists in the first principal thoroughfare on their route, Victoria Street. The response of the escorting police was to divert the procession along an alternative route to the city centre, through May Street. This meant that Protestant counter demonstrators caught up with the nationalist demonstrators in the heart of the city's premier shopping district, Castle Street, where windows were smashed during ten minutes of fighting.[12]

The events of Lady Day 1896 made clear that the police and municipal authorities had now to deal with a new demand, for access to the neutral spaces of the city centre to be denied to Catholic and nationalist events. The demand became explicit two years later, when nationalists announced a second march, this time to mark the centenary of the rebellion of 1798. The newly formed Belfast Protestant Association, a militant working-class movement led by the energetic outdoor orator Arthur Trew, announced its intention of opposing by force any attempt by nationalists to march, as they intended, through the city centre from Cromac Square. However, they declared that they would withdraw all objections if the procession began at Smithfield and proceeded directly to Hannahstown.[13] At this point significant differences opened up among the city's Protestants. The Belfast Grand Master of the Orange order, Revd R. R. Kane, called on his followers to ignore 'the rebel processionists': 'the very genius of Protestantism is to allow others as full a liberty as we claim for ourselves'.[14] The mayor, supported by the town's magistrates, agreed that the march should go ahead, and was unwilling to ask for military assistance unless violence actually occurred. The local police commander accused the magistrates of placing undue faith in Kane's ability to speak for militant Protestant opinion, and warned that any procession passing through the town centre would be met with serious violence. Instead he demanded successfully that the march should depart from Smithfield, 'which confines the processionists to their own territory'.[15] Even this, despite the assurances of the Belfast Protestant Association, was not sufficient to avoid serious violence. The marchers came under sporadic attack as they set out from Smithfield on their way to Hannahstown, and a more sustained assault as they returned later that day. After they had dispersed, Protestants began a more general rampage, mounting repeated attacks on the police, wrecking Catholic-owned shops and pubs, and engaging in a further round of forced evictions and workplace expulsions.

The Belfast Protestant Association's attempt to prohibit any public display of Catholic and nationalist identity continued over the next three years. In

1899 Nationalists announced their intention of marking the anniversary of the 1798 commemoration by another march from Smithfield to Hannahstown. Trew promptly announced a counter demonstration, leading to calls for both assemblies to be banned. In the event the Nationalist procession went ahead, reportedly attended by more than half the city's Catholic population. An extensive police presence allowed the event to pass off with only minor outbreaks of stone throwing. But that night there were serious disturbances in Protestant areas, mainly directed at the police.[16] Two years later the Catholic bishop organised a major religious event, a celebration of the festival of Corpus Christi, with hymns and benediction before an open-air altar. The ceremony took place in the grounds of the diocesan college, St Malachy's, on the Antrim Road. To reach it, however, those attending, estimated to number 15,000, made their way to the college from the different Catholic churches 'in processional order ... headed by their spiritual directors'. The route took them past another of the places of symbolic importance that had emerged over the preceding years: Carlisle Circus and nearby Clifton Street were the site both of a large Orange Hall, erected in 1885 and crowned four years later by an equestrian statue of William III, and of a statue of the Protestant controversialist 'Roaring' Hugh Hanna, a central figure in the contests over open-air preaching in 1857. Trew and others had once again circulated handbills calling for a counter demonstration and the Catholic processionists were heckled and spat on as they passed. There was none of the physical violence seen at earlier parades, but the direct assault on a religious event, along with what was reported as obscene abuse directed at nuns, moved the authorities to act. Trew and two others were convicted of conspiracy and sentenced to terms of six and twelve months' imprisonment.[17]

In assessing the establishment's response to the Protestant exclusivism headed by Trew, it is important to be alert to potential differences between centre and municipality. The Irish executive in Dublin Castle had to consider the balance of nationalist and unionist interests in Ireland as a whole. The Irish constabulary stationed in the town, equally, took their orders from this executive. That, along with their mixed religious composition, was the reason why their replacement of the town police had caused such lasting resentment and made them the object of repeated attack from Protestant mobs. The Lord Mayor, Council members and most of the local magistrates, by contrast, were drawn from the same exclusively Protestant and Conservative party that had dominated municipal politics from the 1840s, leading to regular accusations of partisanship in the administration of justice. In relation to parades, however, there was no clear-cut difference in approach. The decision to prosecute Trew came from the Irish executive in Dublin Castle. In 1898, on the other hand, it was the police who insisted that the Nationalist march should begin from Smithfield, while the Lord Mayor and magistrates had been prepared, despite the violence of two years earlier, to let it pass through the town. The following year it was the police who once again argued for suppressing both the Nationalist procession and Trew's counter demonstration, while the Council agreed, after prolonged debate, that both should go ahead. Meanwhile William Johnston came forward to insist that he would not have challenged the Party Processions Act 'if he had not been prepared to concede to those who differed from him in politics and religion the same liberty that he claimed for the Orangemen of Ulster'. Orangemen had their own impending anniversary to celebrate, 'and how would they like a counter-demonstration proposed to be got up on July 12?'[18]

Against this background, Trew's campaign for exclusive marching rights failed. Released from prison, he resumed his campaign, telling a crowd at the Custom House steps in September 1902 that he and his followers would not tolerate any 'popish' demonstration in the city.

> The Roman Catholics might assemble in Smithfield or some other out of the way place and tread through the slums of the city as they had done before, but if they attempted to pass through Royal Avenue or any of the leading thoroughfares they would have to face the Protestants of Belfast in their thousands.[19]

Only three years later, however, in June 1905, a visit to the city by the Nationalist leader John Dillon, for the purpose of opening a bazaar in the city's National Club, provided the occasion for just the sort of event Trew had vowed to oppose. Dillon and his wife left their train at Lisburn, and proceeded in an open carriage to the top of the Falls Road, where a large crowd of supporters awaited them. The procession, with music and banners, then entered the city centre from west Belfast, passing down the Falls Road to Divis Street and Castle Street, then turning up Donegall Place to reach Dillon's hotel on Donegall Square. Protestant newspapers complained of 'the sturdy and somewhat militant bodyguard' that accompanied the Dillons, accusing them of threatening bystanders with the ceremonial deacon poles and replica pikes that they carried. At the junction with Dover Street, linking the Falls and Shankill Roads at a point where the two came dangerously close to one another, police successfully held back a hostile Protestant crowd. Later, as the procession entered Castle Street, there was some stone throwing, leading to broken windows in a leading department store, and a young man was stabbed in a scuffle in nearby Fountain Street. But Trew's projected embargo on Catholic or Nationalist demonstration in the city centre had clearly collapsed.[20]

Nationalists also continued to exercise their newly won right to use the Ulster Hall. Dillon and the Nationalist party leader John Redmond addressed a crowd of 3,000 there at the end of November 1904, and Redmond returned with another leading Nationalist, T. P. O'Connor, MP for Liverpool, for a further rally in December 1905. Three months later Nationalists once again took over the hall, this time for a banquet to celebrate the return of the local United Irish League leader, Joe Devlin, as MP for West Belfast.[21]

None of this meant that Catholics and Nationalists had achieved anything resembling equal access to public space. Orange parades, from the end of the 1870s, enjoyed an absolute right to take over the streets of the city centre and their choice among the main arteries leading out of the town. Their nationalist equivalents were at times granted access to the centre, but at others were confined to their own main residential area in west Belfast and the adjacent meeting place at Hannahstown. There seems also to have been a greater awareness of the archaic restrictions on public displays of Catholic religious symbols left in place by the Catholic Emancipation Act of 1829. Before the disputed Corpus Christi procession in 1901 the bishop gave assurances to the Commissioner of Police that the processionists making their way through the streets to the private venue at St Malachy's college would not be carrying any religious emblems.[22] Meanwhile, evangelical preachers, often strongly anti-Catholic in tone, had been allowed to assert their right to monopolise the public platform provided by the Custom House steps.

At first sight such blatant inequalities might seem to recall the concerted action that over half a century earlier prevented Daniel O'Connell from making the case for Repeal. In reality, the contexts were very different, and the progression from one event to the other was far from linear. In 1841 Repealer and anti-Repealer jostled for space and brawled within a crowded, multi-purpose town centre. In 1898, by contrast, nationalist and unionist competed for space in a much-expanded urban landscape newly zoned by function and governed by a formal and elaborate code of behaviour enforced by constant, intensive policing. In that competition the prejudices and preconceptions of the Belfast municipal elite, and the pressures exerted on that elite by a Protestant working class empowered by franchise extension and the decline of deference, combined to deny equality to Catholic and nationalist events. At the same time, Arthur Trew's attempt to create a Protestant monopoly of public space ended in defeat.

The case of Belfast thus represents the preservation, in the teeth of opposition accompanied by considerable violence, of the norms of the liberal state. The new public spaces created by the changing urban landscape were in principle open to all. Yet access depended on conformity to a particular vision of what constituted acceptable behaviour. It was a vision to which the Protestant loyalism of the Orange Order conformed more easily than did Catholic Irish nationalism. Pragmatic considerations of public order also favoured the numerically larger group. But the unfettered access achieved by Orange marches had nevertheless had to be earned by the acceptance of a new ethos of respectability and restraint. And, as Arthur Trew and his confederates discovered, there were boundaries that could not be crossed by members of either party. By the same token, the second-class status imposed on Catholic and nationalist events was never allowed to harden into an absolute prohibition. In this sense Belfast remained, however precariously, within the realm of 'the rule of freedom'.

Defining public space

There was of course more than one way of asserting control of public space. At the same time that they reconstructed and ordered the urban landscape through massive building projects, traffic regulations, by-laws and the establishment of police forces, the civic elites of Victorian Britain gave the spaces they had created a political identity by naming streets and squares, by erecting statues and monuments at strategic locations and by developing a body of ceremonial intended to encourage the whole body of the citizenry to identify with the new civic order and to internalise its values. Some of the same processes can be identified in Belfast. But overall, what is striking is the lack of interest shown by the dominant political faction, in the nineteenth century at least, in setting its specific ideological stamp on the territory it controlled.

Street naming was an unavoidable part of the continual expansion of the built-up area. The late eighteenth-century development schemes promoted by the first marquis of Donegall had already given the town Donegall Street, Donegall Place, Donegall Square and Chichester Street. To these the nineteenth century brought only minor additions: Donegall Road, formerly Blackstaff Road but renamed in 1894, which ran west from Sandy Row, and the nearby Shaftesbury Square, dating from 1884 and named in honour of the seventh earl of Shaftesbury, who had married the third marquis's daughter and whose family took on something of the role of aristocratic patron formerly exercised by the Donegalls. Due deference was also paid to royalty. Victoria Street, Victoria Square and Albert Square, along with Queen's Island, all dated from the fit of enthusiasm created by the queen's visit in 1849. The Queen's Bridge, completed in 1844, was later joined by the Albert Bridge in 1890. Meanwhile different sections of the main road linking the town centre to the suburb round the Queen's College passed through a variety of names (Victoria Place, Botanic Road, New Dublin Road) before the whole became, by the 1860s, Great Victoria Street. Another group of place names reflected the growing international reach of Belfast's trade and its inhabitants' identification with the expanding British empire. A cluster of streets bearing the names Jerusalem, Palestine, Damascus and Cairo gave one southern suburb the nickname The Holy Land. Elsewhere there were streets named for Vancouver, Ottawa, Delhi and other colonial capitals.

Street naming thus conveyed definite political messages. But these were of a conventional and uncontentious kind. The nationalism espoused by the great majority of Belfast Catholics, Repeal and, later, Home Rule was of the moderate variety that did not involve rejection of either monarchy or empire. The Protestant municipal elite, for their part, did not approach the task of thus labelling public space with any apparent degree of passion. The decision to name the showpiece boulevard created on the ruins of Hercules Street Royal Avenue came only after the Council had rejected Donegall Place North as too likely to be confused with Donegall Square North. Another suggestion was New York Street. The transatlantic flavour thus given to the existing name of York Street was probably deliberate, given that there was also a proposal to call the new thoroughfare Garfield Street, after the recently assassinated American president. Even after Royal Avenue had been suggested, the main point of discussion was whether a street without trees could properly be called an 'avenue'.[23]

A lack of concern for the iconography of identity was also evident in the meagre display of civic sculpture. Monuments to national or local figures of distinction were a common feature of the Victorian urban landscape, including that of Dublin and other Irish cities. In Belfast, on the other hand, John Clarke, who had served as the town's second Mayor, complained in 1862 that 'every stranger, in visiting our town, must be struck with the very few public monuments and memorials we have of the past'.[24] At this point Belfast had in fact only one public statue, erected in 1855 to commemorate the popular, philanthropically minded earl of Belfast, who had died prematurely two years earlier. It was joined in 1869 by a four-sided clock tower, 113 feet high, dedicated to the memory of Prince Albert (see Figure 3). Otherwise the erection of memorials to civic dignitaries had to wait until the early twentieth century. A statue to Queen Victoria was unveiled in 1903, in front of the still uncompleted City Hall, while elsewhere in the grounds surrounding the new building there were memorials to three former Lord Mayors, the shipbuilder Sir Edward Harland (1902), the retailer Sir James Haslett (1907) and the property developer Sir Daniel Dixon (1909), as well as to the marquis of Dufferin and Ava (1906), one-time viceroy of India and later of Canada. Harland was by any standards one of the makers of industrial Belfast. The particular claims of Haslett and Dixon are less obvious. Dufferin and Ava was a figure of undoubted distinction, but his connection with Belfast consisted mainly of his sponsorship of an unsuccessful attempt to capture one of its parliamentary seats for the Liberals in 1865. All in all, it seems likely that the impetus for this sudden enthusiasm for statues came less from an urge to memorialise for its own sake than from the creation around the new civic headquarters of a large open space, demanding to be appropriately filled up.

Two other additions to the city's monumental landscape were of greater political significance. In both of these cases, however, the Town Council responded to private initiatives. Following the death in 1868 of the Revd

Henry Cooke, agitation began for a memorial. Cooke had been the most celebrated Presbyterian clergyman of his day, but was also a strident political controversialist. The president of Belfast's Queen's College, himself a Presbyterian minister, described the sponsors of the memorial as 'the high Protestant political party', and refused an application to have a statue erected in the college grounds.[25] Instead, the memorial committee applied to the Council to have a statue of Cooke erected on the site of the 1855 memorial to Lord Belfast, which had weathered badly and had been removed from its open-air position to the Town Hall. The Council's agreement divided opinion. The Liberal *Northern Whig* and the Catholic *Ulster Examiner* attacked the enthronement in a public place of a noted Conservative and Protestant champion. On the other hand, Bernard Hughes, the town's most prominent Catholic businessman, supported the proposal on the grounds of Cooke's services to religion and philanthropy, as did the otherwise quite pugnacious Catholic bishop Patrick Dorrian. The statue was duly unveiled in 1876, providing the occasion for a huge Orange rally that played a part in the unravelling of attempts to exclude such demonstrations from the town.[26] A second statue, in 1894, commemorated an even more divisive figure, the anti-Catholic controversialist 'roaring' Hugh Hanna. Again, the cost was met by public subscription, but the Lord Mayor performed the opening ceremony. This time there was no bipartisanship. The *Irish News* condemned the unveiling as 'one of those periodical demonstrations of Orangeism and religious bigotry' with which Belfast was 'unhappily only too familiar'.[27]

Alongside this clear-cut example of sectionalism can be noted one dog that did not bark in the night. In 1864, during the controversy over the inauguration of the O'Connell monument in Dublin, the *Belfast News Letter* floated the idea of erecting in Belfast a statue to William III, whose foundation stone could be laid with the same ceremony displayed by nationalists in Dublin. The paper dutifully noted that a statue to the defender of political and religious liberty would be in any case a worthy project. But in the event, once the provocation offered in Dublin had come and gone, no more was heard of the project.[28] A fine equestrian statue of William subsequently appeared on the top of Clifton Street Orange hall. But Belfast, emerging as the capital of Irish Orangeism, remained without a civic memorial to its most distinctive hero.

Where public ceremonial is concerned the record is equally thin. The Donegall clique that had governed the town in the early nineteenth century had arranged elaborate civic events to mark the coming of age of the earl of Belfast in 1818 and the accession of a new monarch two years later. The new elite installed by municipal reform acquitted themselves creditably, in their own eyes, during the queen's visit in 1849. (The queen herself had been less impressed, commenting privately that the reception had been less well organised than in Dublin, and the management of the crowds of spectators less smooth.²⁹) In the second half of the century there were further ceremonial events. The Lord Lieutenant visited in 1884 to lay the foundation stone of the public library on Royal Avenue; his successor returned in 1888 to open the building. The Prince and Princess of Wales visited in 1885, receiving loyal addresses in the Ulster Hall. The appearance of Queen Victoria's grandson Albert Victor, to lay the foundation stone of the new Albert Bridge in 1889, inspired the *Belfast News Letter* to recall the visit of Victoria herself four decades earlier, and to pronounce the prince's reception 'worthy of the reputation of the capital of the loyal province of Ulster'.³⁰ Not all events, however, went smoothly. In particular, the death of Queen Victoria in 1901 saw Belfast signally failed to rise to the occasion. The reading of the proclamation announcing the accession of Edward VII was lost in the noise from a disorderly crowd, and the press of numbers became so great that the military guard of honour had to climb onto the platform to escape the crush. One observer compared the disorder to that created by the sectarian riots of 1886.³¹ All of these public occasions, moreover, were the conventional response to the visits of royalty or its representatives. There was no attempt to develop a body of specifically local ritual, like the ceremonies that elsewhere accompanied the installation of a new lord mayor, or the celebrated Colchester Oyster festival.³² Instead it was the Twelfth of July, enjoying a privileged status but not part of the official civic calendar, that provided Belfast's main ceremonial occasion.

Why did the Belfast civic elite not make more extensive use of the well-established methods – street names, statues, public ceremonial – by means of which their counterparts elsewhere imposed a political identity on the urban spaces they controlled? Some allowance must be made for local culture. Presbyterian religious scruples may have contributed to a lack of interest in statuary (although this did not seem to extend to what became the fixed practice of commissioning mayoral portraits), while numerous observers commented in more general terms on the dour, undemonstrative demeanour characteristic of the city's population. But there is also the question of civic identity itself. The Belfast that welcomed Queen Victoria in 1849 happily adopted a conventional iconography of union jacks and crowns interspersed with harps and shamrocks. In the decades that followed, however, cultural Irishness was appropriated by an increasingly aggressive nationalism. Already in 1875 the antiquarian Samuel Ferguson complained that it was not possible to have the vacant chair of Irish in the Queen's College filled, because 'an idea exists that it is inexpedient to encourage anything tending to foster Irish sentiment'.³³ It was no longer possible to present Belfast as an Irish town, distinguished from others on the island only by being loyal, hard working and well run. At a later stage a new civic identity was to appear, foreshadowed in the *Belfast News Letter*'s reference to 'the capital of the loyal province of Ulster'. But for now the unadorned nature of public space testified to the limitations of a self-definition conceived primarily in negative terms, as a rejection of Catholic Irish nationalism.

The same limitations were evident in another missing element of the development of nineteenth-century Belfast: the absence of an interest in local history. A common feature of the rising self-confidence of the provincial cites of Victorian Britain was the publication of solid chronicles of their origins and growth. Victorian Belfast did in fact produce a highly accomplished local historian, George Benn, whose *A History of the Town of Belfast* (1877) summarised a lifetime's work. (A first sketch had appeared as early as 1823.) Within Belfast itself, however, the work had little resonance; many, indeed, preferred to take pride in the claim that Belfast was a town without a past, created out of nothing within the past few decades. The *Belfast News Letter*, celebrating its promotion to city status in 1888, proudly announced that 'Belfast greatness began within living memory'.[34] Claims that Belfast's history went back no further than the early nineteenth century usefully emphasised the extent to which its spectacular growth and current prosperity had taken place under the union of Ireland and Great Britain. They also had the advantage of eclipsing an earlier period in which Belfast's history had been closely tied up with that of the rest of Ireland, and of a moment in the 1780s and 1790s when the town had been the capital of Irish radicalism, of joint political action between Catholic and Protestant and, ultimately, of a revolutionary movement dedicated to the cause of separatist republicanism. But such wilful historical amnesia deprived Belfast of another significant component in the process of self-fashioning that characterised so many Victorian urban communities.

Towards the closure of public space

Between the 1840s and the early twentieth century the management of public space in Belfast developed along lines that were in many respects typical of the Victorian and Edwardian city. Municipal reform had completed the transfer of control from an aristocratic proprietor to an elected council drawn from the leaders of the town's commerce and industry. As elsewhere, this new civic elite used the widening tax base of the expanding city to support extensive schemes of urban development. The late nineteenth- and early twentieth-century clearance of the last inner-urban courts and alleyways completed the transition to a non-residential city centre. Broad new thoroughfares – Victoria Street, Royal Avenue, Ormeau Avenue – facilitated the movement of people and traffic across a more open urban landscape. Large and ornate public buildings provided visible symbols of authority, order and civic pride. Public parks made available to all amenities formerly to be enjoyed only in the private park or gentleman's demesne, although in practice access to this railed and landscaped version of nature depended on adherence to strict codes of behaviour and deportment.

In other respects, however, Belfast's development failed to conform fully to the Victorian urban model. Most obviously, the city's deep religious and political divisions created a fissure at the heart of municipal life, making it impossible to promote a sense of shared identity. The brief show of communal harmony inspired by Queen Victoria's visit in 1849 was not sustained. But even among the majority Protestant population there were obstacles to the development of a fully rounded civic identity expressed in public ceremonial, civic statuary or the sense of a communal past. The sharp discontinuity in Belfast political life following the Act of Union, and the growing sense of disconnection from other parts of Ireland, discouraged an engagement with the city's long-term history. The politicisation of what had once been a non-contentious enthusiasm for Gaelic language and antiquities closed off other options. From one point of view the outcome was a stunted and impoverished civic culture. Belfast's monuments were the shipyard and the towering modern edifices of the commercial centre; its history was reduced to a narrative of industrial triumph across a few recent decades. From another perspective, however, the lack of impetus to develop a distinctive municipal culture, in the context of a divided city, preserved a degree of openness. The Orange order, unionist and militantly Protestant, supplied Belfast's main repertoire of public ceremonial. By the late nineteenth century it had secured for itself, partly through violence or the threat of violence, a privileged level of access to public space. Yet it was not part of the city's body of official civic ritual; its iconography, the statues and murals commemorating King William III and his victory at the Boyne, decorated the residential areas of Protestant Belfast, rather than the squares and thoroughfares of the city centre. Meanwhile nationalist and Catholic processions and symbolism, while not enjoying anything like equal status, could also demand access to public space.

All this was before the political crisis arising from the introduction in 1912 of the third Home Rule Bill. The early stages of the new round of political controversy followed a familiar pattern, with both sides organising demonstrations and rallies. One episode in February 1912, when Winston Churchill, First Lord of the Admiralty, was prevented from addressing a pro-Home Rule meeting in the Ulster Hall, at first sight recalls the prevention of O'Connell's Repeal meeting seventy years earlier. Once again, however, the apparent parallel is misleading. The booking for the hall had been accepted, confirming once again that Nationalists were not at this point being routinely denied access to Belfast's premier public venue. What stopped the meeting going ahead, equally, was not the naked threat of physical force but an astute piece of moral blackmail. Unionists themselves booked the hall for the day before and announcing their intention of not leaving it. The prospect, as one Dublin Castle official explained, was of 'the spectacle of the First Lord of the Admiralty at the head of an army of police and soldiers trying to evict two thousand religious fanatics from their sacred temple'. Instead the organisers abandoned their plans, and Churchill delivered his address at Celtic Park football ground, in the heart of Catholic west Belfast.[35]

Over the next two years, as a Home Rule Bill for Ireland made its way through a Parliament in which the House of Lords no longer enjoyed a power of veto, conditions in the city deteriorated in ways that made this type of harmless political trickery irrelevant. In July 1912 an attack by members of the Ancient Order of Hibernians on a Protestant school excursion provoked a wave of retaliatory attacks, in which around 3,000 Catholics were expelled from shipyards, linen mills and other workplaces. In January 1913 opponents of Home Rule formed the Ulster Volunteer Force (UVF) with the declared aim of resisting by all means necessary the imposition of Home Rule on Ulster. In April 1914 they added credibility to their threat by importing a consignment of arms from Germany through Larne in County Antrim. Nationalists responded by forming their own military movement, the Irish Volunteers. By July 1914 Belfast had some 3,000 of these Volunteers, organised into three companies, who marched and drilled in the west of the city and in the surrounding countryside. In late August they staged a parade through the Falls Road in front of an estimated 30,000–40,000 spectators.[36]

From one point of view the appearance on the streets of Belfast of two military forces with diametrically opposed political aims was a major step towards the abyss that was to open up from 1919, as Ireland descended into a cycle of armed insurrection, military retaliation and civil war. From another point of view what is remarkable is the degree of freedom allowed to what were in effect two competing armies. Here it is important not to exaggerate. The show of military preparation involved, on both sides, a substantial element of play-acting. Even the superficially impressive Larne gun-running had not yielded anything like the weapons and ammunition that would have been required to make the UVF a credible fighting force.[37] Their Volunteer rivals were less menacing still. Belfast Catholic leaders, strongly inclined towards the constitutional wing of Irish nationalism, had taken up the Volunteer movement only at a late stage, when the parliamentary leader John Redmond had decided that it was safer to take charge of the force than to leave it in more militant hands. The force was drilled by a former British army officer, George Berkeley, a supporter of Home Rule, but one who on the outbreak of war was to rejoin the crown forces. The 160 or so Italian rifles provided through the agency of the West Belfast Nationalist MP Joe Devlin came without ammunition; a Volunteer later recorded sardonically that 'they looked well, however, when used on parade'.[38] Those parades, equally, remained safely within the confines of Catholic west Belfast. The government's strategy of non-interference thus made a good deal of sense. But the licence allowed to these Catholic Nationalists, as well as to their Protestant unionist opponents, to march and counter march, in uniform and bearing weapons, was nevertheless a final, dramatic illustration of the extraordinary, if conditional, permissiveness of the liberal state, a permissiveness that extended, if in sometimes attenuated form, even to divided Belfast.

If the licence allowed to the two Volunteer forces looked backwards to a liberal era on which the sun was rapidly setting, another major public event provided a pointer to future developments. In September 1913 unionist leaders assembled in Belfast to initiate the mass signing of the Ulster Solemn League and Covenant, proclaiming the determination of the Protestants of Ulster to resist Home Rule. The last such mass event had been in 1892, at the time of the second Home Rule Bill. The level of mobilisation had been dramatic, with 12,000 delegates assembling at a grand convention. By later standards, however, the event had been distinctly lacking in a sense of place. The venue was in the southern suburbs, on an area of open land adjacent to Botanic Gardens. Fifteen year later, by contrast, leaders walked from the Ulster Hall to the City Hall, where the Mayor and members of the Corporation conducted them inside to sign the document. The *Irish News* complained that the headquarters of the municipal administration had been transformed into 'the sacred temple of Toryism and Orangeism'.[39] The observation was prophetic. Already before 1914 Protestantism and unionism had enjoyed privileged access to public space. Now, however, Ulster, or at least a large part of it, was beginning to emerge as a potentially separate political unit, with Belfast as its capital in waiting. It was in this new context, no longer purely municipal, that privilege was to harden into monopoly.

Notes

1 For religious divisions in Carrick Hill see *The Times*, 20 August 1880, and for the importance of North Street shopping, *BNL*, 24 April 1893.
2 *Report by One of the Commissioners of Inquiry, 1886, Respecting the Origin and Circumstances of the Riots in Belfast* (PP 1887 [C.5029] 18), p. 57; *BNL*, 24 April 1893.
3 *Belfast Morning News*, 15 July 1879; *Riots Enquiry 1857*, p. 32; Mark Doyle, *Fighting Like the Devil for the Sake of God: Protestants, Catholics and the Origins of Violence in Victorian Belfast* (Manchester: Manchester University Press, 2009), p. 145.
4 Irish College Rome, Kirby Papers 1866/282, John P. Leahy, bishop of Dromore, to Tobias Kirby, 18 October 1866.
5 Janice Holmes, 'The role of open-air preaching in the Belfast riots of 1857', *Proceedings of the Royal Irish Academy*, 102C:3 (2002), 47–66. Doyle, *Fighting Like the Devil*, p. 104, n. 44, assumes that the 1857 disturbances took place round the new Custom House. However references to the venue as facing the river (*Riot Enquiry 1857*, pp. 38, 46) make clear that this was the older building.

6 Bob Purdie, 'Riotous customs: the breaking up of socialist meetings in Belfast 1893–6', *Saothar*, 20 (1995), 32–40.
7 *Freeman's Journal*, 27 October 1902, 12 January, 9 February, 9 June, 19 August, 2 November 1903, 27 May 1905.
8 Hansard, *Parliamentary Debates*, HC, vol. 106, cols 480–1 (17 April 1902); *Irish News*, 14 April, 2 May 1902.
9 *Irish News*, 3 October 1901; *NW*, 3 October 1901. For use of the Hall after 1902, see below, pp. 140–2, 147.
10 A. C. Hepburn, *Catholic Belfast and Nationalist Ireland in the Era of Joe Devlin 1871–1934* (Oxford: Oxford University Press, 2008), chap. 2.
11 NAI, CSORP 1896/48779, attached to 1912/11935, printed placard, nd.
12 NAI, CSORP, 1896/48779, attached to 1912/11935, reports of E. Seddall, 11 August 1896, T. Moriarty, 11 August 1896, W. H. Hussey, 28 July 1896.
13 NAI, unnumbered bundle attached to CSORP 1912/11935, report of T. Moriarty, 31 May 1898; Moriarty to mayor, 30 May 1898.
14 *BNL*, 2 June 1898.
15 NAI, CSORP, 1898/9839 attached to 1912/11935, report of T. Moriarty, 3 June 1898.
16 *Freeman's Journal*, 6 June 1899; Neil Jarman and Dominic Bryan, *From Riots to Rights: Nationalist Parades in the North of Ireland* (Coleraine: University of Ulster, 1997).
17 *Freeman's Journal*, 22 June, 24 July 1901. Already in 1872, long before the construction of the Orange Hall, the choice of Carlisle Circus, 'chiefly a Protestant district', as the starting point for the Lady Day parade was subsequently seen as one reason for the violence that had followed: PRONI, LA/7/3DF/1, no. 110, Hartingdon to Savage, 6 January 1873.
18 Jarman and Bryan, *From Riots to Rights*, pp. 25–6; *The Times*, 1 June 1899.
19 *Freeman's Journal*, 9 September 1902.
20 *Freeman's Journal*, 6 June 1905; *Irish News*, 6 June 1905; *BNL*, 6 June 1905; *Belfast Evening Telegraph*, 6 June 1905.
21 *Freeman's Journal*, 1 December 1904, 14 December 1905; *Irish News*, 1 December 1904, 14 December 1905, 27 December 1906.
22 *Irish News*, 24 July 1901. For the extent to which these restrictions had elsewhere become a dead letter, see above, p. 7.
23 I owe these details to the ongoing research of Mr Stuart Irwin.
24 *BNL*, 5 March 1862.
25 BL, Add. MS 77,243, P. Shuldham Henry to John Preston, 12 January 1874, to Earl Spencer, 12 January 1874.
26 Jack Magee, *Barney: Bernard Hughes of Belfast 1808–1878* (Belfast: Ulster Historical Foundation, 2001), pp. 218–25. For the demonstration, see above, p. 104.
27 *Irish News*, 2 April 1894.
28 *BNL*, 3 August 1864.
29 S. J. Connolly, 'Like an old cathedral city: Belfast welcomes Queen Victoria, August 1849', *Urban History*, 39 (2012), 586–7.
30 *BNL*, 22 May 1889.

31 S. J. Connolly and Gillian McIntosh, 'Imagining Belfast', in S. J. Connolly (ed.), *Belfast 400: People, Place and History* (Liverpool: Liverpool University Press, 2012), pp. 13–61, at p. 42.
32 See above, p. 4.
33 Fionntán de Brún (ed.), *Belfast and the Irish Language* (Dublin: Four Courts Press, 2006), p. 97.
34 *BNL*, 15 October 1888. For a fuller discussion see Connolly and McIntosh, 'Imagining Belfast', 15–16.
35 Sir Henry Robinson, head of the Local Government Board, quoted in Leon Ó Broin, *The Chief Secretary: Augustine Birrell in Ireland* (Hamden, CT: Archon Books, 1970), p. 52.
36 Hepburn, *Catholic Belfast and Nationalist Ireland*, pp. 160–5.
37 Alvin Jackson, 'Unionist myths, 1912–85', *Past and Present*, 136 (1992), 164–85.
38 Bureau of Military History, Dublin, witness statement no. 183, Liam Gaynor, 21 October 1948.
39 *Irish News*, 30 September 1912.

6

Public space and the Protestant state

Public politics in a new state

On 22 June 1921 the royal yacht *Victoria*, bearing King George V and Queen Mary, arrived in Belfast harbour, accompanied by an imposing flotilla comprising two battleships, two cruisers and a formation of destroyers. The royal party disembarked at Donegall Quay. From there the king and queen, escorted by mounted cavalry, proceeded in an open, horse-drawn carriage along High Street and Castle Place, and then through Donegall Place to the City Hall, where the king presided over a short ceremony to mark the first session of the new Parliament of Northern Ireland. After an elaborate lunch he went on to the Ulster Hall to receive a succession of loyal addresses before returning to the royal yacht. The event attracted huge crowds. 'Every window of every house, shop and office', the *Irish Times* reported, 'was packed to overflowing … every available square inch of space along the sidewalks was alive with excited and expectant sight-seers'. Others had thronged the banks of the harbour, or gathered on the hills to the north of the town, from where they could watch the arrival and departure of the royal flotilla. The wife of Sir James Craig, first Prime Minister of the new polity, noted approvingly that 'even the little side streets that [the king and queen] will never be within miles of are draped with bunting and flags'.[1]

In several particulars – the sea-borne arrival, the route through the town centre, the enthusiastic crowds – George V's expedition to Belfast had clear echoes of the visit just over seventy years earlier of Queen Victoria.[2] In other respects, what was apparent was the changes that, over the intervening period, the city had undergone. Much had been learned, for example, about the staging of major crowd events. In preparation for the day, the authorities had employed 500 extra workmen to decorate the streets and clean the City Hall. But observers were also impressed by the efficiency of the arrangements for managing the expected crowds, including the distribution of water and the presence of nurses and stretcher bearers for those overcome by the crush or the June heat. Boy Scouts sold printed programmes, while overhead four aeroplanes, still a novel sight, entertained the crowd with aerial acrobatics. Most important of all, there was the transformation of the physical environment. In place of the unsatisfactory channel and cramped dock at which Victoria had landed, there was now the sprawling harbour and what was popularly claimed to be the world's largest shipyard. The king's destination, replacing the modest, utilitarian Linen Hall that the queen had paused to admire, was the baroque magnificence of the City Hall. The municipal authorities in 1849 had worried that their town had no distinctive sights or imposing buildings to impress the royal visitor. The *Belfast News Letter*, in 1921, had no such qualms. The City Hall, 'the architectural symbol of the progress and greatness of Belfast', standing in a square created by four broad thoroughfares lined with tall business premises, provided 'an unrivalled theatre upon which to stage a scene in this great act of Ulster's constitutional development'.[3]

That constitutional development was, of course, the other major aspect that set George V's visit to Belfast apart from that undertaken by his grandmother. Plans for Home Rule, and for counter action by Ulster Protestants, had been put to one side following the outbreak of war in August 1914. In December 1920, however, the Government of Ireland Act provided for the establishment of not one but two devolved administrations and Parliaments, one based in Belfast with control of the six Ulster counties with Protestant majorities or near-majorities, the other based in Dublin and responsible for the remaining twenty-six Irish counties. The Act was in response to the revolution that had taken place in Irish nationalist politics. By the end of 1918 a new and more radical movement, Sinn Féin, had largely displaced the constitutional nationalists of the Irish Parliamentary Party, and from the start of the following year its military wing, what came to be the Irish Republican Army (IRA), had begun a campaign of violence directed against the police, army and other agencies of the state. Against this background the focus of the Government of Ireland Act was entirely on the southern Parliament, and the hope that the substantial instalment of self-government that it offered would be enough to detach moderate nationalist opinion from Sinn Féin. The extension of the same provisions to six Ulster counties and a Belfast Parliament was a political gesture, intended to demonstrate to both Irish and world opinion that Great Britain did not seek to rule any group of Irishmen against their will. In the event, the southern Parliament never functioned. Sinn Féin candidates stood unopposed for 124 of the 128 seats and boycotted its proceedings. Instead it was Belfast that now became in law what it had already been in practice: the capital of an assertively British Northern Ireland comprising two-thirds of Ulster.

The royal visit was thus the product of a failed political settlement introduced against a background of mounting violence. The presence of the king, who used the occasion to make a plea for a peaceful settlement, encouraged the organisers to avoid blatant partisanship. The loyal addresses presented in the Ulster Hall carefully avoided mention of any political organisation. Cardinal Michael Logue, Catholic archbishop of Armagh, received an invitation to attend alongside the heads of the other religious denominations. However, he stood aloof, as did other leading representatives of local nationalism. Instead the proceedings were dominated by the Ulster Unionist establishment. Among the honours conferred during the king's visit, for example, were CBEs (Commander of the Most excellent Order of the British Empire) for Fred Crawford, celebrated as the organiser of the Larne gun-running that had turned the UVF into an armed force, as well as for Sir Basil Brooke and Wilfred Spender, both likewise closely associated with the UVF, and also leading figures in the formation of a Special Constabulary to counter the IRA threat. The part-time or 'B' section of this force, widely perceived by nationalists as the UVF under another name, was prominently deployed during the royal visit. Another significant episode was the presentation of loyal addresses by delegates representing the city's shipyard workers, long regarded as the shock troops of Protestant unionism, a reputation consolidated by the violent expulsion of the minority of Catholic workers from both shipyards that had taken place in July 1920. There were also other telling gestures. Members of the Royal Irish Constabulary, still an all-Ireland force and three-quarters Catholic, were on duty alongside the B Specials, but the guard of honour they provided for the king was composed entirely of men from the six counties of the new Northern Ireland. The secretary to the new cabinet likewise stipulated that all of the musicians performing at the lunch in the City Hall, though recruited through a Dublin agency, 'should be Ulstermen and should be Loyalists'.[4]

The emphasis on a separatist unionism based on a distinct Ulster homeland, with Belfast as its capital, that thus crept into the ceremonial surrounding the royal visit was not wholly new. The ostensible aim of unionism in the period 1912–14 was to keep all of Ireland under the Westminster Parliament. But as early as September 1912 the carefully staged proceedings of Ulster Day, focussed on the municipal institutions of Belfast, made clear where the real focus of resistance lay. Since then, as negotiations had continued about a possible compromise settlement, it had become increasingly clear that 'Ulster' would no longer mean the nine counties of the historic province. Meanwhile the concept of a distinctive Ulster allegiance had received powerful reinforcement from another quarter. At the beginning of the war members of the UVF enlisted as a body in what became the 36th Ulster division. On 8 May 1915 the division, on its way to a training camp in England, marched past the City Hall, where the Mayor and Corporation assembled to salute them in a demonstration that combined imperial, unionist and municipal pride. The appalling carnage on the Somme just over a year later, when nearly 2,000 officers and men were killed in the first day of fighting, laid the foundations for a long-standing memory of heroic, and again distinctively Ulster, sacrifice. In 1919 Belfast Corporation insisted on organising the city's celebration of the signing of the post-war treaty, Peace Day, in August rather than on 19 July, ostensibly to avoid a clash with the Twelfth of July festivities but also ensuring, whether by accident or design, that the event did not coincide with that held in Dublin.

After 1921 the movement towards the development of a separate Ulster-based identity gained new momentum. Contemporaries differed on how to categorise the new polity. 'Province' and 'region' were two frequent terms; nationalists resorted to the derisive 'statelet'. Northern Ireland was undeniably something less than a state. At the same time the Government of Ireland Act, introduced with an eye to the aspirations of southern nationalists, had created structures wildly out of proportion to the needs of a region of 1.5 million inhabitants: a bicameral Parliament and prime ministerial and cabinet government with six separate government departments.[5] With the installation of the personnel and premises of this top-heavy administrative and legislative structure Belfast became an administrative as well as a commercial centre. Consciousness of this new status was evident in the construction of the first monumental civic building of the new era, the Royal Courts of Justice erected on Chichester Street between 1928 and 1933. The expense, under the Government of Ireland Act, was to be borne by the British treasury. But when its economy-minded officials insisted on a brick façade the Northern Ireland Government used its own resources to fund a facing in Portland stone.[6]

The political context also encouraged a sharp sense of separateness. The new Northern Ireland defined itself primarily against the nationalist-dominated Irish Free State which by 1922 had emerged in the other twenty-six counties and which continued to deny the legitimacy of its neighbour. But there was also a distinct wariness in relations with the rest of the United Kingdom. The initial unionist mobilisation against Home Rule had been in defiance of the British government and Parliament, mounted by Ulster Protestants no longer prepared to leave the issue in the hands of their allies in the Conservative party. Later, as thoughts in London turned to a compromise with Sinn Féin, Craig and his ministers were all too aware of the need to ensure that peace was not purchased at their expense. There are also signs that they recognised that, in the event of what for a time looked like a wholly possible assault on their territory by the forces of the southern IRA, London would be deeply reluctant to commit troops to a new civil conflict in Ireland.[7]

What all this meant in practice was a wholly new approach to the regulation of public space. Up to 1914, despite the recurrent and sometimes lethal episodes of violence that arose out of disputes over parades and processions, the principle of access to streets, squares and public buildings for the expression of competing political and religious allegiances had continued to be respected to a surprising degree. The new Unionist Government, however, abandoned all pretence of even-handedness. A wide-ranging Special Powers Act, introduced in 1922, authorised the government and police, together or separately, to prohibit public meetings likely to cause disorder or 'promote disaffection'. In its immediate context, at a time when IRA units both within Northern Ireland and in the south were engaged in a coordinated campaign to bring about the collapse of the new administration, the measure was understandable. By 1925, however, tough security measures, a ferocious counter offensive by Loyalist paramilitaries and the outbreak of civil war in the new Free State, had brought the IRA offensive to an end. The Special Powers Act nevertheless remained in force, and its provisions were used to prohibit all public expressions of militant Republicanism. In particular, attempts to stage commemorations of the Dublin insurrection of Easter 1916 that had initiated the rise of Sinn Féin were regularly banned and, where necessary, broken up by force. St Patrick's Day and Lady Day parades by the Ancient Order of Hibernians, affiliated to the more moderate heirs to the Home Rule party, were also sometimes banned. Alternatively they were allowed to take place but confined to exclusively Catholic residential areas. Popular Protestant festivals, by contrast, the Twelfth of July and celebrations of the beginning and end of the siege of Londonderry in August and December of each year, now enjoyed unfettered access to main roads and town centres. The inauguration in 1926 of a two-day public holiday across 12–13 July confirmed the event's status as Northern Ireland's main civic ritual. An isolated incident in 1932, when police rerouted a parade in the predominantly Catholic town of Coalisland, County Tyrone, gave rise to a massive outcry against the administration. Three years later the Minister for Home Affairs, responding to the use of firearms in disturbances arising from Protestant parades, introduced a ban on all processions in the city of Belfast, only to retreat in the face of Loyalist outrage. One classic definition of the modern state is that it is the body that claims a monopoly on the legitimate use of physical force. In Belfast and elsewhere in Northern Ireland, the issue was, rather, with major implications for the future, a monopoly on the use of public space.[8]

Nor was it only Nationalists and Republicans who were the victims of this monopoly. In the 1890s the most blatant attempt to deny other allegiances access to public space had been directed not against the supporters of Home Rule but, rather, against the small and cross-denominational Belfast branch of the Independent Labour Party, who had found themselves violently expelled from Custom House Square. Their experience after 1920 was broadly similar. When trade unionists and others planned a protest against unemployment in the city in 1925, the Government invoked the Special Powers Act in order to prohibit the event. On this occasion the Minister for Home Affairs, Sir Richard Dawson Bates, acted only after expressing some initial doubts about the legitimacy (or possibly the political wisdom) of using laws designed to quell Republican attacks on the state as a means of silencing social protest. By October 1932, however, when tens of thousands, from both Protestant and Catholic areas, took to the streets to protest against the miserly provision for those out of work that was being made by the Belfast Poor Law Guardians, any such scruples had clearly disappeared. Invoking the Emergency Powers Act, the government banned planned demonstrations and sent in the police to disperse crowds, take down barricades and impose a curfew. In Catholic areas – though not, as critics pointed out, in Protestant districts – the police used firearms, killing two men and wounding fourteen others.[9] The resort to emergency powers had some claim to justification, in that left-wing politics and Irish nationalism had long been intertwined. Some of the protests banned in the 1930s, for example, involved left-wing nationalist groups like Republican Congress. But an alternative view would be that the government was guilty of simple political opportunism. The main electoral threat to unionism in this period, after all, came not from the permanent minority of nationalists but from the possibility that a Labour movement boosted by economic hard times might split the Protestant vote. But in either case the prescription of left-wing demonstrations reinforced the central point: public space was now reserved for those whose demonstrations endorsed the core values of the new polity.

The same exclusiveness was evident in a new and highly emotive addition to the public ritual of Belfast and its hinterland, the commemoration of the dead of the Great War. Already at the time of Belfast's separate Peace Day in 1919 the overlap between the UVF, formed to resist the threat of Catholic nationalism, and the 36th Ulster Division, whose blood had been shed in France, encouraged a conflation of the two causes. This was to overlook the war service of Belfast Catholics, who had enlisted in numbers roughly proportionate to their share of the city's population, mainly in the 16th Irish division, which had likewise suffered heavy losses at the Somme, Passchendaele and elsewhere.[10] In the polarised climate of the post-war years, however, neither nationalists or unionists were disposed to think in terms of shared sacrifice. Instead it was primarily the Unionist establishment and its supporters that dominated Armistice Day and other commemorative events, using a rhetoric in which events at home and on the Western Front became part of a single continuing demonstration of loyalty to king and empire.[11] In the case of Belfast the dedication in 1929 of a Cenotaph and Garden of Remembrance beside the City Hall drew a protest from the Nationalist *Irish News*, which objected to the presentation of the war dead as defenders of Ulster.[12]

The most dramatic testament to the new status of Northern Ireland was the erection between 1928 and 1931 of a grandiose new parliament building at Stormont, on the southern outskirts of Belfast. The new Parliament had held its first sessions in the City Hall, then leased part of the Presbyterian Assembly's

College, close to Queen's University. The Stormont estate, five miles from the city centre, was in part chosen for the attractions of the site, 200 acres of wooded parkland on a commanding height, and partly because of the lack of an appropriate building in Belfast itself. But there seems also to have been some idea of not seeming to give the city undue influence within the new polity. Once again the bulk of the cost was borne by the British treasury. Pressures for economy led to modifications to the design, notably the omission of a planned dome. However, Craig fought doggedly and successfully for other aspects of the design, notably the costly positioning of the building at the highest point on the site, and the addition of an elaborate approach road, running dead straight for almost a mile from the massive gates to the front of the building. His reply to those who criticised the cost appealed explicitly to Northern Ireland's new status. It would not do to suggest 'that a small, trifling and niggardly treatment of the subject was sufficient for the Ulster people'. The use of the nearby Stormont Castle as an official prime ministerial residence, equally, was needed to show 'that Ulster is not behind the other parts of the empire in the way in which she can receive the distinguished people who visit her shores'. From an opposite political perspective, the Nationalist *Irish News* was equally clear on the representational function of the new edifice, 'this mighty temple wherein the high priests of the political heathenism called Partition may continuously sacrifice the welfare of the people'.[13]

This identification of the new Parliament House with Ulster's stand against the claims of Irish nationalism was strengthened at its formal opening. Edward Carson, charismatic figurehead of the campaign against the third Home Rule Bill, had not chosen to live in the Northern Ireland created by his efforts, preferring his legal career in England. But in November 1932 he was back in Belfast, alongside his former lieutenant James Craig, to see the Prince of Wales inaugurate the new building. The following year a statue of Carson, presented by the Ulster Unionist Council, took its place on a pedestal half way up the long approach avenue, making it an inescapable part of the whole grand vista. When, two years later, Carson died, once again at his home in England, his body was taken to Belfast for a state funeral and entombed in St Anne's cathedral. In a bizarre ritual, soil from each of the six counties of Northern Ireland was placed in his coffin. Edward Carson, the Dubliner whose aim had always been to preserve the whole of Ireland within the United Kingdom, became in death the patron saint of the separatist polity which his efforts had brought into being.[14]

The government of the new Northern Ireland thus created an explicitly British unionist public culture, and took action to exclude from public space those whom it perceived as challenging the legitimacy of the state. What it did not do was accede to the demands of its more extreme supporters, who demanded that that state should be an exclusively Protestant one. In a celebrated incident in April 1934 Craig was provoked, in the heat of debate, to declare his pride in 'a Protestant parliament and a Protestant state'.[15] But this was just two months before his government permitted the staging in Belfast of one of the two most dramatic public displays of Catholic religious commitment that took place during the inter-war period. In 1932 Dublin had hosted a Eucharistic Congress, a spectacular five-day event culminating in a high mass attended by an estimated one million worshippers, with a live papal address from the Vatican broadcast across a public address system that covered the entire city centre.[16] The thirty-first annual conference of the Catholic Truth Society, staged in Belfast in June 1934, was a smaller event. But a crowd variously estimated at between 80,000 and 120,000 faithful attended an open-air mass, celebrated on a high altar surrounded by a glass canopy twenty feet high, in the grounds of Beechmount, a mansion off the Falls Road recently purchased by the Catholic church. Faced with the possibility of Protestant protest, the government took firm action. Armed police were deployed on buses carrying people to this and other events, as well as at railway stations and at points along the track where carriages might come under attack. In the event, a hostile demonstration accompanied by bands and carrying union jacks confined itself to marching from the City Hall to the Protestant Shankill Road, accompanied throughout by police. As the conference closed, the Catholic bishop of Down and Connor thanked the police for their assistance with the staging of the event. BBC Northern Ireland broadcast the main ceremony, and also provided the coverage that was relayed to audiences in the Irish Free State by southern Irish radio.[17]

A related public manifestation of Catholicism did not end so happily. The organisers of the conference had booked the Ulster Hall for the period 19–28 June for an exhibition. The theme was to be a celebration of Catholic overseas missionary work, with exhibits including such uplifting scenes as 'a model in wax of a nun dressing a leper woman', and 'a priest in a typical African scene catechising a group of nigger [sic] children'.[18] Three weeks before the conference was due to begin, opponents organised a protest meeting in the hall. The main auditorium was filled to capacity, while outside a crowd of 5,000 gathered, accompanied by bands and drums. Samuel Hanna, minister of Berry Street Presbyterian church, acting as chairman, set out the case in openly sectarian terms:

> It was their duty as Protestants to protest. This was a Protestant city. Nine-tenths of its business and its industries had been developed by Protestants. At least seven-tenths of the city rates were paid by Protestants and one hundred per cent of its benevolent institutions had been established by Protestants.

Hanna went on to insist that the city offered 'fair play' to all those willing to live in harmony with their surroundings. In this case, however, they were dealing with a group that sought 'to misrepresent their city in the eyes of the world' and 'to flaunt Romish ritual in the face of the people who loathed it'. His complaint focussed on the booking of the Ulster Hall, but the resolution eventually carried by the meeting seems also to have called on the government to ban the Catholic Truth Society conference itself, not just in Belfast but in any part of 'Ulster'.[19] The excited crowds that dispersed following the meeting were mainly kept under control by a strong force of police, although in the religiously mixed waterfront area of Sailortown one rowdy group smashed a window in a Catholic social club.[20]

The protest against the Ulster Hall booking opened up significant divisions within Protestant opinion. The protest meeting was condemned by the Belfast Presbytery of the Presbyterian church in Ireland, and, in a sermon preached in St Anne's cathedral, by the Church of Ireland dean of Belfast. Even the Grand Master of the Belfast Orange institution, in a public letter, wholly disassociated the Order from the proceedings.[21] In the end the organisers, 'in the interests of peace and harmony', withdrew their booking, and the exhibition went ahead instead in the convent of the Dominican Nuns on the Falls Road. How far this surrender may have been due to behind-the-scenes pressure from either the city or the Northern Ireland authorities it is impossible to say. In public, however, the government's stance was uncompromising. Police shorthand note-takers attended the protest meeting in the Ulster Hall and Hanna and another speaker were brought before a special court on a charge of using words calculated to lead to a breach of the peace. Hanna apologised and was given the benefit of the Probation Act. The other defendant, a Mrs Dorothy Harnett of County Down, who had called on the young men present to 'discipline yourselves and get physically fit', and who had met prospective criticism with the call 'For God's sake let us stir up feeling', was bound over to keep the peace.[22]

The vehemence of the opposition provoked by the proposed missionary exhibition arose in part from the venue that had been chosen. The Ulster Hall, Hanna claimed, was a site 'sacred to every Protestant heart, with a thousand memories'. In Parliament the Independent Unionist John William Nixon referred back to the events of February 1912, demanding to know 'whether the Government had changed their policy since the Prime Minister and other members of the Cabinet forcibly seized the Ulster Hall to prevent Mr Winston Churchill from addressing a meeting there'.[23] Yet this notion of the hall as a unionist 'sacred space' was clearly not shared by all. Within a few years, in fact, there was to be serious discussion of having the building demolished, on account of its run-down state. Some of the ways in which it was being used are also difficult to reconcile with the notion of an exclusively unionist space. Just three months before the Catholic Truth Society conference, in fact, it had provided the venue for what was billed as 'an Irish concert', where the city's leading authority on Irish dance, Peadar O'Rafferty, directed troupes of performers, while the Belfast city organist, Captain J. C. Brennan, performed a selection of Irish airs. The firmly unionist *Belfast News Letter* recorded enthusiastically that 'the graceful steps and movements of folk dancing were demonstrated by bands of experts in this ancient Irish accomplishment', while Captain Brennan 'brought us into the atmosphere of old-time Ireland, with its pathos and joy, lament and triumph in native minstrelsy'. The event was one of a series of such concerts during the 1930s, generally staged on a Saturday close to St Patrick's Day, with both O'Rafferty and Captain Brennan appearing as regular performers.[24] These performances, and in particular Brennan's participation, indicate that the official culture of the city was significantly broader than the proceedings at Hanna's protest meeting, taken in isolation, would suggest.

Overall there is little question that the Unionist rulers of the new state of Northern Ireland used their power, in Belfast and elsewhere, to promote what was clearly a sectional identity. At the same time their actions should not be seen in isolation. South of the new Irish border, the Irish Free State remained a Dominion of the British Empire. But its establishment nevertheless saw a thorough purge of public space. Street and town names recalling what was now seen as a colonial past were changed, so that Kingstown became Dun Laoghaire and Queenstown Cobh. Statues of British monarchs were removed or destroyed.[25] A planned memorial to the Irish dead of the First World War, designed by Edward Lutyens for Kilmainham in the western suburbs of Dublin, quickly fell into decay, while celebrations of Armistice Day, inadequately protected from attacks by militant Republicans, were progressively moved away from the city centre. Meanwhile events like the extravagant staging of the Eucharistic Congress openly proclaimed the Catholic character of the southern state. There was also a wider context. Inter-war Europe was the great age of the theatre state, when parades, commemorations and monumental buildings were used to enshrine a particular set of values at the heart of the often unstable and internally divided polities created by the Versailles settlement.[26] Belfast City Hall and Stormont were never the location of demonstrations comparable to those seen at Nuremberg, or even to the less elaborately choreographed gatherings that took place before the balcony of Rome's Palazzo Venezia. Nor can Unionist infringements of civil liberties be compared in any way to the atrocities perpetrated by these regimes. The Nationalist polemicist who in 1946 christened Londonderry 'Ireland's fascist city' exaggerated wildly.[27] But the political theatre of Ulster Unionism, from Ulster Day in 1912 to Carson's state funeral in 1935, nevertheless fitted into a broader pattern as what developed into a mildly authoritarian regime sought to demonstrate a legitimacy based on the mobilisation of the loyal masses.

A divided capital

The 1920s, the decade that saw Belfast acquire a new status as a political capital, were in other respects the beginning of a long period of difficulty for the city. Shipbuilding suffered badly, first from the world-wide glut of almost-new floating tonnage that was a legacy of mass construction programmes during the First World War, and then from the contraction of world trade during the Great Depression. Linen, the other staple industry, also faltered, as changes in fashion and the declining availability of affordable domestic servants led consumers to switch to lighter and more easily managed fabrics. During 1931–32 one in four of the city's working population was unemployed. In 1935 Workman, Clark and Company, the smaller of the city's two shipyards but before 1914 the sixth-largest in the United Kingdom, ceased production.

Alongside industrial collapse the immediate post-war years brought communal violence on a new scale. The two were initially closely linked. Hostilities began with the mass expulsion from the two shipyards of Catholic workers, partly in response to the escalating violence of Sinn Féin and the IRA in the south, but also fuelled by allegations that 'disloyal' Catholics were unfairly holding on to jobs they had taken over from Protestants who had gone to fight for king and country. As the conflict developed, however, the issue became the collapse or survival of the new Northern state, with each side, Republican and Loyalist, using often indiscriminate violence in an attempt to break the will of the other to continue. Between 1920 and 1922 there were an estimated 498 killings in Belfast, representing 90 per cent of cases of lethal violence in the six counties as a whole, as well as 10,000 workplace expulsions, while some 23,000 became homeless through the familiar pattern of sectarian cleansing of residential neighbourhoods. The Catholics, heavily outnumbered, suffered worst. With just under a quarter of the city's population, they accounted for three out of every five casualties recorded, as well as for the great majority of the workplace expulsions. By the summer of 1922 superior Loyalist firepower, reinforced by the efforts of the newly formed Royal Ulster Constabulary (RUC) and the B Specials and by sweeping special powers legislation, had imposed an uneasy peace. Yet the potential for violence remained. A succession of violent incidents from 1933, again coinciding with a period of increased unemployment, reached a climax in fighting following the 1935 Twelfth of July celebrations, leaving ten people dead (seven Protestants and three Catholics), 214 Catholic and 64 Protestant houses cleared of their inhabitants and once again some hundreds of Catholics expelled from their workplaces.[28]

Confronted by this combination of economic and political crisis, the Belfast municipal authorities were poorly equipped to respond. In 1919 the British government, concerned to protect both Catholic and Protestant minorities, had introduced proportional representation in Irish local elections. In consequence the Council elected for Belfast in 1920 was the most diverse ever returned: thirty-seven unionists (six of whom were returned as 'Labour Unionists'), ten nationalists (five each for Sinn Féin and the former Home Rule party), and thirteen Labour. In 1922, however, the Northern Ireland Government restored election by simple majority. In elections the following year the Labour representation was cut to two seats, as compared to fifty unionists (twenty-three of them returned unopposed) and eight nationalists. From then until the end of the Second World War Labour's representation never rose above the three returned in 1929. The duopoly of nationalist and unionist, with unionists in a permanent majority, was effectively restored.[29]

The absence of effective challengers gave the municipal elite little incentive to address the massive problems affecting the post-war city. The most dramatic demonstration of the gulf between rulers and ruled was the very low level of provision for those unemployed not covered by the limited national insurance scheme, the issue behind the riots of October 1932. Here, however, Belfast Council played no significant part. Relief was administered by the separately elected Board of Guardians, while it was the Northern Ireland Cabinet that stepped in, once things got out of control, to force the introduction of more generous provision. In one area for which it was responsible, education, the Council had a reasonably good record, spending steadily on the construction of new primary schools and introducing medical inspections and free school meals and text-books for poorer children. (This relatively benign outcome was partly due to the personal commitment of a particularly effective committee chairman, but his efforts may also have been aided by the fact that the state schools for which the Council was directly responsible were almost entirely Protestant, Catholic children being provided for by a separate network of grant-aided voluntary schools.) In relation to health, in contrast, Council indifference, and unwillingness to spend money, had dire consequences. By the late 1930s infant mortality stood at 97 per thousand births, compared to 77 in Northern Ireland as a whole, 74 in Liverpool and 69 in Manchester. Deaths from tuberculosis amounted to 21 per thousand population, compared to 12 per thousand across England's urban districts. The likelihood of death in childbirth, meanwhile, had risen by one fifth between 1922 and 1938. In the case of housing, a Council responsibility from 1919, the record was also poor. Of some 28,000 houses constructed within in the county borough between the wars, fewer than 2,600 were built by the Council, and these were generally sold or rented at a price that placed them beyond the reach of the average working-class family.[30]

As well as complacency, a permanent monopoly of power also encouraged corruption. An audit of the Housing Committee in 1925 discovered serious irregularities in tendering and payment for materials, leading to resignations and some prosecutions. A subsequent inquiry into the workings of the Council as a whole gave a scathing account of a dysfunctional system in which councillors attempted to micromanage matters properly left to officials, and in particular devoted far too much time to the distribution of patronage. A withering soundbite suggested that Belfast was attempting to manage its affairs on lines better suited to the running of a village. A local Act in 1930 introduced reforms, but perceptions of the Council as corrupt and ineffective remained widespread. The 1930s, in fact, appear to have seen a tightening of one-party rule, as the city's Unionists developed a more effective political organisation. Their leader, Sir Crawford McCullagh, had been chair of the Housing Committee at the time of the scandal and lost his seat in 1929. However, he had returned to the Council in 1930 and went on to serve as Lord Mayor for the following sixteen years, with one short break in 1942.[31]

The Second World War, coming at the end of two long, grim decades of economic malaise, community divisions and a discredited municipal system, had a mixed effect on Belfast's fortunes. The staple industries quickly expanded to meet war-time demand: the surviving shipyard and the linen mills (converted to the provision of uniforms, parachutes and fabric for aeroplane wings and fuselages) returned to full production, while the one great success story of the inter-war period, the aircraft manufactory established in 1937 by Short Brothers, also saw demand rise to new levels. But the demands of war time also cast a pitiless light on the continued inadequacies of the municipal administration. A series of air raids between 7 April and 6 May 1941 found the city woefully unprepared. There were no shelters for either the industrial work-force or the civilian population. The fire brigade was undermanned, and under prepared for an emergency; in the aftermath of the May raid, fire engines from Dublin arrived in Belfast to help deal with the inferno. The city mortuary was overwhelmed, and St George's Market and the Falls Road Public Baths were used to house the 1,000 or so dead.[32] The following year there was a new corruption scandal, this time focussing on the Tuberculosis Committee. The revelations were depressingly familiar. Members of the committee had lobbied for the choice of an unsuitable and overpriced site for a new sanatorium, and had purchased unsuitable blackout material from a firm with which four councillors had connections. Further enquiries revealed other malpractice, including the widespread use of the Corporation's fleet of cars to convey officials to and from their homes. When the Council failed to come up with credible proposals for reform, the Northern Ireland Government stepped in, placing control of appointments, contracts and purchases in the hands of appointed commissioners for a period of more than three years.[33]

The coming of war also brought back into focus the deeply divided allegiances of the city's population. On 26 May 1941, in response to discussion of the possibility of extending conscription to Northern Ireland, an estimated 7,000 nationalists gathered in the Gaelic Athletic Association's Corrigan Park, on the Whiterock Road, to sign a pledge to resist compulsory military service 'by the most effective means at our disposal, consonant with the law of God'.³⁴ A statement by Cardinal Joseph MacRory dismissed the suggestion that the havoc wreaked by German air raids just three weeks earlier should in any way modify the total rejection of the Northern Ireland state by its Catholic inhabitants.

> That the people of all creeds and classes in Belfast have recently suffered heavily at the hands of the Germans, regrettable as it may be, does not touch the essence of the question, which is that an ancient land, made one by God, was partitioned by a foreign power against the vehement protest of its people, and that conscription would now seek to compel those who still writhe under this grievous wrong to fight on the side of its perpetrators.³⁵

War-time conditions also inspired a sporadic revival of IRA activity in the city. The most serious incident was an ambush on a police patrol in west Belfast on Easter Sunday 1942, leading to the death of a constable. Six men arrested on the spot were sentenced to death but only one, nineteen-year-old Thomas Williams, was actually hanged. On the day of the execution opposing crowds gathered outside the jail. Female supporters of Williams knelt in prayer while nearby a hostile crowd of girls and women sang 'God Save the King', followed by 'Land of Hope and Glory' and 'There'll Always be an England'. Later, nationalist protestors passed through Royal Avenue, some reportedly giving Nazi salutes, and there was sporadic rioting in the main Catholic residential districts. The police responded in force, arresting between 100 and 200 men in dawn raids the following day and deploying armoured cars equipped with machine guns to patrol nationalist areas.³⁶

Old quarrels and new beginnings

In economic and social terms, the post-war years were relatively benign. The war-time boom in the city's major industries, shipbuilding, engineering and linen, continued into the early 1950s, further boosted by the Korean War. Thereafter the traditional staples resumed their slow decline, but new ventures in different types of light industry seemed for a time to be taking their place. Meanwhile the London government had accepted that Northern Ireland's contribution to the war effort entitled it to the financial support necessary to give the region an equal share in the post-war expansion of welfare services.

Where the management of public space was concerned, conflicting forces were at work. On the one hand, some within the Unionist establishment showed signs of a more relaxed approach. In 1948 Edmond Warnock, Minister for Home Affairs, overruling police objections, refused to announce the customary general ban on commemorations of the Easter Rising. In

September he declined to prohibit a celebration of the 150th anniversary of the United Irishmen's insurrection of 1798, 'because I dislike the necessity of interfering with public assembly'. Instead the proposed commemoration was relocated from High Street in the city centre to nationalist west Belfast. (To achieve this rerouting Warnock adopted the curiously cumbersome method of banning *all* parades in the city, exempting only the Catholic parts of west Belfast, a strategy that placed him in an embarrassing position when it was discovered that an Orange parade was also planned for the day in question.)[37] The Estates Committee of the City Council cancelled a booking for a *ceilidh* to be held in the Ulster Hall on 17 September, as part of the same commemoration. However, the Commemoration Committee took its case to the High Court, which ordered that the booking be upheld, with costs awarded against the Council. The *ceilidh* was duly staged, with 1,600 people attending.[38]

Moves towards a more tolerant policy continued under Warnock's successor, Brian Maginess. In 1951 he introduced a Public Order Act imposing new restrictions on parades, as well as creating an offence of 'provocative' conduct designed to cover displays of the Irish Tricolour. But this was an attempt to move away from the less satisfactory procedure of non-statutory restrictions imposed under the much-criticised Special Powers Act, and Maginess, introducing the Bill, emphasised that its provisions were aimed only at a small, extremist minority. The following year, acting on police advice, he prohibited a proposed Orange parade through a Catholic district, the Longstone Road in County Down, although in this case he later backed down in the face of fierce opposition within his own party. Initially Maginess had the backing of the Prime Minister, Sir Basil Brooke, earlier a Protestant militant but now concerned to avoid repressive measures that would open Northern Ireland to international criticism. However, the vision of a more liberal, potentially even a more inclusive, unionism was undermined by political events. In 1948 a new coalition government in the south moved to sever the country's last links with the British Commonwealth and redesignate the Free State as an Irish Republic. The southern political parties and a new grouping of Northern Ireland nationalists also joined in a revived campaign against Partition. The Northern Ireland general election of 1949, seen by both sides as a referendum on Northern Ireland's separate existence, was marked by violent clashes, and over the next two years parades and demonstrations continued to be the occasion for dangerous confrontations. Against this background, Brooke and Maginess faced strong opposition from within their own party, and from sections of the Orange Order, who denounced what they described as the 'appeasement' of nationalist enemies of the state. In the general election of October 1953 the Unionist vote fell sharply. Maginess himself narrowly avoided defeat at the hands of an Independent Unionist candidate.

This was the background to perhaps the most contentious new legislation introduced by the post-war Northern Ireland Government, the Flags and Emblems Act of 1954. The revival of the anti-Partition movement had encouraged more frequent displays of the Irish Tricolour. On 12 August 1946, for example, its appearance alongside another flag at a Socialist Republican parade at Carrick Hill provoked a police baton charge. Once again militant Protestants were outraged, not just by nationalist provocation, but by what they saw as the inadequate response of the authorities. In June 1953, during preparations for celebrations to mark the coronation of Queen Elizabeth II, the Chief Inspector of the RUC had instructed officers to discourage the flying of the Union flag in circumstances where it might lead to a breach of the peace, and the police had in fact intervened to dissuade businesses in nationalist districts of Belfast from putting up flags on their premises. In the aftermath of the election, however, and with protest within the party and the Orange Order continuing, the cabinet approved a new Act making it an offence to interfere with displays of the Union flag. In addition, without specifically mentioning the Tricolour (apparently on the grounds that this would have been a foreign policy matter and so outside Stormont's remit), the Act empowered the police to remove any flags that might cause a breach of the peace.[39]

To nationalists, the legislation of the post-war government was a confirmation of their second-class status within the Northern Irish state. The Public Order Act required organisers of parades to give forty-eight hours' advance notice to police. However, it specifically exempted public processions 'customarily held along a particular route', which in practice meant the parades of the loyal orders. Regardless of its intentions, the Act thus confirmed the long-standing inequality of rights. For loyal Protestants, access to public space was an absolute entitlement; for Catholics (and left-wing Protestants), it remained conditional on the level of challenge they presented to the status quo and the amount of opposition they were likely to encounter. The Flags and Emblems Act, as the Chief Inspector of the RUC pointed out, gave the police no practical powers that they did not already have under the general heading of preserving public order, but it remained a symbolic statement of intent. In practice the handling of nationalist events under the new legislation proved to be variable, with much discretion apparently left to the senior police officers concerned to decide how public order was best preserved. Marches and other gatherings continued to be banned or rerouted, and individuals were at times arrested and prosecuted for the display of Tricolours or similar offences. But other parades and commemorations, with or without displays of the Tricolour, were allowed to go ahead unhindered, and the general trend in the late 1950s and early 1960s was towards a greater degree of toleration. Orange events, however, retained their privileged status. In 1958, another Minister for Home Affairs, W. W. B. Topping, banned a proposed Orange parade in Dungiven,

County Londonderry, only to find himself heckled at the subsequent Twelfth of July gathering and dropped from the cabinet soon after.[40]

One further indication both of the continuing division of allegiances within Northern Irish society, and of the more relaxed tone that nevertheless seemed to be creeping into public life, was the visit in July 1953 of the newly crowned Elizabeth II. The comparison here is not just with the visit of George V, made against a background of civil war in June 1921, but with the visit of his son, George VI, following his coronation, in 1937. For the unionist population, at a low point in Belfast's economic fortunes, that nine-hour visit provided a welcome splash of colour. In 1937 as in 1921, the king and queen began their visit with a short progress from Donegall Quay to the City Hall for the presentation of royal addresses. Thereafter, however, the use of a motor car rather than a horse-drawn carriage permitted a more expansive itinerary: to Hillsborough in County Down, residence of the Governor General, back to Balmoral in south Belfast to review 30,000 assembled Boy Scouts, Girl Guides and other representatives of uniformed youth organisations, and then to Stormont for a garden party. The return journey to the royal yacht took the couple along the Newtownards Road, allowing them a glimpse of drab working-class streets transformed by flags and bunting. *The Times* put the total number of spectators lining the twenty miles covered by the royal car at a million, leading it to conclude that 'large numbers of theoretical opponents of Partition were sufficiently interested in the pageantry of the visit to merge with the multitude which gave the King and Queen so tumultuous a greeting'.[41] But the celebrations had a darker underside. In preparation for the visit, police had carried out pre-emptive arrests in the Falls Road and other nationalist areas and had made a sweep through the city's boarding houses, questioning visitors about the reason for their presence. On the night before the visit IRA units attacked and destroyed customs posts on both sides of the border, and planted a bomb on a railway bridge near Dundalk in an unsuccessful attempt to sever the Belfast–Dublin link. Another failed railway-bridge bomb, in County Antrim, appears to have been aimed at a train carrying police back from special duty in the city. There was also an explosion in Belfast itself, in Academy Street, timed to coincide with the presentation of the loyal addresses.[42]

Sixteen years later, when George VI's daughter made her first visit as queen, the same political divisions were on display. Nationalist leaders boycotted the event, as they had done earlier visits. There was a recurrence of the squabbles over Union flags and Tricolours that had taken place during the coronation the previous month, and that were to lead to legislation the following year. The IRA once again bombed the Dublin–Belfast railway line, apparently in an attempt to disrupt the plans of a group of ex-servicemen travelling north to meet the queen.[43] Meanwhile the government took the precaution of drafting no fewer than 1,300 RUC officers, one third of the entire force, into Londonderry to ensure that the queen did not encounter any hostile demonstrations during her time there.[44] Yet, despite this background of conflict, the three-day visit was the most elaborate royal performance Northern Ireland had so far seen. The queen and prince consort arrived by air, spending their first night in the Governor General's residence at Hillsborough. The next day was devoted to Belfast, with visits to Queen's University, City Hall, the annual show at Balmoral and the Parliament House at Stormont. On the last day, in a new departure, the queen travelled by train to beyond Coleraine, stopping at stations along the way, then proceeded by sea to Londonderry. The proceedings brought to Northern Ireland the mixture of deliberately archaic pomp and new-style accessibility that was to be the hallmark of the 'new Elizabethan' monarchy. The royal couple came accompanied by a detachment of the Yeomen of the Guard and a group of state trumpeters, but every stage of their three-day progress was designed to bring them as close as possible to the large and enthusiastic crowds that gathered for the occasion. The result was a colourful and exhilarating blend of official and populist loyalism. The Prime Minister, now Viscount Brookeborough, set the tone when he interrupted his journey to the airport to inspect the decorations on some of the 'little streets'. Later, when the royal couple made an impromptu appearance on the balcony of Government House at Hillsborough, they were greeted not just by cheering crowds but by the pounding of the Lambeg drums that were a centrepiece of Orange parades.

For the United Kingdom as a whole the accession of the young queen brought a moment of glamour, and a promise of better times to come, to a society just emerging from the bleak sacrifices demanded by war time. For Northern Ireland it had an additional significance. It provided the occasion, after the challenge of the anti-Partition campaign, to reaffirm an alternative unionist narrative, in which Protestant Ulster's long record of unwavering loyalty confirmed its place within the British state. It was a narrative powerfully reinforced by Northern Ireland's participation in the sacrifices of the Second World War, in contrast to the neutrality of the Free State. The *Belfast Telegraph*, for example, saw the arrival in Lough Foyle of the queen's frigate as evidence of 'Londonderry's new-found place as one of the principal naval bases in the United Kingdom'. Two days earlier, in an even more telling juxtaposition, the same paper had accompanied its report on the royal tour with an article for the anniversary of the Battle of the Somme, with the heading 'When Orange sashes were worn by the British army'.[45]

'Positive Protestantism'

The royal visit of 1953 was a triumphant assertion of Northern Ireland's Protestant unionist public culture. Within a decade, however, the rigid framework within which the region's public life had been conducted began to show signs of becoming more flexible. In 1963 Viscount Brookeborough, veteran of Ulster's resistance to Home Rule before and after the First World War, resigned as Prime Minister. His successor, Captain Terence O'Neill, adopted a new rhetoric, speaking of the need to replace a 'negative' with a 'positive' Protestantism, defined by what it stood for rather than what it opposed. He also referred, in terms wholly lacking in specifics but nevertheless deeply unsettling to traditionalists, of the need to reconcile the Catholic minority to its place in a reformed Northern Ireland. A similar transition had already taken place in the Irish Republic, where Sean Lemass, succeeding as Taoiseach in 1959, had abandoned the protectionist economic policies of the preceding three decades in favour of a strategy of directly encouraging foreign investment. Along with the commitment to modernisation came a more pragmatic attitude to Partition, symbolised when he and O'Neill exchanged official visits, first in Belfast and then in Dublin, in January and February of 1965.

An important part of the background to these developments was the abject failure of a new attempt to revive the tradition of physical force Republicanism. From the end of 1956 IRA activists based in the Republic staged a series of attacks across the border, striking at police stations and customs posts. The violence was real enough: in all, six members of the RUC and twelve Republicans were killed. But the campaign, though not formally called off until 1962, had already lost momentum several years before. Its defeat was in part achieved through the internment of Republican activists in both north and south. But also important – and in terms of the long-term consequences, most important – was the general failure of the Catholic population north of the border to support the return to armed action. This in turn ensured that the Protestant response to the renewed IRA challenge was proportionate. There was increased police activity, some of it involving the notoriously partisan and heavy-handed B Specials. But there was no resort to the indiscriminate sectarian killings, or the mobilisation of Protestant paramilitary vigilantes, that had taken place in the early 1920s. The sense that Catholic attitudes had shifted towards some form of acquiescence, however grudging, in the existence of a separate Northern Irish state was confirmed when, in 1965, the Nationalist party accepted the role of official opposition in the Stormont Parliament.

A changing political climate had implications for the use of public space. Defenders of the Orange tradition have frequently claimed that their parades, prior to the political conflict that erupted in the late 1960s, were a generally accepted part of Northern Irish life, attended by Catholics as well as Protestants. Such claims are, in some cases, self-serving. But there are indications that in the more relaxed circumstances of the late 1950s and early 1960s the annual Twelfth of July parade, in Belfast at least, did in fact lose some of its sectional and potentially aggressive character. The Belfast solicitor Charles Brett, a Labour party activist highly critical of unionism in all its guises, recalled touring parts of Sandy Row and the Shankill Road, in company with left-wing friends, Catholic as well as Protestant,

> joining in the dancing or the bonfire parties as we went, taking a bottle of stout first in this pub, then in that. ... No questions were asked; a Catholic was as welcome as a Prod; it really seemed that, at long last, the Orange celebrations had cast off their anti-Catholic associations, and were developing into a folk celebration of a harmless and delightful kind.[46]

Oral testimony relating to the same period, collected from Catholic working-class respondents, confirms that some among them turned out to enjoy the spectacle of the passing parade, if not necessarily the alcohol-fuelled festivities of the nights before and after.[47]

A changing political climate also affected the handling of nationalist events. Here the O'Neill era began with what at first sight looked like a reaffirmation of the traditional policy of repression. In the run-up to the general election of October 1964 police smashed their way into the offices of one of the Republican candidates for West Belfast, located on Divis Street at the bottom of the Falls Road, to remove a Tricolour displayed in the window. Their action provoked the worst rioting seen in the area since 1935. The police, however, had acted reluctantly, under pressure from O'Neill's most prominent critic, the Revd Ian Paisley, who had threatened to lead his own militant Protestant followers in a raid on the office if the authorities did not act. The display was indeed a breach of the Flags and Emblems Act of 1954. But Paisley's intervention was clearly directed at a pragmatic official view that minor breaches taking place in the heart of nationalist areas were best ignored.

The extent to which that view prevailed became evident two years later, with the anniversary of the Easter Rising of 1916. In the south the Dublin government organised an elaborate series of commemorative events, driven partly by genuine national pride but also by a fear that to do otherwise would leave the field open to Sinn Féin and the IRA, allowing them to pose as the true heirs of the revolution that had given birth to the state. But it made no attempt to extend the commemoration north of the border. Instead it was the Dublin-based leadership of Sinn Féin that urged Belfast Republicans to use the occasion to assert their continued relevance, despite the defeat of 1955–62. The resulting celebrations were elaborate. On Easter Sunday, Republicans staged their traditional march to Milltown cemetery, with 5,000 marchers and 20,000 spectators. The following Sunday, 17 April, a much larger crowd of 70,000 turned out to watch a procession make its way along the Falls Road to the Gaelic Athletic Association football ground at Casement Park. The event involved figures from all shades of nationalist opinion, including the moderate constitutionalists of the Nationalist party. But the dominant symbolism was that of armed-force Republicanism. Marchers carried Tricolours and banners of the executed leaders of the 1916 rising, while IRA veterans and members of Cumann na mBan, the Republican women's organisation, turned out in berets and military-style uniforms.[48]

For O'Neill's Unionist administration, these west Belfast commemorations presented an acute dilemma.[49] A substantial element within his party made clear their disquiet at these open celebrations of a Republican tradition that explicitly denied the legitimacy of the state. It was also becoming clear that Paisley's rabble-rousing had the potential to undermine the party's popular support. On the other hand, several prominent Unionists openly declared that the proposed celebrations, however deplorable, had to be tolerated in the name of free speech. O'Neill himself was influenced by the fear that any attempt at suppression would give Republicans an excuse to commence a new round of anti-state violence. He was also acutely aware of the damage that anything that looked like heavy-handed repression would do to Northern Ireland's image in the rest of the United Kingdom. On this basis his government allowed the commemorations to go ahead without interference, although in a sop to Protestant opinion (and possibly out of genuine security concerns) it imposed restrictions on north–south rail travel over the weekend of 16–17 April. With hindsight the decision to stand aside can be seen as a step on the road to the violent divisions that were to appear from 1969. Four days after the Casement Park event a reconstituted UVF announced that it was going to war against what it identified as the IRA, and went on to carry out two murders. Meanwhile, large popular demonstrations testified to Paisley's rising status as the champion of a mainly working-class Protestant militancy. At the time, however, the new moderate unionism seemed to be in the ascendant. Three organisers of the Falls Road procession on 17 April were prosecuted for not having sought police permission for the event and, when they refused to pay their fines, were arrested. But in June Paisley was also arrested, and jailed for three months, for having organised a similarly unauthorised march that had led to violent clashes when it passed through the Catholic Cromac district, while in the same month the UVF was declared illegal.

All this took place in a society that was entering a period of rapid social change. With the post-war rise in living standards, underpinned by an expansion of public sector employment and the extension to Northern Ireland of a new range of welfare provision, came a boom in the city's leisure industries. Cinemas, clubs and dance halls proliferated and thrived, encouraging the spread of new fashions in dress, hairstyles and music. Many of the new styles were American in origin, reinforcing an influence that had begun with the arrival during the war years of large numbers of United States servicemen (and – even more of a shock to local expectations – uniformed servicewomen). Television was another major influence; Northern Ireland got its own commercial station, UTV (Ulster Television), in 1959. What had been a closed, provincial society was opening itself to a wider world.[50] One consequence, by the 1960s, was the appearance on the streets of Belfast of new types of gathering, representing movements that for a time seemed to pose a real challenge to the established dichotomy of nationalist and unionist, Catholic and Protestant.

Notes

1 *Irish Times*, 23 June 1921; Lady Craig quoted in Gillian McIntosh, *Belfast City Hall: One Hundred Years* (Belfast: Blackstaff Press, 2006), p. 109.
2 See above, pp. 70–1.
3 *Irish Times*, 23 June 1921; BNL quoted in Gillian McIntosh, *Belfast City Hall*, p. 109.
4 Gillian McIntosh, 'The royal visit to Belfast, June 1921', in D. G. Boyce and Alan O'Day (eds), *The Ulster Crisis 1885–1921* (Basingstoke: Macmillan, 2006), pp. 259–78, at pp. 270, 275. For the honours conferred see *The Times*, 23 June 1921.
5 Nicholas Mansergh, *The Unresolved Question: The Anglo-Irish Settlement and its Undoing 1912–72* (New Haven and London: Yale University Press, 1991), p. 244.
6 Alan Greer, 'Sir James Craig and the construction of Parliament Buildings at Stormont', *Irish Historical Studies*, 31:123 (1999), 373–88, at p. 381, n. 40.
7 Brian Barton, *Brookeborough: The Making of a Prime Minister* (Belfast: Institute of Irish Studies, 1988), p. 56.
8 Keith Jeffery, 'Parades, police and government in Northern Ireland, 1922–69', in T. G. Fraser (ed.), *The Irish Parading Tradition: Following the Drum* (Basingstoke: Macmillan, 2000), pp. 78–94; Neil Jarman and Dominic Bryan, 'Green parades in an Orange state: Nationalist and Republican commemorations and demonstrations from Partition to the Troubles, 1920–70', in G. Fraser (ed.), *The Irish Parading Tradition: Following the Drum*, pp. 95–110. The government banned a planned Orange counter demonstration in County Fermanagh in 1938, but this was uncontentious as the order also prohibited the meeting against which they had intended to protest.
9 Jeffery, 'Parades, police and government', pp. 80–2; Jonathan Bardon, *A History of Ulster* (Belfast: Blackstaff Press, 1992), pp. 527–9.
10 Catholics made up 23 per cent of the male population of Belfast. In 1914 they contributed 23 per cent of the city's recruits and in 1915, 27 per cent. See Eric Mercer, 'For king, country and a shilling a day: Belfast recruiting patterns in the Great War', *History Ireland*, 11:4 (2003), 29–33. Richard S. Grayson, *Belfast Boys: How Unionists and Nationalists Fought and Died together in the First World War* (London: Continuum, 2009), suggests that in West Belfast, where Catholics accounted for 35 per cent of men, they contributed 37 per cent of recruits across the whole period of the war. However, his calculations are criticised by David Fitzpatrick, who suggests that the true figure for recruits was 29 per cent, indicating 'moderate under-representation of Catholics': David Fitzpatrick, 'West Belfast exceptionalism: Richard S. Grayson's *Belfast Boys*', *Irish Economic & Social History*, 38 (2011), 106.

11 Keith Jeffery, 'The Great War and modern Irish memory', in T. G. Fraser and Keith Jeffery (eds), *Men, Women and War* (Dublin: Lilliput Press, 1993), pp. 136–57, at pp. 150–1.
12 McIntosh, *Belfast City Hall*, p. 102.
13 Greer, 'Sir James Craig and the construction of Parliament Buildings', pp. 385–7.
14 Gillian McIntosh, 'Symbolic mirrors: commemorations of Edward Carson in the 1930s', *Irish Historical Studies*, 32:125 (2000), 100–9.
15 Craig's remark is much quoted, but the context is rarely given. He had just declared his commitment, during a debate on Catholic grievances, to seeing 'that fair play was meted out to all classes and creeds without any favour whatever on my part'. The Nationalist MP George Leeke interjected, 'What about your Protestant Parliament?', leading Craig to remind him that 'in the South they boasted of a Catholic State. They still boast of Southern Ireland being a Catholic State. All I boast of is that we are a Protestant Parliament and a Protestant State. It would be rather interesting for historians of the future to compare a Catholic State launched in the South with a Protestant State launched in the North and to see which gets on the better and prospers the more.' *Northern Ireland Commons Debates*, vol. 16, cols 1095–6 (29 April 1934). Craig's comments must be clearly distinguished from those of Sir Basil Brooke, then a government whip, now Minister for Agriculture, who the previous year had called on employers to hire 'good Protestant lads and lassies' rather than disloyal Catholics. On the other hand, Craig did not, when challenged, disavow his cabinet colleague's comments. See Bardon, *A History of Ulster*, pp. 538–9.
16 Rory O'Dwyer, 'On show to the world: the Eucharistic Congress, 1932', *History Ireland*, 15:6 (2007), 42–7.
17 *Anglo-Celt*, 30 June 1934. The figure of 80,000 is given in *Irish Times*, 25 June 1934, which also reported the arrangements for the broadcast. For the higher total of 120,000 see Oliver Rafferty, *Catholicism in Ulster 1603–1983: An Interpretative History* (Dublin: Gill and Macmillan, 1994), p. 236.
18 *Anglo-Celt*, 30 June 1934.
19 *Belfast Telegraph*, 25 May 1934.
20 *NW*, 25 May 1934.
21 *BNL*, 30 May, 4 June 1934; *NW*, 2 June 1934.
22 *Belfast Telegraph*, 12, 13 June 1934.
23 *Irish Examiner*, 27 June 1934. Much of Nixon's intervention was ruled out of order, and this part of his remarks does not appear in the official parliamentary record (*Northern Ireland Commons Debates*, vol. 16, cols 2247–50, 26 June 1934).
24 *BNL*, 20 March 1934. See also *BNL*, 31 January 1930, 12 March 1937.
25 Yvonne Whelan, 'The construction and destruction of a colonial landscape: monuments to British monarchs in Dublin before and after Independence', *Journal of Historical Geography*, 28:4 (2002), 508–33.
26 Eric Hobsbawm, 'Foreword', in Dawn Ades et al., *Art and Power: Europe under the Dictators* (London: Thames & Hudson, 1996), pp. 11–15.
27 Frank Curran, *Ireland's Fascist City* (Londonderry: Derry Journal, 1946).
28 Alan Parkinson, *Belfast's Unholy War* (Dublin: Four Courts Press, 2004); A. C.

Hepburn, 'The impact of ethnic violence: the Belfast riots of 1935', in Hepburn, *A Past Apart: Studies in the History of Catholic Belfast 1850–1950* (Belfast: Ulster Historical Foundation, 1996), pp. 174–202.
29 Ian Budge and Cornelius O'Leary, *Belfast: Approach to Crisis* (London: Macmillan, 1973), pp. 136–56, 186–7.
30 W. A. Maguire, *Belfast, a History* (Lancaster: Carnegie Press, 2009), pp. 144–7; Jonathan Bardon, 'Governing the city', in F. W. Boal and S. A. Royle (eds), *Enduring City: Belfast in the Twentieth Century* (Belfast: Blackstaff Press, 2006), pp. 124–40, at pp. 128–34.
31 Budge and O'Leary, *Belfast*, pp. 143–53. See also Susan B. Cunningham, *Sir Crawford McCullagh: Belfast's Dick Whittington* (Donaghadee: Ballyhay Books, 2016), chap. 12.
32 Brian Barton, *The Blitz: Belfast in the War Years* (Belfast: Blackstaff Press, 1989).
33 Budge and O'Leary, *Belfast*, pp. 153–4; Bardon, 'Governing the city', pp. 135–6.
34 *Irish Press*, 24 May 1941.
35 Liam Canny, 'Recruiting in the Irish Free State and Northern Ireland for the British armed forces during the 1939–1945 war' (M.A. dissertation, Queen's University, Belfast, 1995), p. 58.
36 *Irish Times*, 3, 4 September 1942; Steven Moore, *Behind the Garden Wall: A History of Capital Punishment in Belfast* (Antrim: Greystone, 1995), pp. 167–78.
37 Jeffery, 'Parades, police and government', pp. 88–9.
38 Peter Collins, *Who Fears to Speak of '98? Commemoration and the Continuing Impact of the United Irishmen* (Belfast: Ulster Historical Foundation, 2004), pp. 70–2. In subsequent years the status of the Ulster Hall remained, in some minds at least, an issue of concern. In 1959 the Council, in a belated triumph of ideology over aesthetics, removed the coat of arms, bearing generically Irish images of a deer and a wolfhound, that had adorned the building since its erection in 1862, and replaced it with a crude slab bearing the traditional red hand emblem of Ulster. See C. E. B. Brett, *Buildings of Belfast 1700–1914* (2nd edn, Belfast: Friar's Bush Press, 1985), p. 38.
39 Henry Patterson, 'Party versus order: Ulster Unionism and the Flags and Emblems Act', *Contemporary British History*, 13:4 (1999), 105–29.
40 Neil Jarman and Dominic Bryan, *From Riots to Rights: Nationalist Parades in the North of Ireland* (Coleraine: University of Ulster, 1997), pp. 36–42; Dominic Bryan, *Orange Parades: The Politics of Ritual, Tradition and Control* (London, 2000), pp. 74–6.
41 *The Times*, 30 July 1937.
42 *The Times*, 28, 29 July 1937; *Irish Independent*, 28 July 1937.
43 *Irish Independent*, 3 July 1953.
44 A Nationalist meeting to condemn the visit was, however, permitted in Meenan Park in the Catholic Bogside district, well away from the route of the procession. *Fermanagh Herald*, 4 July 1953.
45 Gillian McIntosh, 'A performance of consensus: the coronation visit of Elizabeth II to Northern Ireland, 1953', *Irish Studies Review*, 10:3 (2002), 315–29.
46 C. E. B. Brett, *Long Shadows Cast Before: Nine Lives in Ulster, 1625–1977* (Edinburgh: John Bartholomew & Son, 1978), p. 82.

47 Sean O'Connell, 'An age of conservative modernity 1914–68', in S. J. Connolly (ed.), *Belfast 400: People, Place and History* (Liverpool: Liverpool University Press, 2012), pp. 271–315, at p. 273.
48 Margaret O'Callaghan, '"From Casement Park to Toomebridge" – the commemoration of the Easter Rising in Northern Ireland in 1966', in Mary Daly and Margaret O'Callaghan (eds), *1916 in 1966: Commemorating the Easter Rising* (Dublin: Royal Irish Academy, 2007), pp. 86–147.
49 Catherine O'Donnell, 'Pragmatism versus unity: the Stormont government and the 1966 Easter commemorations', in Mary Daly and Margaret O'Callaghan (eds), *1916 in 1966: Commemorating the Easter Rising* (Dublin: Royal Irish Academy, 2007), pp. 239–71.
50 O'Connell, 'An age of conservative modernity 1914–68', pp. 310–15; Marianne Elliott, *Hearthlands: A Memoir of the White City Housing Estate in Belfast* (Belfast: Blackstaff Press, 2017), chap. 6.

7

New directions? The 1960s

In 1965, marchers from the nationalist district of Ballymurphy descended upon Belfast City Hall, some of them brandishing placards that compared the Unionist-controlled City Council to Belsen, the Nazi concentration camp. In the same year, students holding a thirty-four-hour vigil outside the American consulate sang songs from the African-American civil rights campaign and proudly proclaimed that their model of agitation was directly influenced by the radical students of Berkeley. In 1968 students protesting at the participation of American sailors in the Lord Mayor's Parade hoisted a North Vietnamese flag in the city centre.[1] These very brief vignettes from the Belfast of the mid- and late 1960s have two things in common. First, all three actions took as their point of reference events outside Northern Ireland. In this they reflected the greater openness to outside influences that had begun with the Second World War and continued and deepened in the new era of relative prosperity and optimism that followed. Second, none of the three movements involved could be fitted neatly into the simple two-part division of unionist and nationalist, Catholic and Protestant, that had for so long dominated public life. Instead the 1960s were to see a short-lived but significant opening up of public space to new expressions of identity and aspiration by groups who made their own claims to access to the symbolic locations of the City Hall and the city centre.

The civil rights movement and the denial of public space

Discussion of the issue of public space in 1960s Northern Ireland has been dominated by the proceedings of the Northern Irish civil rights movement (CRM), a loose and broad-based movement formed in 1967 to campaign on a range of issues, most notably on discrimination in employment and housing, the gerrymandering of electoral wards and the reform of the B Specials. The declared aim of the movement was to challenge the abuse of power within Northern Ireland, rather than to seek an end to Partition. The extent to which such claims can be taken at face value continues to be debated.[2] To many unionists, however, the issue was clear cut: 'civil rights' was a mere flag of convenience, masking a renewed attempt by nationalist opponents of the state to advance their goal of a united Ireland. Such fears were heightened by the movement's use of street politics. This was particularly the case in Belfast, where physical space historically reproduced ethno-national boundaries between nationalists and unionists.[3] 'Occupations, squattings, marches' might, as R. F. Foster has noted, 'appear the simple mechanics of the international student protest; but within Ulster they represented symbolic invasion of ancient territory and the assertion of an illegitimate right to "walk".'[4] Thus, the CRM's challenge to the status quo was not only through its perceived political objectives, but through its demand for access to the key symbolic, and even sacred, spaces of unionism in Belfast.[5] Indeed, the right to enter these spaces became a fundamental goal of protests and, as such, a crucible for conflict between protestors and the security forces. For example, on 9 October 1968, civil rights demonstrators marched from Queen's University Belfast with the aim of holding a protest in the grounds of Belfast City Hall. When the security forces denied access, the demonstrators held an impromptu three-hour sit-down protest.

This focus on the issue of access to the city centre was to continue in subsequent years, as civil rights gave way to an explicitly nationalist agenda, challenging the legitimacy of the Northern Irish state. The right of access to the space of the City Hall and to other locations became a spatial analogy for the wider struggle for group rights, and the associated discourses of equality and inclusion, that undergirded the violent conflict in Belfast. In 1973, for example, the socialist-republican organisation People's Democracy demanded authorisation from the security forces to march into the city centre. The Minister of State, in consultation with the security forces, prohibited the march from 'within a radius of half-a-mile from the City Hall, Belfast'.[6] Refusing to adhere to the ban, People's Democracy confronted the security forces, which responded by firing plastic bullets into the crowd attacking the barricades. For many nationalists, their continued exclusion from the city centre was seen as the spatial confirmation of inequality. On this issue, a nationalist leader wrote in 1973: 'one thing goes on forever – the ban on … any anti-unionist organisation marching to the City Hall in Belfast'.[7] For Irish nationalists, the City Hall became framed as an 'impenetrable bulwark of a "Protestant state for a Protestant people"'.[8]

Notably, when the first Irish nationalist parade was granted permission to enter the city centre in 1993, the Irish Republican organisers called the event a 'Nationalist Rights Day'.[9] Speaking prior to the parade, Alex Maskey, a leading member of Sinn Féin, stated that one of the main injustices experienced by nationalists in Belfast 'was not being allowed into our own city centre unhindered. We're now taking that step.'[10] At the conclusion of the event,

Gerry Adams, the president of Sinn Féin, addressed the crowd outside the City Hall, 'you have the right to your city, the right to your City Hall'.[11]

Other feet and other voices

Repeated confrontations between civil rights marchers, the security forces and, on occasion, Protestant counter demonstrators, in Belfast and elsewhere, form an important part of the chain of events leading up to the explosion of lethal violence that took place in 1969 and after. But they were initially only one part of the street politics of the 1960s. Other movements that cannot be fitted into that narrative, of the kind with which this chapter began, have largely been elided in the subsequent academic literature. Yet there are a number of important reasons why these movements, and in particular the claims they made to public space, merit illumination.

First, as seen in the preceding chapters, the idea that Belfast is a historically divided city is certainly true. This division has been apparent in the patterns of residential segregation separating Catholics and Protestants, sporadic periods of intense sectarian violence and high levels of endogamy. Such divisions would appear to be indicative of Lustick's classic definition of a 'divided society', in which levels of intergroup distrust and hostility are high and group boundaries are sharp enough so that 'membership is clear and, with few exceptions, unchangeable'.[12] Yet, the expression 'divided city' risks naturalising in an ahistorical way the shifting ethno-national cleavages and forms of political mobilisation that have occurred in the city. The concept of the 'divided city', therefore, generates a picture in which competing ethnic identities appear frozen, locked in unending antagonistic conflict.

Through uncritically deploying the concept of the divided city there is a danger of lapsing into what Rogers Brubaker has called 'groupism': 'to take discrete, sharply differentiated, internally homogeneous and externally bounded groups as basic constituents of social life, chief protagonists of social conflicts, and fundamental units of social analysis'.[13] Accordingly, we should shy away from simply assuming the permanency of ethnic groups and 'ethnic identities as given *ex ante*, automatically salient, fixed ... and predictive of individual political behaviour'.[14] Rather than places in which mutually exclusive renderings of ethnic identity are apparent, divided cities can provide dynamic political and social contexts wherein such identities and expressions of community can be negotiated and transformed.

The existence of groups that do not easily fit into the binaries of the nationalist/unionist two-community model generates important insights into why ethnicity may not be the primary basis for political and cultural mobilisation at particular historical junctures in divided cities. Equally, the history of non-sectarian movements may also reveal how so-called ethnic identities and divisions become constructed over time and/or at a specific moment. In particular, if we accept that ethnicity is not primordial and enduring, but can be constructed, within reason, then it is necessary to understand the conditions and socio-political processes through which ethnicity is forged. Non-sectarian movements, in other words, can be seen as relational, permitting an examination of how they interact and negotiate with the traditional ethno-national politics in the city, and even challenge their saliency. In divided cities, like Belfast, virtually all politics is practically subsumed by the wider ethno-political conflict over state legitimacy, or at least reduced to sectarian interests. Few non-sectarian movements are able to advance political issues and communal identities without being seen as automatically aligned with a particular ethnic party or agenda. Thus, paradoxically, while it is important to analyse how groups advance intercommunal politics that challenge the simple notion of the divided city, it is also apparent that these groups find it difficult to escape the parameters of traditional ethno-politics. In the case of Northern Ireland this situation became critical towards the end of the decade as politics became increasingly radicalised and non-sectarian movements were under threat of co-option from ethno-political movements.

Second, the relationship of these groups to the city centre is significant as it reveals how this 'sacred space' was open to protest by a wide variety of groups, none of whom were clearly articulating nationalist or unionist politics. This importance is further illuminated through longitudinal research on the decade of the 1960s. Rather than viewing the advent of the CRM as the point at which public space began to be contested in Belfast, the various movements explored in this chapter demonstrate how the city centre was already identified by groups, even during the early 1960s, as a crucible in which the institutions of governance and state power could be confronted. Such contestation could be reasonably subtle. Notably, while nationalist symbols and rituals were *de facto* proscribed under the Flags and Emblems Act – which meant that applications for nationalist events in the city centre were banned by the security forces – many protests and rituals by non-sectarian movements in the city centre featured members from Irish nationalist districts. The reform which these groups sought in the public and institutional arena, including demands for changes in the production of social goods and public services, was not viewed by the state authorities as necessarily articulating a direct threat to unionism. Significantly, most of the movements examined here were granted permission by the security forces to enter the confines of the city centre, a space viewed as the historical preserve of unionism.

This chapter advances by exploring three examples of non-sectarian movements that held protests and/or annual displays in Belfast city centre during the 1960s: the ban-the-bomb movement, public housing associations and the trade union May Day demonstration. Although these movements were generally distinct, advancing particular goals and politics, there was often a strong link between them, including overlapping membership and many shared forms of street politics. Through tracing these groups' protests and annual parades during the 1960s, key insights into the issues noted above are exposed. Most especially, these movements reveal the range of politics and identities in the city at that time, their complex relationship to nationalist and unionist groups and to the state authorities, and how the city centre was a stage that dramatised these shifting identities, politics and multiple relationships.

The Northern Ireland Campaign for Nuclear Disarmament

'Tools of communists'

The Northern Ireland Committee of the Campaign for Nuclear Disarmament (NICND) was formed in 1958.[15] The organisation broadly took its lead from the central British branch of the Campaign for Nuclear Disarmament (CND), which began in 1957, and NICND regularly sent a delegation to the annual four-day Easter march from London to Aldermaston (the site of the Atomic Research Establishment). NICND initiated its own annual parade from Customs House Square to Belfast City Hall in May 1960, which attracted 400 marchers. Led by a banner proclaiming 'Ban the Bomb: Without Vision the People Perish', the march was organised by NICND's chair, Revd Alex Watson, minister of Lambeg and Seymour Hill Presbyterian church, located in Belfast's southern suburbs.[16] Newspaper coverage of a 1961 parade in the city centre emphasised that the march was 'an exceedingly orderly one, proceeding through the city in a sedate and unobtrusive manner, without any shouting or gesticulation on the part of the demonstrators'.[17] Other reports noted the broad range of participants, which 'included housewives, students, members of the trade union organisations, the Society of Friends, the Communist Party, the Socialist Youth Group ...'.[18] Reports of the 1962 parade also favourably noted that a delegation from the Irish Republic, led by southern Irish parliamentarian Noël Browne, participated.[19]

NICND also mobilised around the impact of nuclear weapons on Northern Ireland. In 1960 a US naval nerve centre was moved from London to Clooney, near Derry, and NICND claimed that the post acted as a control mechanism for Polaris submarines in the Atlantic.[20] Although initially the US consulate in Belfast denied that the post existed,[21] the US military subsequently revealed that the base was a vital communications link for the US commander-in-chief in the Eastern Atlantic and Mediterranean to keep in constant touch with US warships and aircraft.[22] In 1961 NICND members waged a campaign outside the US consulate against the establishment of the Derry base. Protestors in Belfast were recorded holding placards stating: 'No To Death Signals from

Derry', 'Ulster Stands Firm Against Polaris Post' and 'Polaris Will Sink Us, Not Save Us'.[23]

NICND's local purview also turned on the Unionist government at Stormont. In 1960, Lord Brookeborough, Northern Ireland's Prime Minister, was asked in a political debate if his government intended to establish a Polaris base in Northern Ireland. Brookeborough replied: 'we would be prepared to accept one if it meant more employment'.[24] In response, NICND wrote to Brookeborough demanding that a Polaris post would not be based in Northern Ireland 'to off-set the rising incidence of unemployment'.[25] Belfast, however, was to be excluded from the proposed lucrative contracts for the building of the UK's Polaris submarine fleet. In 1963 Terence O'Neill, by then Prime Minister, wrote to Henry Brooke, the British Home Secretary, to request that he put pressure on the Admiralty to award Polaris contracts in Belfast, given that 'the employment outlook in our shipbuilding industry is causing great concern and further redundancy is forecast for the summer'.[26] The request was rejected and the contracts were awarded elsewhere.

Although NICND was willing to critique the local Unionist administration and the Westminster government for their policies on nuclear weapons, the organisation was simultaneously at pains to portray the movement as non-political and non-confrontational. NICND protestors were quick to distance themselves from the more direct forms of collective action utilised in some anti-nuclear demonstrations in England and Scotland during the early 1960s. One NICND member, involved in an overnight protest outside the City Hall during the Cuba crisis in October 1962, stated that 'we won't be lying down in protest or anything ... If we sit down, it'll be to rest and not to be arrested.'[27] The organisers also sought to maintain the movement's autonomy from regional party politics. For example, when members of the Young Socialist Society unfurled banners at the Easter 1963 march, proclaiming 'Socialism, Not War', and 'Out with Tory Bombs and Labour to Power', the Revd Alex Watson implored them to put the banners away from public view.[28]

Despite attempts to present a peaceful and non-aligned image in regard to party politics, the ban-the-bomb movement was also occasionally the subject of critique and distrust. Criticisms often centred on the movement's wide-ranging membership and its perceived anti-government politics. As such, NICND generated some degree of suspicion by dint of existing in a society where all forms of political mobilisation are almost inevitably positioned within the wider context of Northern Ireland's constitutional position. For example, in the aftermath of NICND's protests outside the US consulate in Belfast city centre during the Cuba crisis, Albert McElroy, the president of the Ulster Liberal Association, wrote to the *Belfast Telegraph* accusing the protestors of being 'the tool, if not the front organisation, of the Communist Party'.[29] Notably, such accusations were commonly levelled by some unionists, including McElroy, against the civil rights campaign in the late 1960s. As such, the epithet 'communists' became synonymous with anti-state sentiments, and especially with holding an affiliation to Irish Republicanism, which was accused by many unionists of covertly directing the CRM.[30] The feeling that NICND was anti-state and opposed to the Unionist government of Northern Ireland appeared confirmed when the movement protested against the possibility of Polaris submarines being built in Belfast's shipyards. At a period when Northern Ireland was experiencing high unemployment due to the post-war collapse of heavy industry – felt especially severely in Belfast's shipyards – such a contract could have acted to cauterise the haemorrhaging of industrial jobs, especially Protestant jobs. Notably, the main political party to support NICND was the Northern Ireland Labour Party (NILP), left leaning and, in aspiration at least, a cross-community movement. In the early 1960s, NILP increasingly threatened the Ulster Unionist Party's political hegemony by attracting working-class Protestant voters disaffected by the economic recession. As part of their attempts to win back Protestant voters, Unionist leaders sought to undermine the NILP by attacking not only its socialist – and thus apparently anti-state – politics, but the negative impact of such policies on working-class Protestants. Thus, NILP's support for NICND was framed as identical to a lack of support for jobs in the shipyards.[31]

NICND was also distrusted by some due to the character of its membership. As noted above, the newspapers often complimented the movement's good behaviour and commented favourably on the wide range of individuals and groups that participated. At the same time, the fact that the movement clearly comprised both Protestants and Catholics was a threat to the stability of existing ethno-religious boundaries in Northern Irish society. In a letter to the *Belfast Telegraph* in 1962, a reader signing himself Pastor Douglas wrote to express his 'disdain at those boys and girls of the "Ban the Bomb" movement'. Douglas's objection was not so much to the anti-nuclear campaign per se, as to the day on which NICND had protested: 'Sunday to Protestant Ulster is the Lord's Day, the Sabbath ... An evening of church service, instead of their Sunday march, would have done more good ...'[32] NICND members replied that some 'ministers and other religious people', like the letter writer, are 'happy to continue a cold war between Protestants and Roman Catholics'.[33] Another NICND member wrote to ask: 'since when have people like Mr. Douglas had permission to split up our community into the grades of religion, i.e. "Protestant Ulster", "Catholic Ulster" etc?'[34]

Changing direction

By the mid-1960s, the ban-the-bomb movement in the UK began to change its emphasis by embracing a range of new issues. This change was stimulated by two interrelated factors. First, the threat of imminent nuclear devastation had somewhat abated after the end of the Cuba missile crisis and the signing of the Partial Test Ban Treaty, under which the US, the Soviet Union and Britain banned nuclear testing in the atmosphere.[35] Thus, the initial fervour of radicalism that had inspired many members had somewhat waned and CND was under pressure to kindle interest and membership by mobilising on new issues.

Second, CND's position as a relevant social movement was challenged by the ongoing restructuring of the post-war New Left in the West.[36] Seeking to go beyond what they viewed as an outdated, economic-determinist variant of Marxism, socialists in the First World became inspired by struggles against colonialism and exploitation in the Third World. The fight for liberation by communists in Vietnam, South Africa, Cuba and Algeria demonstrated to Western radicals that, contrary to orthodox Marxist theory, a ripened capitalism was not an essential precondition of successful revolution. Revolution was an act of will rather than the predetermined product of a particular stage in the development of a society's economic structure. The attainment of revolution in the Third World had an additional benefit: it could help to precipitate revolution in the First World by overstretching Western capitalist states.[37] Under pressure from socialists in the organisation, CND began to prioritise non-nuclear campaigns in the mid-1960s, such as opposition to the war in Vietnam, support for the African-American civil rights campaign, and the campaign against apartheid in South Africa.

In line with this ideological change, the ban-the-bomb movement began to evolve its street politics and protest tactics. Initially, the movement had been profoundly influenced by the international pacifist movement.[38] In the 1950s peace groups such as the Peace Pledge Union began working on a Non-Violent Commission to examine the use of direct action in campaigning, including non-violent civil disobedience.[39] Leading protagonists in CND, such as the public intellectual Bertrand Russell, simultaneously became influenced by Gandhi's philosophy of *satyagraha* or non-violent action, which while refusing to cooperate with unjust laws seeks to avoid at all costs an ever-growing escalation of violence.

In 1960 CND supporters of non-violent direct action, dissatisfied with CND's hitherto non-confrontational street politics, set up a break-away organisation, the National Committee of 100. The Committee argued that mass civil disobedience, replete with sit-ins and blockades, was utterly justifiable, even if it broke the law and led to the arrests of practitioners.[40] In February 1961, 4,000 ban-the-bomb protestors in London sat down outside the Ministry of Defence in Whitehall, and in September 1,300 campaigners were arrested in Trafalgar Square. NICND received a first-hand lesson in non-violent direct action when Pat Arrowsmith, field secretary for the National Committee of

100 and the organiser for the Aldermaston marches, visited Belfast in 1962 to participate in a march and give a speech to Belfast dockers.[41] Shortly afterwards, Queen's University formed a branch of the National Committee of 100. Arrowsmith subsequently, in the 1970s, became an active member of the Troops Out Movement, an organisation which espoused Irish unity.

Belfast's left-wing groups began to develop a wider array of non-violent direct action tactics inspired by global radical movements. In October 1965, for example, the youth wing of NICND held a thirty-four-hour vigil outside the US consulate to protest against America's military intervention in Vietnam. The idea of the vigil, claimed the protestors, was motivated by the students at Berkeley University, California, who had written to the Belfast movement imploring them to join in spirit with their ongoing protests.[42] The students at Berkeley came to prominence in 1964 for their 'Free Speech Movement', which demanded that the university authorities should recognise the students' right to free speech, on-campus political activities and academic freedom. Due to the tactics of civil disobedience practised by students, the protest politics at Berkeley have been seen as a precursor of the student uprisings of the *enragés* of Paris in May 1968.[43] Such student radicalism has also been identified as providing a model for People's Democracy, the socialist-leaning civil rights group in Northern Ireland.[44]

The new radicalism of NICND occasionally brought it into conflict with the security forces in Belfast city centre. An example of this was in September 1965 when members of NICND were arrested during a protest over US policy in Vietnam outside the US consulate in Belfast city centre. As the organisers had failed to give the authorities notice of their plan to parade with political placards, the police decided to move the protestors, who were holding up traffic. In an precursor of civil rights tactics, protestors were recorded singing protest songs and strumming guitars, with some lying down to blockade the street. NICND later complained about the conduct of the RUC after it was alleged that 'several demonstrators were pushed and kicked by the police, who had in addition used '"obscene language"'.[45]

By the late 1960s, NICND was 'a focus for co-operation between young Republicans, socialists and communists'.[46] An example of this was in 1968 when members of NICND decided to protest against US intervention in Vietnam. When a group of US sailors stationed in Belfast on the warship USS *Keppler* were invited to participate in the Belfast Lord Mayor's Show, NICND decided that the occasion provided an ideal platform to make a public demonstration. On the morning prior to the parade, members of the Communist Youth League erected a North Vietnamese flag in the city centre. Following complaints by the US sailors, the flag was removed by the police.[47] Then, during the parade, six protestors ran out onto the road waving a North Vietnamese flag before lying prostrate in a line, blocking the path of the US sailors as they passed by the City Hall. However, the demonstrators failed to make the desired impact, as the sailors simply stepped over them and continued with the parade.[48]

The radicalism of NICND increasingly became overshadowed by the emergence of the civil rights campaign. Many members of NICND were now leading members of civil rights or radical socialist groups. Eamonn McCann was a member of NICND and participated in the 1965 Aldermaston march; John McGuffin, an anarchist and leading member of People's Democracy, was the chairperson for Queen's University branch of NICND during 1964–65. Other young civil rights leaders, such as Cyril Toman and Michael Farrell, also belonged to NICND.

It is important to note that, in the specific case of Belfast,, the emergence of the CRM in late 1960s was largely dominated by People's Democracy. Based at Queen's University, People's Democracy transcended the initial mandate of civil rights as articulated by the Northern Ireland Civil Rights Association, which was to address issues of discrimination in the region via a reformist approach. Somewhat like NICND, which was dominated by young socialists in the mid-1960s, People's Democracy looked to tap into the Trotskyite agenda for global transformation at the local scale. Would-be revolutionaries who had participated in NICND protests against the Vietnam War and the apartheid regime in South Africa were now organising demonstrations under the auspices of People's Democracy and were, according to civil rights leader Eamonn McCann, further linking themselves to the 'black struggle in the US, the workers' fight in France ... the uprising against Stalinism in Czechoslovakia'.[49]

Tenant associations

'Ban the increase'

The Amalgamated Committee, Belfast Corporation Tenants Association, was formed in 1961 from representatives of the large public housing estates in the city.[50] Similar committees already had a long tradition in the UK, beginning with the Glasgow rent strike of 1915, which was organised by tenants' committees and women's associations.[51] The Glasgow rent strike, which called for subsidised housing and restrictions on rent rises, concluded with a series of government legislative Acts establishing rent control for low-cost housing and a mandate for local government to build houses for working-class families.[52] From that point, a number of housing committees sprung up across UK cities to try to control speculators and to demand decent and affordable public housing and convenient free urban services.

Belfast too had a history of protest by municipal housing tenants. In 1936, for instance, a huge crowd of nationalist and unionist tenants, MPs and councillors descended on City Hall to force Belfast Corporation to halt an attempt to rescind a motion to reduce rents by two shillings per week.[53] In the early 1960s, Belfast's Corporation tenants, frequently supported by elected politicians, increasingly mobilised into grassroots pressure and protest groups. In August 1961, members of the Amalgamated Tenants Committee and nine council members marched to the City Hall in an unsuccessful attempt to stave off increases in rent on 11,000 council dwellings after the Corporation's Housing Estate and Markets Committee found itself in deficit by £97,000. Many of the several hundred marchers were recorded brandishing placards bearing slogans like: 'Back to the Hungry 30s'.[54]

During the early 1960s, Belfast Corporation faced annual shortfalls in its housing budget. The major reason was inflationary loan charges linked to the Corporation's policy of borrowing to cover the costs of building and maintaining housing stock. In order to cover the debt, the Corporation repeatedly proposed rent increases, stimulating protests by public housing tenants. A protest in September 1962 against further rises, containing 500 members of the Amalgamated Tenants Committee, included one protestor holding a placard which made an analogy between the campaigns of the tenants and nuclear disarmament: 'Ban the Increase, Ban the Bomb'.[55] The rises primarily impacted upon tenants living in substandard public housing – often without a hot-water tap or an indoor toilet. This situation angered tenants, who noted that not only were they funding the construction of new homes but the construction costs of these homes were chronically over-inflated. To add insult to injury for many, the rent increases for pre-war Corporation houses were often higher than those for new-build post-war houses and flats. The proposed rise in 1961, for instance, increased rent for pre-war homes by 2s 6d per week, while post-war homes increased by 2s.[56]

At a time when nationalist-related events, especially demonstrations, were *de facto* proscribed from the city centre under the Flags and Emblems Act, tenants' street protests in the early and mid-1960s were a medium through which nationalists could enter the centre to protest. A protest march to the City Hall in November 1963 by the Amalgamated Tenants Committee was recorded by the *Irish News* as specifically involving 500 placard-holding nationalist residents.[57] Many nationalist estates, like Ballymurphy, Turf Lodge and Andersonstown, formed their own tenants' groups, which came under the jurisdiction of the Amalgamated Tenants Committee. Another protest march to the City Hall against proposed rent increases of four shillings per week in August 1965 was afforded great preparation by the Ballymurphy Tenants Association, which concocted slogans to outline its grievances. As the *Irish News* remarked, 'some of the slogans were not without a biting humour'. One placard in the parade of 400 protestors read: 'Higher Rents, Higher

Bus Fares, Higher Food Prices – Why Not Just Change the Name Belfast to Belsen?'[58]

The CRM and housing

The development of the civil rights campaign in the late 1960s changed the context within which issues involving public housing were pursued. While organisations like the Amalgamated Tenants Committee had previously protested solely to limit rents and improve the quality of public housing, the CRM adopted the issue of perceived inequalities in the distribution of public housing between Catholics and Protestants. Thus, the question of public housing was now indivisible from the larger question of discrimination within the polity.

The CRM's adoption of housing as a central rallying point was, to some extent, an unintended consequence of the Stormont government's post-war drive to expand its stock of public housing. Between June 1944 and December 1964, 124,878 new dwellings were built by a combination of local government, the Northern Ireland Housing Trust (NIHT) and the private sector.[59] However, many of these homes were allocated on a blatantly partisan basis, as Unionist-dominated councils used public housing as a form of political patronage and sought to confine Catholic applicants to a limited number of overcrowded areas as a means of minimising the impact of their votes. (The NIHT, by contrast, allocated the properties under its control on a non-sectarian basis, but its houses, and the associated rents, were tailored to the better-off sections of the working class, in which Catholics were under-represented.)[60] It was this malpractice, particularly widespread west of the River Bann, where large Catholic electorates had to be contained by every means possible, that led the CRM to make housing a central part of its campaign of protest. Complaints of sectarian misallocation were in fact less prevalent in Belfast, which was heavily industrialised and thus a major centre for the construction of new homes. Between June 1944 and December 1966, Belfast Corporation built 10,020 dwellings in the city alongside the NIHT's 17,000 and 25,000 homes contributed by private builders. But the wider problem of housing in the city was an acute one. A three-day series of special reports in the *Belfast Telegraph* in March 1967 pointed out that, despite the programme of house building, 8,000 homes needed to be urgently built and that, rather than the programme speeding up, the number of house completions had slowed.[61] While Belfast had fared better in terms of new houses than other areas of Northern Ireland, the report noted that it lagged behind similar-sized cities in England. Alongside this, the report highlighted that 'nearly half the population of Belfast is living in condemned or near-condemned property' and that building costs had risen 50 per cent between 1958 and 1965 as builders sought to maximise profits. Public housing tenants were quick to note that these inflationary housing costs were being passed on to them via rent increases.

As noted earlier, the initial medium for protests in Belfast over rent rises and the poor standard of public housing in the early to mid-1960s was the Amalgamated Tenants Committee. By the late 1960s, public housing issues were increasingly directed away from the Tenants Committee and into the CRM's sphere of influence. During 1969, in particular, the CRM initiatives made a number of interventions in the city's housing protests. One example of this was when an organisation called the Belfast and District Civil Rights Committee tried to resist the eviction of a family 'living in a two-roomed "hovel"' in a nationalist area of Belfast. In a statement, the committee asserted 'that those who saw no need for civil rights in Belfast should look at the housing situation in the city'.[62]

The main expression of CRM in Belfast was People's Democracy, which, as noted earlier, was a student-based revolutionary socialist grouping. People's Democracy quickly speculated that the issue of housing conditions in Belfast provided a medium to build links with the industrial working class. In early 1969 a 'one-issue'[63] branch of People's Democracy formed in the nationalist Cromac district, stating that it would take immediate action over the 'disgraceful housing conditions in the area'.[64] A march to the City Hall in April, organised by the Cromac People's Democracy Housing Action Committee, ended in confrontation when 200 Loyalists, led by Major Ronald Bunting, Ian Paisley's deputy, descended on the City Hall to carry out a counter demonstration against an organisation which they identified as a cloak for Irish Republican radicalism.[65]

Despite People's Democracy's desire to act as the revolutionary vanguard of the city's nationalist working class, the People's Democracy Cromac Housing Committee's tenure was brief, as it was unable to muster more than thirty people for its protests. Thus, the relative failure of People's Democracy to co-opt tenants' committees demonstrated that the movement's strategy of seeking coalescence by absorbing grassroots pressure groups was only marginally successful. Moreover, as People's Democracy moved inexorably towards the revolutionary left and away from a broader reformist agenda, campaigning against rent rises was seen by many members as contrary to radical ideals. This concern is broadly indicative of the Marxist-Leninist doctrine that increasingly became the outlook of People's Democracy. According to this view the working class, without the leadership of the revolutionary, intellectual elite, could not by itself expedite a radical consciousness; instead, it would limit itself to immediate economic issues. Certainly, prior to the advent of the CRM, the Amalgamated Committee called for a moderate approach to rent. A deputation of tenants to the Estates Committee in 1965, for instance, suggested that one way the Corporation could avert fiscal mismanagement engendered by inflated building costs was by ensuring that houses were built at a contracted rate with money borrowed at a fixed rate of repayment.[66] For People's Democracy, on the other hand, as their manifesto of February 1969 made clear, reducing rent was not the ultimate aim: instead People's Democracy prioritised the requisitioning of vacant housing and the cancellation of Housing Trust debts to the central banks.[67]

Irish Republicans in the city also became increasingly involved in the tenants' campaigns to oppose rent rises and poor housing conditions during the late 1960s. For example, in April 1969, a group calling itself the Belfast Housing Action Committee delayed traffic for thirty minutes on Divis Street, west Belfast, where a family of eight was squatting in a Housing Trust maisonette. The *Irish News* reported that the Action Committee was led by a young Gerry Adams, who stated 'that with the full support of the people of the district they would continue their campaign'.[68]

The environment of radicalism that characterised street politics in the city during the late 1960s also influenced the Amalgamated Committee. Under pressure from attempts by People's Democracy and Republicans to co-opt the movement, the Amalgamated Committee moved away from advancing its hitherto moderate approach to housing and promoted more confrontational measures. After the Belfast Corporation yet again found itself in deficit in 1969, this time to the tune of £210,000, it was proposed that rents would rise by seven shillings. A meeting in response by the Amalgamated Committee demonstrated that the tenants were now willing to utilise subversive street tactics to oppose the rise, including threatening a sit-in at the City Hall and a sit-in at the home of the Housing Trust's head.[69]

May Day and trade unionism: 'Bury the old shibboleths'

As a major industrial centre, Belfast had a long history of labour organisation. The craft unions active throughout the second half of the nineteenth century were joined in its closing years by the 'new unionism' of the unskilled. In 1907 industrial action on the docks and elsewhere brought the city's commerce to a near standstill, and for a time seemed to hold out the prospect that joint action by Catholic and Protestant workers would allow the politics of class to supplant the politics of ethnicity and religion.[70] Over the next two decades, on the other hand, vicious communal conflict, including episodes such as the mass expulsion of Catholics from the shipyards, threatened to destroy the labour movement altogether. In the event, a reasonably effective trade union movement survived the period of crisis. Although the great majority (by the late twentieth century 90 per cent) of trade union members belonged to organisations whose headquarters were in the United Kingdom, overall direction of trade union affairs in Northern Ireland was left in the hands of the Northern Ireland Committee of the Dublin-based Irish Congress of Trade Unions (ICTU). It was a compromise sustained by the convention that this Northern Ireland Committee, recruited from Northern Ireland and including both Catholics and Protestants, should confine itself strictly to labour matters, avoiding any involvement in the politics of unionism, nationalism and Partition.[71]

The other main voice of labour, the NILP, attempted a similar policy of neutrality on questions of nationality, but as a party forced to compete for votes in a starkly polarised electoral system it enjoyed less success. In the Stormont election of 1949, which the recent declaration of an Irish Republic in the south allowed the Unionist party to frame as a referendum on Partition, the party failed to win a single seat. In the apparently changing Northern Ireland of the late 1950s and early 1960s, however, its prospects seemed suddenly to improve. In the Stormont election of 1958 it won four seats, and held on to these, with increased majorities, in the next electoral contest, in 1962. It was against this background that the annual May Day parade of trade unionists and other labour activists assumed a new significance as a public assertion of class solidarity above divisive sectarian allegiances.

Suspended during the period of violence that accompanied Partition, the Belfast May Day parade had resumed in 1931, after a gap of ten years. The form varied. In 1934, for example, participants paraded in the main streets of the city centre with flags and banners before gathering to hear speeches in front of the Custom House. In 1938, on the other hand, there was a meeting in the same venue, but no procession.[72] In the years of political marginalisation during the 1950s, internal divisions brought disruption. In 1955 the NILP withdrew from the event which it had previously organised jointly with the Belfast Trades Council, in protest at the inclusion among the speakers of the prominent Communist Party member Betty Sinclair; in 1958 the party organised its own rival demonstration on the same grounds.[73] In the early and mid-1960s, however, May Day took on a new life. The processions attracted up to 20,000 participants, led by as many as thirty brass bands and with each union carrying a huge representative banner. The pageant would wind its way through the city centre and then conclude at 'Blitz Square', a large expanse of wasteland at the bottom of York Street still vacant following the devastation caused by the Luftwaffe's bombs in 1941. Here, the trade unionists would gather to listen to the various leaders give fiery speeches. Given its identity as a socialist space, 'Blitz Square' also attained the popular sobriquet of 'Red Square'.[74] Newspaper coverage of the 1961 demonstration noted: 'Large crowds of shoppers lined the side walks in the city centre to watch the colourful parade.'[75] Similar to the ban-the-bomb parades of the early 1960s, the organisers of the May Day parade were proud of their links to fraternal organisations in the Irish Republic. For instance, the 1961 demonstration was led by the band of the Irish Transport and General Workers Union from Dublin.[76]

The clear purpose of this revived series of May Day events was to provide what can be seen as a ritual of unity – an expression of *communitas*, the 'communion of equal individuals'[77] – wherein the divisions that permeate everyday life are temporarily abandoned in favour of unmediated and egalitarian association among individuals.[78] This unifying identity was particularly evident in the speeches given by leading trade unionists after the parade. A speech by Frank Cousins, general secretary of the Transport and General Workers Union, at the end of the 1962 May Day demonstration declared that the trade union movement in Northern Ireland was 'against sectarianism. That was trade unionism, and labour thinking.'[79] A speech by another leading trade unionist, Harry Campbell, after the 1966 May Day demonstration implored Northern Irish society to 'bury the old shibboleths' that differentiated nationalist and unionist workers, insisting that it was up to 'socialists and trade unionists to shove them into the grave'.[80] As such, the trade union movement could be seen as subscribing to what Gellner famously called the 'wrong address' theory of nationalism: a conviction that the spirit of human consciousness made a terrible error by delivering the awakening message to nations instead of classes. The task for socialists, in this view, was 'to persuade the wrongful recipient to hand over the message, and the zeal it intends, to the rightful and intended recipient', the working classes.[81]

The trade union organisers of May Day zealously guarded the demonstration's identity as a display of class unity unblemished by sectarian or factional political interests. For this reason, the organisers were quick to proscribe any grouping that they perceived as being in contravention of that spirit. In 1965 they stopped members of the Irish Nationalist Party marching as a separate unit. In 1966 and 1967 the Young Socialists, a small grouping of Trotskyists affiliated to the NILP, were also banned from participating as an individual unit. The ban on the Young Socialists became especially fractious when the organisers became embroiled in minor scuffles with members of the group.[82]

The proscription of the Young Socialists was a harbinger of the major schisms that were to characterise the May Day demonstration during the civil rights era and the subsequent outbreak of violent conflict in the city. Although the Young Socialists were again debarred from participating in the 1968 parade as an individual unit, members tried to defy the ban by joining in the parade after it had started. Although parade stewards quickly removed the socialists, they rejoined later with placards calling for 'Victory to the Vietcong' and 'Democracy in Derry', the latter a clear reference to the struggle for civil rights that was then taking place in Northern Ireland's second city.[83] As such, the trade union movement, via the May Day parade, was increasingly being challenged to embrace issues, especially civil rights, that had the potential to embroil it in politics in a way that might appear sectarian, or would at least threaten its claim to class cohesiveness.

This threat became reality in 1969 when People's Democracy called on its members to 'join in the May Day parade organised by the Irish Congress of Trade Unions ... to demand full rights for trade unionists and the basic demands of one man, one job, and one family, one house', a clear reference to core CRM objectives.[84] In response, the May Day organisers attempted to rearticulate its unifying, intercommunal values. The then chair of the Northern Ireland Committee, Stephen McGonagle, stated that it was the movement's purpose to 'shun any form of bigotry and sectarianism' and called on People's Democracy to march as members of their respective trade unions and not as an individual political grouping.[85]

Nevertheless, reports of People's Democracy demanding that its members should participate in the 1969 May Day demonstration generated Loyalist counter action, especially from Ian Paisley and his followers. Paisley had taken it upon himself to destroy CRM after declaring it to be little more than a barely concealed Irish Republican plot.[86] Thus, according to the *Irish News*, 'a dozen Protestant militants' turned up at the head of the [May Day] parade with union flags to protest'. The leader of the 'extremists', John McKeague, remonstrated 'against the Papists and anarchists behind us'.[87] In the following days and weeks, via the medium of their newspaper, the *Protestant Telegraph*, hard-line unionists expressed outrage at the May Day organisers, accusing them of banning the Union flag: 'Communists and rebels are welcomed but the flag of my country is rejected.'[88]

The struggle of the May Day organisers to maintain unity was finally broken in 1970 in the aftermath of serious sectarian violence in Belfast the previous summer. In response to the violence, the ICTU decided to cancel the 1970 May Day parade 'as a gesture towards peace in the community'.[89] However, two different organisations – NILP and the People's Democracy – decided to hold their own unofficial May Day parades in the city centre. The People's Democracy parade was reported as involving 300 participants, some of whom held placards stating 'Workers of the World Unite'. As the parade passed Shaftesbury Avenue, led by a car with a loud-speaker playing 'The Internationale', a group of Loyalists greeted the marchers by chanting 'UVF' and 'go home you bums'.[90]

For the next few years, as Belfast and the wider region experienced increasing levels of violence, May Day continued to be characterised by factionalism, with as many as four separate parades occurring in the city on the same day in 1972. Apart from the official ICTU-organised demonstration, there were parades by the NILP, People's Democracy and the Loyalist Association of Workers, a militant outfit that cajoled Protestant trade unionists into exclusively identifying with the Loyalist cause. Given the rising trajectory of violence in the city, alongside the widening sectarian schism of the trade union movement, the ICTU often cancelled May Day demonstrations in the early 1970s. In 1973, for example, the ICTU called on its members to take part in a march, led by the Citizens United for Reconciliation and Equality, which called for an end to violence and for reconciliation to take root in the beleaguered society.[91]

Conclusion

The 1960s was clearly a period of transformation and crisis for Belfast's polity and society. While the eruption of extreme sectarian violence in the city during the summer of 1969 is often bookmarked as the chronological start of the Troubles, it is nonetheless deeply problematic to see the violence as the end point of a long teleological process. In this synopsis, the civil violence that began in 1969 was the inevitable consequence of Northern Ireland's underlying sectarian divisions and inequalities. Such grievances and divisions, in themselves, do not automatically convert into intercommunal conflict. Moreover, as this chapter has shown, rather than a city and political culture completely defined by permanent and well-defined cleavages, Belfast in the early to mid-1960s hosted a relatively rich variety of protest movements that advanced a range of political objectives and identities outside the traditional framework of ethno-politics.

On the one hand, the existence of these movements challenges the historical narrative of Belfast as a terminally divided city characterised by extreme ethnic fractures that made conflict appear certain. Groups could mobilise and develop political opinions on issues that concerned all members of society regardless of their ethnic or religious affiliation. On the other hand, a longitudinal assessment of these movements over the decade also demonstrates the difficulty that they had in trying to carve out a neutral space in a society where practically all politics was subsumed by sectarian interests. Groups that proudly organised on non-sectarian lines could be a target of suspicion and distrust. These movements risk being framed as anomalous, distortions that confuse and upset normal categories underlying ethnic distinctions in divided societies. Such anomalies are thus potentially transgressive, constituting pollutants that contaminate the boundaries that demarcate 'us' and 'them', 'friend' and 'enemy'. As Mary Douglas noted, societies try to cleanse anomalies or reorganise them by inserting them into the established modes of thinking and social order.[92] In some cases groups could be accused of being covert nationalist or unionist fronts, and thus an object of censure and critique. A longitudinal analysis also reveals how these movements were an object of co-option and assimilation by more radical nationalist and unionist groups, especially towards the end of the 1960s.

It is also significant that the non-sectarian movements discussed in this chapter identified the City Hall and the surrounding city centre as a key space to hold their protests. This is important, as it calls into question the assumption that these spaces were merely the sacred spaces of unionism and therefore an unalloyed property of unionist power and hegemony, at least until the challenge provoked by the civil rights protests at the end of the decade. The city centre and the City Hall attracted the demonstrations of trade unionists, ban-the-bomb movements, anti-war protestors and housing tenants' movements which preceded the CRM. Thus, while the city centre was a site of social centrality that appeared to legitimise political power for unionism, it was, by the early to mid-1960s, a space in which such power could be, at least, questioned. As Friedland and Hecht note: 'conflicts over the social order will ramify in its sacred centre'.[93] With this in mind, it has been the intention of this chapter to illuminate and analyse the wide-ranging and complex character of political performance in the dramatic arena of Belfast city centre during the 1960s.

Notes

1 John Nagle, 'From "Ban-the-Bomb" to "Ban-the-Increase"': 1960s street politics in pre-civil rights Belfast', *Irish Political Studies*, 23:1 (2008), 41–58.
2 See Bob Purdie, 'Was the Civil Rights Movement a Republican/Communist conspiracy?' *Irish Political Studies*, 3 (1988), 33–41; Simon Prince, *Northern Ireland's '68: Civil Rights, Global Revolt and the Origins of the Troubles* (Dublin: Irish Academic Press, 2007).
3 Paul Bew, Peter Gibbon and Henry Patterson, *Northern Ireland 1921/2001: Political Forces and Social Classes* (London: Serif, 2002).
4 R. F. Foster, *Modern Ireland 1600–1972* (London: Allen Lane, 1988), p. 588.
5 For 'sacred spaces', in this context, see above, p. 12.
6 *Irish News*, 10 February 1973.
7 *Irish News*, 10 February 1973.
8 Thomas Hayden, 'Foreword', in Mairtin O'Muilleoir (ed.), *Belfast's Dome of Delight: City Hall Politics, 1981–2000* (Belfast: Beyond the Pale, 1999), pp. i–ix.
9 John Nagle and Mary-Alice Clancy, *Shared Society or Benign Apartheid? Understanding Peace-building in Divided Societies* (Basingstoke: Palgrave Macmillan, 2010), p. 73.
10 F. Boyle, 'Nationalist city centre march looks set for approval', *Irish News*, 7 August 1993. For a more detailed discussion of the admission of nationalist events to the city centre, see below, pp. 184, 193–4, 214–15.
11 Boyle, 'Nationalist city centre march'.
12 Ian Lustick, 'Stability in deeply divided societies: consociationalism versus control', *World Politics*, 31:3 (1979), 325–44.
13 Rogers Brubaker, 'Ethnicity without groups', *Archives Européennes de Sociologie*, 43:2 (2002), 163–89.

New directions? The 1960s 177

14 Stathis N. Kalyvas, 'Ethnic defection in civil war', *Comparative Political Studies*, 41:8 (2008), 1043–68.
15 *Irish News*, 16 May 1960.
16 Ministers from the Church of Ireland also often participated in marches. In fact, in 1962 the General Synod of the Church of Ireland narrowly voted in favour of a motion calling on the UK government to end tests on nuclear weapons. See *BNL*, 21 May 1962.
17 *BNL*, 9 October 1961.
18 *BNL*, 14 May 1960.
19 *Belfast Telegraph*, 21 April 1962.
20 *Belfast Telegraph*, 9 December 1960.
21 *BNL*, 21 February 1961.
22 *Belfast Telegraph*, 30 August 1962.
23 *Irish News*, 21 February 1961.
24 *Northern Ireland Commons Debates*, vol. 47, cols 753–4, 29 November 1960.
25 *Belfast Telegraph*, 2 December 1960.
26 PRONI, CAB 4/1225, Cabinet Meeting, 21 March 1963.
27 *Belfast Telegraph*, 26 October 1962.
28 *Belfast Telegraph*, 13 April 1963.
29 *Belfast Telegraph*, 2 November 1962.
30 Purdie, 'The Civil Rights Movement', p. 156.
31 *Belfast Telegraph*, 2 November, 1962.
32 *Belfast Telegraph*, 10 January 1962.
33 *Belfast Telegraph*, 16 January 1962.
34 *Belfast Telegraph*, 16 January 1962.
35 Kate Hudson, *CND: Now More Than Ever. The Story of a Peace Movement* (London: Vision, 2005), p. 87.
36 Simon Prince, 'The global revolt of 1968 and Northern Ireland', *The Historical Journal*, 49: 3 (2006), 851–75.
37 Prince, 'The global revolt'.
38 Prince, 'The global revolt', p. 862.
39 Hudson, *CND*, p. 34
40 Hudson, *CND*, p. 73
41 *Belfast Telegraph*, 1 December 1962.
42 *BNL*, 14 October 1965.
43 Prince, 'The global revolt', p. 861.
44 For an analysis of the role of student activism in the CRM, see Paul Arthur, *The People's Democracy: 1968–1973* (Belfast: Blackstaff, 1974).
45 *BNL*, 20 September 1965.
46 Niall Ó Dochartaigh, *From Civil Rights to Armalites: Derry and the Birth of the Irish Troubles* (Basingstoke: Palgrave Macmillan, 2005), p. 55.
47 *Belfast Telegraph*, 2 August 2003.
48 *BNL*, 20 May 1968.
49 Eamonn McCann, *War and Peace in Northern Ireland* (Dublin: Hot Press, 1998), p. 4.

50 *Irish News*, 21 July 1961.
51 C. Pickvance, 'Marxist approaches to the study of urban politics', *International Journal of Urban and Regional Research*, 1:1–3 (1977), 219–55.
52 Manuel Castells, *The City and the Grassroots: A Cross-Cultural Theory of Urban Social Movements* (London: Edward Arnold, 1983), p. 27.
53 *Irish News*, 24 May 1936.
54 *Irish News*, 2 August 1961.
55 *Belfast Telegraph*, 22 September 1962.
56 *Irish News*, 2 August 1961.
57 *Irish News*, 16 November 1963.
58 *Irish News*, 3 August 1965.
59 Bob Purdie, *Politics in the Street: The Origins of the Civil Rights Movement in Northern Ireland* (Belfast: Blackstaff, 1990), p. 83.
60 The evidence on the extent of malpractice in the allocation of public housing is carefully reviewed in J. H. Whyte, 'How much discrimination was there under the Unionist regime, 1921–68?', in Tom Gallagher and James O'Connell (eds), *Contemporary Irish Studies* (Manchester: Manchester University Press, 1983), pp. 1–35. For the Northern Ireland Housing Trust see Marianne Elliott, *Hearthlands: A Memoir of the White City Housing Estate in Belfast* (Belfast: Blackstaff Press, 2017), chap. 2.
61 *Belfast Telegraph*, 3 March 1967.
62 *Irish News*, 19 July 1969.
63 Arthur, *People's Democracy*, p. 93.
64 *Irish News*, 20 April 1969.
65 *Irish News*, 21 April 1969.
66 *Irish News*, 4 March 1965.
67 Arthur, *People's Democracy*, p. 46.
68 *Irish News*, 17 April 1969.
69 *Irish News*, 17 April 1969.
70 John Gray, *City in Revolt: James Larkin and the Belfast Dock Strike of 1907* (Belfast: SIPTU and the Linen Hall Library, 2007).
71 Terry Cradden, 'Trade unionism, social justice, and religious discrimination in Northern Ireland', *ILR Review*, 46:3 (1993), 480–98.
72 *BNL*, 4 May 1931; *Irish Press*, 7 May 1934; *BNL*, 2 May 1938.
73 *Irish Press*, 6 May 1955; *Sunday Independent*, 4 May 1958.
74 Nagle, 'From Ban-the Bomb'.
75 *Irish News*, 8 May 1961.
76 *Irish News*, 8 May 1961.
77 Victor Turner, *The Forest of Symbols: Aspects of Ndembu Ritual* (New York: Cornell University Press, 1967), p. 100.
78 John Nagle, '"Everybody is Irish on St Paddy's"': ambivalence and alterity at London's St Patrick's Day 2002', *Identities: Global Studies in Culture and Power* 12:4 (2005), 563–83.
79 *BNL*, 7 May 1962.
80 *BNL*, 2 May 1966.

81 Ernest Gellner, *Nations and Nationalism* (New York: Cornell University Press, 1983), p. 129.
82 *BNL*, 6 May 1968.
83 *BNL*, 6 May 1968.
84 *Irish News*, 1 May 1969.
85 *Irish News*, 3 May 1969.
86 Purdie, *Politics in the Street*, p. 156.
87 *Irish News*, 5 May 1969.
88 *Protestant Telegraph*, 12 May 1969.
89 *BNL*, 2 May 1970.
90 *Belfast Telegraph*, 2 May 1970.
91 *BNL*, 6 April 1973.
92 Mary Douglas, *Purity and Danger: An Analysis of Concepts of Pollution and Taboo* (London: Routledge, 2003).
93 Roger Friedland and Richard Hecht. 'The bodies of nations: a comparative study of religious violence in Jerusalem and Ayodhya', *History of Religions*, 38:2 (1998), 101–49, at p. 147.

8

Violence and carnival: renegotiating public space 1970–2008

On 21 July 1972 twenty-six bombs exploded within minutes of each other in central Belfast. Nine people died and 130 were injured. This appeared to be a response by the IRA in Belfast to Bloody Sunday in Derry/Londonderry on 31 January, when soldiers had killed thirteen demonstrators at an anti-internment demonstration, and an attempt to demonstrate its capacity to undermine any semblance that the city was working under normal conditions. As this book tries to explore, the nature of civic space is constantly being created and recreated under changing social, economic and political circumstances. Who has access to the city, how they present themselves, what they do and the influence this in turn has on those around them is at the heart of the urban story. The violent context that engulfed Northern Ireland was inevitably going to play itself out in civic spaces as competing groups struggled for political recognition and the state and civic institutions strove for versions of normality. The negotiation over civic space was mediated through a struggle for control and security.

By the 1960s, in common with many other industrial cities across western Europe, and particularly within the United Kingdom, Belfast had started a process of economic decline. Across the Irish Sea, Liverpool experienced industrial and commercial decline in the 1970s and 1980s. Its civic arena was marked by significant political turmoil, and people in certain residential areas experienced bouts of rioting.[1] Glasgow experienced similar industrial decline and gained an enhanced reputation for violence related to gangs. These same processes were evident in Belfast, but the violence and division experienced by its people were of another order altogether. As geographer Fred Boal characterised, Belfast became a polarised city where 'simple service delivery questions and planning decisions regarding the use of space are transformed into conflicts'.[2]

The perpetrators of violence were the increasingly influential locally based paramilitary groups, Republican and Loyalist, and institutions of the state, the

RUC and, after August 1969, the British Army. In certain residential areas of the city the state was no longer seen as the legitimate arbiter of the use of force. The legitimacy of policing functions had long been questioned by Irish nationalists. But the development of an insurgency with significant levels of popular support was something not seen since the early 1920s. The emergence of the Provisional IRA in 1970 dramatically changed the use of public spaces and the meaning people gave to those spaces. The context also became problematic with the development of the UVF in 1966 and the vigilantism of the Ulster Defence Association (UDA) from 1971, reflecting reduced faith in the capacity or willingness of the state to sustain and protect Protestant areas.[3] Alternative policing functions, including the use of force, developed in working-class Protestant areas just as they did in working-class Catholic areas. From 1969 a complex, deeply problematic relationship has evolved between Loyalist paramilitaries, unionist politics and the institutions of the state that has been no less damaging to a stable, peaceful city than Republican use of violence. Residents of parts of the city may proactively support these groups, but perhaps more significantly many simply recognise that they offer certain services more effectively than the state. Thus the position of these paramilitary groups is not sustained simply by active support but also by the weakness of the state.

As well as replacing some of the policing and social functions of the state these groups look to be legitimised through representations in the public, civic sphere. So, for example, while the Unionist government in 1966 almost immediately made the UVF illegal, Loyalist paramilitaries were gradually able to present themselves in the public arena as part of broader unionist representations in events like the Twelfth of July parades. In contrast, Republicans struggled to achieve the same visibility and implied status because many of their symbolic representations had long been restricted or banned by the state. Nevertheless, Republicans also began the development of ritual and symbolic events in public spaces that entered the centre of Belfast.

This chapter identifies some key ways in which civic space in the city has been transformed by this new context. The changes in residential patterns, particularly the increased sense of territory, with the consequent enhancing of physical boundaries through the building of interfaces such as walls, or the restructuring of road and infrastructure networks to separate Catholic and Protestant areas, have been identified by a number of writers.[4] The territorial and physical landscape was invested with new meaning as violence created spaces of fear and safety.[5] Frank Burton describes the situation he encountered while undertaking sociological research in west Belfast in the early 1970s.

> In Belfast one generally walks round parked uninhabited cars with suspicion, casts unnerving glances at unattended parcels, scrambles to get home before it

gets too dark, maps out safe and dangerous journeys, all in an effort to evaluate risks which previously could be ignored.[6]

Paramilitary groups searching for legitimacy and power demarcated space by the use of violence, but also by defining areas of control through forms of protection. This included undertaking some of the welfare functions of the state as well as those of policing. But it also included marking space symbolically through displays of flags and murals and the development of ritual events such as commemorations and parades to represent their existence.[7] These predominated in working-class areas but were not uncontested. So, for example, attempts to display Irish Republicanism at the funerals of members of the IRA by the use the Irish Tricolour flags, paramilitary symbols on the coffin and displays of firearms at the cemetery were contested by the forces of the state, albeit often unsuccessfully, with their own displays of force to restrict the events. As murals became more common in areas of Republican strength, particularly after the 1981 hunger strikes, they were frequently defaced by other groups within and outside an area and by the forces of the state.[8]

By no means, and at no point, did any group enjoy uncontested support in any residential area of Belfast. These places were highly competitive arenas for hegemonic control. In addition, boundary areas were particularly contested and sites of struggle. By contrast, the spaces of the centre of Belfast were different. The violence dramatically changed the physical infrastructure and people's relationship with the city centre, but there was an existing civic space, broadly unionist but not without points of contest and alternative political displays. The City Hall reflected Britishness, Empire and the industrial history of the city. The largest annual public event was the Twelfth of July parade, but the annual Lord Mayor's Show reflected a less overtly political representation of Northern Ireland, while the May Day parade provided an example of an alternative political configuration from that of unionism and nationalism. This chapter examines changes that took place in that public realm, identifying not only the way the civic sphere became a point of struggle in a polarised political system but also ways in which it provided 'shared space', offering some reimagined views of the city. Through this period the balance of power within Belfast City Council altered, reflecting the entry of Sinn Féin into local politics and the proportionate growth of the city's Catholic population relative to Protestants.

It is possible to identify three significant changes between 1969 and 2008 that impacted on the public sphere. The first involves those existing expressions of unionism, reflecting both the divisions within mainstream unionism, as seen in the development of Paisleyite politics and the growth of the DUP, and the appearance of the UVF and the UDA as significant contributors to the cause of Ulster Loyalism. While each of these groups has developed its own forms of representation in the public sphere through parades and protests, for unionist legitimacy they have attempted to appropriate existing unionist events, most obviously the Twelfth of July. The Twelfth of July parades became part of the political contestation within unionism, but particularly the vehicle for new Loyalist formations to present themselves in public.[9] This was most obvious as some of the marching bands that accompanied the Orange lodges were increasingly of the 'blood and thunder' variety, coming from Protestant working-class districts and, through music, uniforms and flags, showing direct support for the paramilitaries.[10] When combined with the contesting of Orange parade routes in some residential areas of Belfast, these parades began to become much more problematic for the forces of the state. While the full consequences of this shift did not become clear until the 1990s, even in the late 1960s and 1970s a more conflictual relationship between loyal order parades and the state was apparent.

The second identifiable shift might best be described as a shrinking of the civic space. Put simply, the violence and securitisation of the centre of Belfast reduced activity in the area (Figure 10). It is of course difficult to evidence this very accurately and to identify exact causes, but events such as the Lord Mayor's Show became smaller and reduced in popularity. It can be contrasted not only with the less contested civic arena of the 1950s and 1960s but, in retrospect, with the flourishing of civic events after the 1998 Good Friday or

10 The security gates at the entrance to Donegall Place, with Christmas tree in front of City Hall, 13 December 1977.

Belfast Agreement. Belfast, caught in economic decline and violent polarised politics, experienced a decline in public, civic activity.

The third broad change took place in the 1990s and involved the opening of civic space to Irish nationalism and Republicanism. At the start of the 1980s, boosted by support during the hunger strikes in 1981, the Provisional IRA evolved a political strategy that worked alongside its violent campaign.[11] Participating in local and national elections, it refused to take seats won in the United Kingdom Parliament but did take seats on local councils. In Belfast this meant that, by the start of the following decade, Sinn Féin had become a significant political force in the City Council. This shift in power within the municipal institutions, although the role of the Council is limited compared to authorities in other parts of the UK, made a change in the management of the civic arena inevitable. Since 2001 the varieties of unionism no longer constitute a majority of councillors. It is also interesting, given that the major paramilitary groups called cease-fires in 1994, that in 1993 the first major Republican event was given access to the centre of the city. This was followed by a number of events in the city reflecting varieties of Irish nationalism, but most outstanding was the introduction of St Patrick's Day events in the city centre in 1998.

The physical spaces of central Belfast altered dramatically as a result of violence, securitisation and economic decline. But this was accompanied by changes in the way the civic space was used. The remainder of this chapter will examine these processes by looking at the Twelfth of July, the Lord Mayor's Show and St Patrick's Day.

The Twelfth of July

The Twelfth of July parades had been a key marker for unionism throughout the history of Northern Ireland. Ulster Unionist politicians routinely spoke at the 'field', the destination of a Twelfth of July parade, where religious and political speakers reflected on the politics of the day. Ministers from the Northern Ireland Government were often viewed as honoured guests. There were inevitably political tensions, but until the 1960s the Ulster Unionist Party (UUP) was broadly hegemonic. This began to break down in the 1960s and effectively came to a shuddering halt in 1972 when, with increasing political violence, the Northern Ireland Parliament at Stormont was prorogued by the British government. From this point on the Twelfth of July began to take on more elements of a ritual of resistance, reflecting disunity within unionism and increasing disenchantment with the forces of the state.[12]

The Twelfth of July as an event in Belfast has a number of narratives running through it, depicted through symbol and image on banners, flags and uniforms, reflecting the political breadth of unionism. There is a historical narrative that picks out key moments from Irish and British history, particularly 1690, the Battle of the Boyne, and 1916, the Battle of the Somme. In addition, themes encompassing the varieties of the Protestant faith, locality and work-place, abstinence and temperance are common on lodge banners, as well as issues from contemporary politics.[13] In that sense the parade provides plenty of diversity which lodges and bands can negotiate with in order to present their own variety of Loyalism.

The parades have always had an awkward relationship with civic Belfast. Despite constant attempts by organisers to profile the respectable and religious elements of Orangeism, and a strong seam of temperance and abstinence present amongst lodges, parades have a history of riotous clashes with authorities, with rough, drunken behaviour present in many events.[14] Authority within the Orange Order in Ireland is diffuse and the parades reflect political culture in local areas. Sections of the parade from working-class districts of the city frequently reflect forms of behaviour that could be described as carnivalesque as well as sometimes overtly sectarian, both of which civil authorities can find difficult to manage.

From the late 1960s, in the context of conflict over civil rights marches, Orange and other loyal order parades became more contested in residential areas, particularly in west Belfast. The White Rock parade, on the last Saturday of June, which has a route from the Shankill Road to the Springfield Road, now crossed an interface that runs through west Belfast. Parades on the upper part of the Crumlin Road that passed the Ardoyne area were to become problematic well beyond the peace process. The 'blood and thunder' marching bands that are hired by the Orange lodges increased in number, with rudimentary uniforms, but by the 1980s their clothing and drums reflected paramilitarism, as did the increased carrying of flags. Such public displays inevitably were a challenge to the police and to those in Orangeism, probably the majority, who rejected support for Loyalist paramilitaries. Given the tense security situation, Orange parades were no longer treated as unproblematic and the police, the British Army and the state were prepared to block and occasionally re-route events. The first police officer to be killed in the conflict was enforcing a ban on a loyal order parade.[15]

Pressure on the changing nature of the parades was internal to the Orange Order as Paisleyite and Loyalist politics increasingly played a role in the events. Some quite dramatic new versions of Loyalism attempted to become part of the parade. Most significant was the increasing profile of paramilitaries through some bands. So, for example, the UVF, formed in 1966, saw itself as the heir of the UVF formed in 1913 to resist Home Rule and whose members joined the British Army as part of the 36th Ulster Division in 1914, playing significant roles at the Battle of the Somme and elsewhere. Therefore, through the symbolic repertoire of historic unionist resistance to Home Rule and sacrifice in the First World War, the contemporary UVF, despite being an illegal organisation, was able to develop a presence within the Twelfth of July parade in Belfast.[16] The same is true, though in a more limited way, for the UDA, with the symbolic use of the Red Hand and the naming of bands using terms such as 'Defenders'. One contemporary band names itself Ulster First Flute, with the same initials as the fighting arm of the UDA, the Ulster Freedom Fighters (UFF). There were nuances to these displays, as the UVF could more easily incorporate a symbolic narrative, given the historic relationship of the UVF of 1913 to the First World War. Thus it shared a history with the Orange Order and, indeed, with the British state. This allowed for the use of a range of symbols reflecting that common history that was a more easy fit with the range of Orange banners and flags. The UVF of the 1970s onwards was able to appear in the parades through reference to historic events. The UDA was made illegal only in 1992 but its paramilitary wing, the UFF, was proscribed in 1973. Nevertheless the appearance of UFF regalia was also not uncommon, with the symbol of the clenched red fist appearing on uniforms and flags. Loyalist paramilitary groups effectively gained access to civic space in central Belfast through Orange parades. While the Orange Order in Belfast had rules about the displays of flags that could be carried in a parade these were never strictly adhered to, and by the 1980s and 1990s symbolic representation of the UVF and UDA in the Twelfth of July parade was commonplace.

So, while the Twelfth of July parades in the city of Belfast had always displayed a tension between respectable religious and political displays and the 'rougher', somewhat carnivalesque and drunken behaviour of some of the bands and Orangemen, the existence of Loyalist paramilitarism offered a more direct challenge to a civic space. The parades were also showing increasing signs, reflected in working-class loyalism, of resistance to the state. The sentiments of Sir John (Jack) Hermon, Chief Constable of the RUC from 1980 to 1989, capture the relationship of the Twelfth of July with civic space.

> By mid-May 1985, the Force [the RUC] was fully prepared to address the smouldering problem of Loyalist parades. Over almost half a century, these had been given a special position in Northern Ireland and appeared to have acquired a sort of temporal sanctity. Participants believe they can march wherever and whenever they choose. Their marches epitomised the right to civil and religious liberty, so long as the religion in question was Protestantism... I was not alone in believing that the superior attitude of the Loyalists in respect to their marches, had to be changed.[17]

This goes to the heart of the process of negotiation around what might be considered the civic. That is the civic as a set of broadly accepted rules that provide space for social interaction and the conduct of citizenship. How that space is defined, or negotiated, changes over time. The Twelfth of July in Belfast, for the first seventy years of the twentieth century, was civic, although not unproblematically, in that it would have involved large numbers of people seen as civic leaders, such as unionist councillors and religious ministers. It was not directly funded by the City Council but it was certainly facilitated in terms of cleaning up after the event and provision of facilities. It sat slightly uncomfortably within the civic, because some of the performances and behaviour threatened what might be seen as normatively acceptable, and potentially because the event by definition excluded many members of society. It did, however, reflect dominant and mainstream political positions within Northern Ireland through that period.

Events less overtly political, and perhaps more directly civic, than the Twelfth of July also showed signs of stress in this period. An example of such a civic occasion would be the annual Lord Mayor's Show.

The Lord Mayor's Show

In the 1960s the annual Lord Mayor's Show was a reflection of a combination of commercial self-advertisement and an implicit unionism, a measure of how well Belfast and Ulster were doing. In 1961, the *Belfast News Letter* described the event, organised by the Junior Chamber of Commerce, as presenting 'in a tangible form the results of the wonderful skill, industry and imagination of local businessmen'. That year the 'Lord Mayor and Lady Mayoress of Belfast' travelled in the 'County Antrim Grand Jury Coach' pulled by four 'magnificent grey horses', brought over from Luton in England, which had previously 'taken part in royal ceremonies and [been] hired out for film work'. The ninety-five floats stretched for over two miles and included twelve marching bands. Amongst the floats were entries from hospitals, the police, departments from Belfast Corporation, Belfast Museum, the British Army and Royal Navy, various charities, major companies including Gallaher Tobacco, International Computers and Tabulators Ltd, the Milk Marketing Board, the Ulster Bank, the Irish Linen guild, the Co-Op and numerous vintage cars. As the parade passed by the dignitaries at the City Hall, including Home Affairs Minister Brian Faulkner, the crowd were treated to a fly-past from helicopters from the Royal Navy 719 Squadron.[18]

The first Lord Mayor's Show appears to have taken place in 1956,[19] and throughout the 1960s newspapers give the impression of a large and vibrant event. In 1962 the BBC had a commentator in an aircraft overhead, with 100,000 spectators expected at an event themed as 'Ulster in Action'.[20] The military played a significant part in the parades, including the use of a Centurion tank, as did the Boy's Brigade, Boy Scouts and Girl Guides.[21]

> The floats decorated with flowers, pretty girls and bunting, each received a cheer from the crowd, but the most popular item of all appeared to be the Cheshire Regiment under attack by Redcoat soldiers in 17th-century uniform.[22]

The route came from the Ormeau Park embankment area down the Ormeau Road, up Donegall Pass and Dublin Road and past the front of City Hall, finishing at the Lagan bank.[23] In 1964 Princess Margaret and her husband, Lord Snowdon, attended, while in 1966 the *Belfast News Letter* headlined the fact that six floats from Eire, as it termed the Irish Republic, were taking part. The themes for each year had a clear commercial angle: 'Buy Ulster Goods' (1963), 'Pride in Progress' (1964), 'Enterprise '65''', 'Opportunity and Partnership in 1966' 'Ulster Week' (1967) and 'Tomorrow's World'.[24] In 1968, as described in the previous chapter, a contingent of US sailors from the *USS Keppler* took part in the event but were met by anti-Vietnam War protestors who threw themselves in front of the marching servicemen.[25] In 1969 a beauty contest was introduced, although the *Belfast News Letter* seemed to recognise a potential threat of civil disturbances.

> The Show Organisers, Belfast Junior Chamber of Commerce, said yesterday that in spite of the disturbances in Northern Ireland, industrial, commercial and other concerns have been very keen to enter floats.[26]

It is also interesting that later that year the Civil Rights Association announced on 6 September that it wanted to hold a protest over high unemployment and poor housing in the city, to take the same route, along the Ormeau Road, as the Lord Mayor's Show.[27]

In 1970 there were seventy-two floats and twelve bands but the RUC and British Army had to seal off the Dublin Road as it appeared that fifty women from the Shankill Road were to lie in front of the parade as a diversion to allow a float from the Shankill Development Committee to become part of the parade.[28] The event theme was 'Prosperity for the Seventies'.[29] A military regimental band led the parade and RAF Ballykelly was also involved, as were commercial contributors such as Esso and Coca Cola. The following year the show was part of the Ulster 71 celebrations recognising fifty years of the Northern Ireland state, with 100 floats taking part, and the event included a parachute drop by members of the Parachute Regiment into Ormeau Park and a fly-past by the Shorts Skyvan aircraft.[30]

> Many floats, notably those entered by the GPO [General Post Office] and the Milk Marketing Board, were decorated with beautiful Irish colleens dressed in mini skirts and hot pants.[31]

However, the apparent attempt at optimism is in contrast to the following year, when the parade was cancelled due to the security situation, and in 1974 the events took place under the slightly pleading theme of 'Your Ulster – Your Future'.

> Even the gloom of the Loyalist strike which blacked out much of the city and the constant rain and drizzle failed to depress the occupants of dozens of gaily coloured floats which wound towards City Hall ...[32]

By 1975 the route of the parade had shifted from the lower part of the Ormeau Road and instead went from the Ormeau Park, up Stranmillis Road, through the area of Queen's University. Musical accompaniment for the claimed eighty floats, under the theme 'We will Build', was provided by the 7th City of Belfast battalion of the Ulster Defence Regiment. At the Lord Mayor's Show Banquet held at City Hall the Lord Mayor, Sir William Christie, discussed the impact of violence on society and the cost of compensation.[33] In 1976 the theme seemed to shift to a need to build a sense of community with the theme of 'Participation', with seventy floats.[34] Secretary of State Merlyn Rees joined the dignitaries and there was still a fly-by by a locally manufactured Shorts plane. The following year only 4,000 spectators watched while 'Belfast went Mardi Gras ... and for several hours at least forgot all its troubles', the theme again being 'Tomorrow's Belfast'. Even given the likely exaggeration of spectator figures in the 1960s, the drop in numbers appears considerable. The organisers noted that fewer schools were taking part.[35] Councillor Bill Jeffrey noted that 'the whole show adds a little Mardi Gras atmosphere to a pretty dead town and it is lots of fun', and in the speech after the show Councillor Stewart noted that 'the long suffering citizens of Belfast have been able to keep the wheels of trade and commerce turning to a remarkable degree'.[36] The list of prizes for the floats suggests a reduction in the number of commercial entrants. In 1979 the newspapers claimed fifty floats to be an increase in the number, with the Royal Irish Rangers leading the parade.[37]

The diminishing size of the event and the lack of commercial interest becomes obvious in the 1980s. In December 1980 Bill Kohner, the president of the Junior Chamber of Commerce, announcing the following year's theme 'Our effort – Our Show', appealed for the big employers to return to the event.[38] Organisers in 1981 claimed the fifty-three floats to be more than in previous years and were 'encouraged by the visit of mayors from Cardiff, Dublin, Westminster and Waterford'.[39] Indeed the *Belfast News Letter* hopefully claimed that this was 'the biggest ever Lord Mayor's Show'.[40] Lord Mayor Carson in his speech described a recent trip to America when he was able to let people know that they in Northern Ireland 'were not all bigots and murderers'.[41] The sense of desperation in the events was recognised in 1982 when the Lord Mayor, Grace Bannister, called for a restoration of civic pride under the theme of 'Build a Better Belfast'. Organisers claimed that 100,000 people had turned out the previous year and that 'half a million watched the highlights on television'.[42] The president of the Chamber of Commerce hoped that the theme would 'plant a seed in people's minds'.[43] And, for the first time, the 1982 event had a Youth for Peace Group putting a float in to 'bring the two communities together'.[44] As part of 'Civic Festival' the 1983 event was themed 'Helping Belfast through Team Effort'. The fifty-three floats and fifteen bands included the Boys' Brigade, and a War on Want float was joined by schools as well as 'covered wagons, cowboys and Indians, complete with wigwam, from the Department of Economic Development ...'.[45] A military band still headed the parade. The slightly desperate themes in the years that followed included 'Our Faith in the Future of Belfast' and 'Caring Belfast'.[46] By 1988 the parade was noted as being shorter than usual and, while there were some commercial floats and the UDR and RUC bands amongst others, the role of civic society, the 'efforts of charities, voluntary organisations, trade unions and the City Council' were noted. In 1989 reporter Charles Fitzgerald, discussed the forty floats and twenty bands and suggested that 'surely it is time it [The Lord Mayor's Show] received some help from the City Council and the Department of the Environment to make it a show worthy of our premier city?'[47]

The event in 1990 looked forward to the forthcoming European Single Market under the concept of a 'new Europe' and drew an estimated crowd of 10,000.[48] In 1991 community groups and charities such as War on Want and the Multiple Sclerosis Society, a Chinese dragon and a seven-foot dinosaur joined the commercial floats to total about fifty entrants.[49] By 1992 the event seemed to be down to thirty floats.[50] Interestingly, and a sign of things to come, in 1993 the theme was Belfast as a carnival city, and in the following year the director of the Lord Mayor's Show boasted that they had added new activities so that it could be described as a 'civic festival'.[51] The direct commercial element of the parade seems to have disappeared altogether.

In 1995, in a strange precursor of events to come, members of the Republican prisoners group Saoirse attempted to introduce a float into the event, and when they were blocked protested at the statue of Henry Cooke in College Square. It was claimed that the protestors booed participants from community groups in the Catholic working-class areas of Poleglass and Twinbrook.[52] Previously a spokesperson for Saoirse, Phil McCullough, argued that RUC involvement in the event evidenced the political nature of the content, but suggested that his group was not politically aligned.[53] That this group showed any interest in the event at all suggests a shift in the civic space. It shows that the type of participation had changed since the 1960s and that the previously unthinkable idea that Republicans might take part had become at least conceivable. It suggests a shift in the negotiated politics of the civic space which would lead to members of Sinn Féin in time becoming mayors in the city and thus leading the annual parade.

In 1998, reflecting significant shifts in the balance of power at City Hall, the first nationalist mayor of Belfast, Alban Maginness of the Social and Democratic Labour Party (SDLP), led the parade. But contestation continued. Protestors from the predominantly working-class Protestant area of Donegall Pass objected to a float entered by the Lower Ormeau Residents Action Group. Protestors claimed that a Tricolour was to be carried, although the group denied that this was the case. The Lord Mayor's show was rerouted away from the Donegall Pass.[54]

These incidents at the end of the 1990s are an interesting indicator in the changes taking place to public spaces around Belfast. However, the most profound change in the civic and public arena was the political agreement reached on 10 April 1998. The Good Friday or Belfast Agreement, followed by the St Andrews Agreement on 13 October 2006, dramatically changed the legislative context within which public authorities worked, the relationships between British and Irish governments and between the political parties in Northern Ireland and, crucially, the definition of citizenship within Northern Ireland. The Good Friday Agreement contained a commitment by the British and Irish governments to 'recognise the birth right of all the people of Northern Ireland to identify themselves and be accepted as Irish or British, or both, as they may so choose ...'.[55] The related legislation, the Northern Ireland Act 1998, including section 75 on equality and 'good relations', had a major impact on how agencies such as local councils engaged in public and civic space.

Tension was high in 1998, as the Agreement had been concluded in April and the referendum on its terms took place on 22 May, just days before the Lord Mayor's Show. Perhaps more directly, the Lower Ormeau Residents Action Group had been engaged in protests aimed at preventing parades by the Orange Order, Royal Black Institution and Apprentice Boys from taking a route from the upper part of the Ormeau Road through the 'lower' Ormeau Road to Donegall Pass. The move to a more community-based event, with groups coming from different Protestant and Catholic residential areas of Belfast, had thus introduced a new political dimension to the organisation of the show. An event that had been largely based in the commercial life of Northern Ireland was now resting its legitimacy on local communities and local involvement. That new focus unavoidably meant the involvement in the event of areas that were Catholic and, indeed, Republican.

To accommodate this shift and recognise the diversity of the city the idea of 'Carnival' became one selling point of the event. In 1999 the Belfast Lord Mayor's Show actually had participants from London's Notting Hill carnival, and the press release in 2001 promised a carnival spectacular.[56] In particular, the involvement of the Beat Initiative, an art-based non-governmental organisation that specialises in carnival and costume-type events, was to mark the parade over the following years. The theme in 1999 was 'Belfast Celebrates', followed by 'Creating the Future' in 2000, 'Our City – Our Belfast' in 2001 and 'Energy' in 2002.[57] In 2003 Belfast City Council invested £50,000 around the theme 'Our Belfast – Don't Waste It'.[58] The parade was led by the mayor, Sinn Féin's Alex Maskey.

At the start of the new century the Lord Mayor's Show in Belfast was smaller, more community orientated and politically diverse. It was no longer

11 The Lord Mayor's Show, rebranded as Belfast Carnival, 28 June 2008. Rory the Lion makes his way as part of the procession.

imagining the commercial life of the city, but the diverse life of the urban community. It had become reconceived as a carnival. At around the same time, the civic life of the city had a new 'carnival' entry.

St Patrick's Day

While the Lord Mayor's Show has long been part of a civic presentation of Belfast, in contrast there is no history of St Patrick's Day parades in the centre of the city. There were patchy celebrations in west Belfast but no sustained parading tradition. This makes the discussions around holding a city centre event in the late 1990s so interesting. The status of St Patrick as the founder of Irish Christianity was recognised by all of the major religious denominations. St Patrick's Day, 17 March, was likewise a global expression of Irishness that had moved well beyond religious or national boundaries.[59] This potential is made clear by Belfast Councillor Nelson McCausland, then Ulster Unionist but later to move to the DUP, in a Council committee in 1994:

> Patrick brought the Christian faith to Ulster and established the ancient British Church in this part of the British Isles. It is therefore appropriate that St. Patrick's Day should be marked in this manner by the Council in the capital city of Ulster.[60]

Discussions over a potential event took place through the 1990s. In 1998, the year of the Good Friday Agreement, a parade was proposed by people based at Féile an Phobail, the West Belfast Festival. Féile an Phobail started in 1988 as a cultural response by Republicans to their political struggle in the west of the city. It provided a range of musical and theatrical events, as well as a parade, which were entertaining but frequently politically engaged. The potential St Patrick's Day parade was thus, at one level, an extension of a Republican political agenda and, at another level, part of the peace process. Mairtin O'Muilleoir, who fifteen years later became a Sinn Féin mayor of the city, provides a telling description, from a Republican perspective, of the 1998 event.

> The tens of thousands who turned Belfast city centre black with green on Tuesday were doing more than scribbling footnotes, more than even contributing chapters to our history. They were shredding the pages of past wrongs, binning the Belfast of the pogroms and second-class citizenship, erasing the painful memory of too many Twelfths on the wrong side of the swagger stick ... and proudly painting their own prologue: we've arrived. We've not forgotten how just a few short years ago, we were banned from our own city centre. Didn't this very paper record how, in the searing agony of the 1981 hunger strike, a handful of protesters were beaten by the RUC for daring to attempt to march to City Hall. (On Tuesday a pus [a contemptuous Irish word for 'face'] as long as Royal

Avenue on every RUC man's face – not to mention the absence of even a single sprig of shamrock on their caps – told its own tale of changed times.)⁶¹

Parts of the parade started in all of the key working-class nationalist areas of the city and met at the city centre, very much in the style that the Twelfth of July parade starts from working-class unionist areas and meets in central Belfast. The parade contained a large number of Tricolours and was led by west Belfast Black Taxis. Throughout the conflict London-style black cabs had acted as an alternative to public buses in west Belfast and thus were symbolic of resistance. Despite organisers' claims to the contrary, there was little chance of significant cross-community support for this event.

Here was the quintessential annual global public expression of Irishness, making a claim on the civic space precisely at a time when political power appeared to shift in the city and just twenty-four days before political parties and the British and Irish governments produced the Good Friday Agreement. Although unionists had resisted Sinn Féin's position on key committees, its claim to a greater role in the management of the city was becoming irresistible.

What is interesting is that right through this process there were attempts from all political parties to explore St Patrick's Day as a cross-community event. At an early stage in the preparations for a parade in 1999 there were negotiations to obtain cross-party agreement and funding for the event.

> It was agreed that to censor flags, of any type, could be counter-productive and nugatory but it was agreed that the official flag for the carnival should be a St Patrick's flag with Belfast City Council tourism promotion logo superimposed. These flags would be distributed to participants and spectators as a promotional item for the event. As was the case this year no political slogans or emblems would be permitted in the parade.⁶²

In the end no agreement was reached and the event went ahead without Council backing. Over the subsequent years an annual debate took place over possible Council funding for a St Patrick's Day event. Serious attempts were made by organisers to change the event, including coming up with symbols that might replace the use of Tricolours. These new flags were handed out for free in the streets prior to the event starting.

Nevertheless the event continued to reflect Republican politics. The unionist-leaning *Belfast News Letter* described the 2002 event in the following way:

> Men dressed in black berets and dark glasses, a form of garb worn by the IRA at funerals and demonstrations, added a sinister aspect to a St Patrick's Day parade yesterday. The men waved to the crowds in Belfast city centre as they drove along in a white car marked 'Garda' on the side. Although the stunt was good-humoured, it added a deeper shade of green to an event which has largely failed to appeal to Protestants.⁶³

Driven by Council policies that now oriented towards funding 'shared' events and 'good relations'; the new political and legal context; a desire by organisers to access funding and see St Patrick's Day as part of the civic life of the city; and the general recognition that St Patrick's Day was of interest to some Protestants, the annual discussions at the Council continued and attempts to make the event more palatable to Protestants were reviewed. In addition, politics in the Council had now significantly changed, with the nationalist parties, the SDLP and Sinn Féin, constituting the largest group, though not a majority, while the Alliance Party held the balance of power. Consequently, key posts at the Council were now rotated and in 2002 Alex Maskey became the first Sinn Féin Mayor of the city.

It was not only the political balance of the Council that had gone through a dramatic change. So had the broader legal and policy context in which the Council worked. The 1998 Good Friday Agreement introduced the idea of 'parity of esteem' into the policy regime. The major political parties, with the exception of the DUP, endorsed the commitment made by the British and Irish governments that the power of the sovereign government with jurisdiction

> shall be exercised with rigorous impartiality on behalf of all the people in the diversity of their identities and tradition and shall be founded on the principles of full respect for, and equality of, civil, political, social and cultural rights, of freedom from discrimination for all citizens, and of parity of esteem and of just and equal treatment for the identity, ethos, and aspirations of both communities.[64]

Apart from the contradictions between the 'diversity' mentioned at the start of the paragraph and the implication of just two communities at the end, this section provided the basis for legislative changes found in the rest of the Good Friday Agreement. At face value the only other minor paragraph that relates to public space talked about the use of symbols. Under the section of the Agreement entitled 'Rights, Safeguards and Equality of Opportunity: Economic, Social and Cultural Issues', the participants to the Agreement recognised the importance of 'tackling the problems of a divided society', increasing respect for linguistic diversity in Northern Ireland and sensitivity over the use of symbols in public spaces.

But a much more important change in the nature of the civic space was to be introduced through human rights and equality legislation. The Good Friday Agreement also committed the British government to incorporating the European Convention on Human Rights into UK law, which was completed in 2000, and to creating a statutory obligation on public authorities in Northern Ireland to carry out all their functions with due regard to the need to promote equality and to draw up formal assessments of the implications for equality of changes in policy. This was recognised in section 75 of the

Northern Ireland Act 1998, which had enormous impact on the workings of local councils and will be discussed in the next chapter.

Given that local councils play a central role in defining civic spaces, these changes were of major significance. In 2003 Belfast City Council produced a Good Relations Strategy called 'Building our Future Together'.[65] It reflected the work of a Good Relations Steering Panel and a Good Relations Working Group, as well as of a Cultural Diversity Sub-Committee that had been established in March 1998.[66] The strategy highlights the duty of the Council to promote 'equality of opportunity', 'tolerance and understanding' and good relations.[67] It bluntly describes the city over which it has authority:

> The segregated patterns of life in the city are marked at all levels – on the whole, people live in separate residential areas, go to separate schools, to different churches and social clubs and celebrate different traditions. These divisions dominate the landscape and the nature and scale of the problem is evident, often being expressed in physical form – through for example flags, gable end murals and kerb painting.[68]

The strategy sets out a model of 'equality, diversity and interdependence' that was being worked on by the Community Relations Council.[69] Festivals are identified as a key part of the strategy and it was proposed that 'the Council should consider in particular their aims and how they would increase the confidence of the community, enhance the understanding of the traditions of people from different backgrounds and ensure that each event was enjoyable'.[70] Importantly, 'in considering the provision of grant aid, it was generally agreed that the criteria should specify that any event should be open, inclusive, non-party political and the promoters must be accountable in respect of the outcome'.[71]

This was the context in which St Patrick's Day was being discussed. The Council voted not to fund the outdoor festival in 2004 that culminated outside City Hall. The organisers got into some difficulty when the former Pogues singer Shane McGowan drank alcohol on stage at what was supposed to be an event aimed at children, and there were some public order incidents later in the day.[72] On 21 January 2005 the Policy and Resources Committee agreed criteria to be used in allocating Council funding for an outdoor public event to mark St Patrick's Day that included 'inclusivity and broad participation', 'evident commitment to encouraging understanding and celebrating cultural diversity' and 'avoidance of use of symbols and signage that may regarded as offensive or triumphalist'.[73] Relations between Belfast City Council and the organisers saw an improvement. The organisers had made attempts to make the event more cross-community, such as the adoption of a multi-coloured shamrock as the event's official symbol. A £30,000 grant to the carnival had also been approved in principle, but eventually the committee voted against funding the event directly.⁷⁴ The event on 17 March 2005 was more oriented towards children, and although there were plenty of Tricolour flags on display the multi-coloured shamrock offered an alternative emblem.⁷⁵

The St Patrick's Day celebration in 2006 marks a specific change. In the light of the 2005 experience it was decided that the Council should take the lead in delivering an 'inclusive' outdoor event. The Council invested £70,000 and an additional £25,000 was offered by the Arts Council. While there was to be a parade there was also an entertainment held in the newly refurbished Custom House Square, site of many public meetings in nineteenth-century Belfast. While the parade was to have participation from local communities the content was largely to be delivered by Beat Initiative, the same charity already involved in recasting the Lord Mayor's Show as a carnival event. Over the following years this would help to define what a St Patrick's Day, delivered by the Council as a civic day, would look like.

In the months before the event an interesting debate took place over the plans which the Council might have for controlling the symbolic content of the events. A number of newspapers carried reports that Tricolours and shamrocks might be banned.⁷⁶ On 4 January the Council voted by the narrowest of margins to go ahead with the funding of St Patrick's Day. This was variously reported as a positive decision to back the event;⁷⁷ a failed attempt to stop funding;⁷⁸ and the defeat of the unionist side of the chamber.⁷⁹ In all articles the debate was represented as a sectarian dispute with unionist concerns about security and inclusivity pitted against arguments from Alliance, SDLP and Sinn Féin that the event would be inclusive and safe.

This tension defined the event over the following years and is an indicator of the developing nature of civic space in the city. To make St Patrick's Day a shared event organisers needed to reduce the number of Tricolours and Celtic football shirts and concentrate on content that was carnivalesque and multicultural. Cultural symbols that were potentially politically Irish were deemed a problem. The irony of this was that St Patrick's Day in 1998 had seen the introduction of the Tricolour to the city centre, whereas now the civic authorities were trying to usher it back out again.⁸⁰

At 'The St Patrick's Day Carnival' in 2006 Council workers distributed 5,000 shamrock T-shirts and 8,000 flags that had either the cross of St Patrick or a multi-coloured shamrock on them. In the previous year's events, feeder parades had walked to the centre of town from nationalist areas of the city: the Newlodge, the Falls Road, the Short Strand and the lower Ormeau Road. In 2006 this took place only from Short Strand, and after a dispute at City Hall this group left the city centre before the main body of the parade. In using these routes from different parts of the city participants had effectively been mimicking the feeder parades that the Orange Order take on the morning of the Twelfth of July in Belfast.⁸¹ Of course the Orange Order feeder parades come from Protestant areas of the city. This gives the events significant connections to residential areas, as supporters follow parts of the parade from their area. Since 2006 the route of all sections of the St Patrick's Day parade has been within the centre of the city.

Participants and spectators were not permitted into the area around City Hall with Celtic football shirts or Tricolours and instead spectators were offered a Belfast St Patrick's Day T-shirt and a choice of small flags displaying a multi-coloured shamrock or the cross of St Patrick. This attempt to discourage the use of the Tricolour became a feature over the years that followed. Strategies included the handing out of replacement items and attempting to remove people selling cheap Tricolours in the centre of the city. In sites like the City Hall and Custom House Square, where a staged event takes place, people were asked by stewards to put Tricolours away. The key change, however, was that the core of the parade itself was organised by an outside body, the Beat Initiative. The parade itself therefore had no flags but, rather, a multicultural and creative feel to it.

At the staged event in Custom House Square performances included Irish and Scottish dancers, Indian dances and Chinese martial arts. It was probably most noticeable for the use by an Ulster Scots band of the iconic Lambeg drums, more often associated with rural Orange events. The crowd of around 3,000 included teenagers waving Tricolours which in this, the first year of the Council-run event, the stewards did little to deal with. In the years that followed stewards became more confident in asking people to put away their Tricolours, on the basis that they were entering a cross-community event.

These changes reflect the rules that Belfast City Council developed to accompany its events. These require that 'flags, emblems or paraphernalia of a political, sectarian, racist or partisan nature will not be permitted on site' and that there are to be 'no football jerseys'.[82] In 2006 researchers counted ninety-eight Tricolours in all entering the site, mostly small flags, with about twelve larger Tricolours draped over the shoulders of teenagers.[83] These were very visible at the event but clearly constituted a small number in relation to the overall size of the crowd and the flags handed out by the Council.

The management of this aspect of the event was never straightforward. Does a green, white and orange inflatable hammer constitute a political symbol? But the broad approach reflects the wider legal and policy environment that had developed in Belfast after the 1998 Agreement and as a result of a shift in the balance of political power. In the years that followed, the stewarding of the event became more assertive, with the distribution of Council-designed flags and attempts to ask people not to display Tricolours. The Beat Initiative, also providing floats for the Lord Mayor's 'Carnival', provided a variety of costumes and floats to give the parade diversity. Large figures of local golfers, clever floats of the large cranes Sampson and Goliath that overlook Belfast

Harbour and dinosaurs might make unlikely content for many St Patrick's Days around the world. Many carnival-style events in the world are connected to acts of resistance and control of space by those at the lower end of the social scale. In Belfast 'carnival' provided a multicultural and cosmopolitan environment for an event struggling to be civic.

A new civic ethos

In 2008 the Mayor of Belfast, Ulster Unionist Councillor Jim Rodgers, led the tenth St Patrick's Day parade to take place in the city centre. Later that year, 28 June 2008, the position of mayor had changed hands and the Lord Mayor's Show, that year rebranded the Belfast Carnival, was led by Sinn Féin Councillor Tom Hartley. The St Patrick's Day events had moved from being an event where the Tricolour was being carried into the city to a 'carnival' type event which was on the civic calendar of the Council and where 'political' flags were being discouraged. The Lord Mayor's Show, over a much longer period of time, had moved from representing the economic well-being of Northern Ireland in the 1960s to an event struggling with a city ridden by violence and in economic decline, only to be renewed as a multicultural community-led carnival in the gradually more confident city of the 1990s and 2000s. Even the Orange Order make attempts to negotiate their position in the civic space. A raft of policies, the introduction of a range of new events, and the development of longer-standing events suggests an expansion of the public arena around the centre of Belfast from the city that struggled in the 1970s and 1980s. The context for these different developments was not just the shift that had taken place in the balance of political power within the Council, but also the impact upon the city of a new political and legal context within Northern Ireland as a whole. The political and policy lexicon began to resonate with ideas of 'parity of esteem', 'good relations' and 'shared space'. The process of peace building, like the violence before it, had a dramatic impact on civic space.

Notes

1 Jon Murden, 'City of challenge and change: Liverpool since 1954', in John Belchem (ed.), *Liverpool 800: Culture, Character and History* (Liverpool: Liverpool University Press, 2008), pp. 383–485, at pp. 440–5.
2 Fredrick W. Boal, 'Encapsulation: urban dimensions of national conflict', in Seamus Dunn (ed.), *Managing Divided Cities* (Keele: Keele University Press, 2004), pp. 30–40, at p. 31.
3 Richard Reed, *Paramilitary Loyalism: Identity and Change* (Manchester: Manchester University Press, 2015).

4 Peter Shirlow and Brendan Murtagh, *Belfast: Segregation, Violence and the City* (London: Pluto Press, 2006); Frederick W. Boal, *Shaping a City: Belfast in the Late Twentieth Century* (Belfast: Institute of Irish Studies, 1995); S. A. Bollens, *Urban Peace Building in Divided Cities: Belfast and Johannesburg* (London: Routledge, 1999); Dominic Bryan 'Titanic town: living in a landscape of conflict', in S. J. Connolly (ed.), *Belfast 400: People, Place and History* (Liverpool: Liverpool University Press, 2012), pp. 317–53.

5 Frank Burton, *The Politics of Legitimacy: Struggles in a Belfast Community* (London: Routledge and Kegan Paul, 1978); Allen Feldman, *Formations of Violence: The Narrative of the Body and Political Terror in Northern Ireland* (Chicago: The University of Chicago, 1991), p. 37.

6 Burton, *The Politics of Legitimacy*, p. 20.

7 Neil Jarman, *Material Conflicts: Parades and Visual Displays in Northern Ireland* (Oxford: Berg, 1997); Dominic Bryan, *Orange Parades: The Politics of Ritual, Tradition and Control* (London: Pluto Press, 2000).

8 Bill Rolston, *Politics and Painting: Murals and Conflict in Northern Ireland* (London and Toronto: Associated University Press, 1991).

9 Bryan, *Orange Parades*.

10 Bryan *Orange Parades*; Gordon Ramsey, *Music, Emotion and Identity in Ulster Marching Bands: Flutes, Drums and Loyal Sons* (Bern: Peter Lang, 2011).

11 Richard English, *Armed Struggle: The History of the IRA* (London: Pan Macmillan 2004), pp. 206–7.

12 Bryan, *Orange Parades*.

13 Neil Jarman, *Material Conflicts*; Neil Jarman, *Displaying Faith: Orange, Green and Trade Union Banners* (Belfast: Institute of Irish Studies, 1999).

14 Bryan, *Orange Parades*.

15 David McKittrick, Seamus Kelters, Brian Feeney and Chris Thornton, *Lost Lives: The Stories of the Men and Women and Children Who Died as a Result of the Northern Ireland Troubles* (Edinburgh: Mainstream Publishing 1999), p. 42.

16 Dominic Bryan and Stuart Ward 'The "deficit of remembrance": the Great War revival in Australia and Ireland', in Katie Holmes and Stuart Ward (eds), *Exhuming Passions: The Pressure of the Past in Ireland and Australia* (Dublin: Irish Academic Press 2011), pp. 163–86; Dominic Bryan, 'Forget 1690, remember the Somme: Ulster Loyalist battles in the twenty first century', in Oona Frawley (ed.), *Memory Ireland: The Famine and the Troubles* (New York: Syracuse University Press, 2014), pp. 293–309.

17 John Hermon, *Holding the Line: An Autobiography* (Dublin: Gill & Macmillan 1997), pp. 171–2.

18 *BNL*, 20 May 1961.

19 *BNL*, 20 May 1961.

20 *BNL*, 5 May 1962.

21 *BNL*, 19, 21 May 1962.

22 *BNL*, 21 May 1962.

23 *BNL*, 18 May 1963.

24 *BNL*, 20 May 1964, 20 May 1965, 21 May 1966, 22 May 1967, 8 May 1969.

25 *Belfast Telegraph*, 18 May 1968.
26 *BNL*, 15 May 1969.
27 *Irish News*, 1 August 1969.
28 *BNL*, 25 May 1970.
29 *BNL*, 23 May 1970.
30 *BNL*, 15 May 1971. For an interesting discussion of Ulster '71 see Gillian McIntosh 'Stormont's ill-timed Jubilee: The Ulster '71 Exhibition', *New Hibernia Review*, 11:2 (2007), 17–39.
31 *BNL*, 17 May 1971.
32 *BNL*, 20 May 1974.
33 *BNL*, 12 May 1975.
34 *Irish News*, 2 December 1975; *BNL*, 24 May 1976.
35 *BNL*, 15 May 1978.
36 *BNL*, 15 May 1978.
37 *BNL*, 14 May 1979.
38 *Irish News*, 4 December 1980.
39 *Irish News*, 8 May 1981.
40 *BNL*, 11 May 1981.
41 *BNL*, 11 May 1981.
42 *BNL*, 26 November 1981.
43 *BNL*, 28 November 1981.
44 *BNL*, 8 May 1982.
45 *BNL*, 7, 16 May 1983.
46 *BNL*, 12 May 1984, 18 May 1987.
47 *BNL*, 16 May 1988, 8 May 1989.
48 *Belfast Telegraph*, 5 May 1990.
49 *BNL*, 6 May 1991.
50 *BNL*, 11 May 1992.
51 *BNL*, 3 May1993, 9 May 1994.
52 *BNL*, 8 May 1995; *Belfast Telegraph*, 5 May 1995.
53 *Belfast Telegraph*, 5 May 1995.
54 *BNL*, 25 March 1998.
55 *Good Friday Agreement*, Part 1 section (iv).
56 *BNL*, 24 May 1999, 5 April 2001.
57 *Belfast Telegraph*, 24 May 1999; *BNL*, 6 May 2000; *Belfast Telegraph*, 26 May 2001, 24 May 2002.
58 *Irish News*, 24 April 2003.
59 Mike Cronin and Daryl Adair, *The Wearing of the Green: A History of St Patrick's Day* (London: Routledge, 2002).
60 Belfast City Council Minutes, Nelson McCausland, Policy and Resources Committee, 21 January 1994.
61 'Glorious Green Gridlock', *Andersonstown News*, 2 March 1998.
62 Belfast City Council Minutes E657, May 1998.
63 'Men in black cast shadow on green day', *BNL*, 18 March 2002.
64 *Good Friday Agreement*, Part 1 section (v).

65 Belfast City Council, *Building our Future Together* (Belfast: Good Relations Unit, Belfast City Council, 2003), www.belfastcity.gov.uk/nmsruntime/saveasdialog.aspx?lID=2795&sID=2346 (accessed 15 February 2018).
66 Belfast City Council, *Building our Future Together*, p. 9.
67 Belfast City Council, *Building our Future Together*, p. 9.
68 Belfast City Council, *Building our Future Together*, p. 11.
69 Karin Eyben, Duncan Morrow and Derick Wilson, *The Equity, Diversity and Interdependence Framework: A Framework for Organisational Learning and Change* (University of Ulster, 2001), www.files.ethz.ch/isn/136965/edi_report.pdf (accessed 2 May 2018)
70 Belfast City Council, *Building our Future Together*, p. 45.
71 Belfast City Council, *Building our Future Together*, p. 45.
72 http://news.bbc.co.uk/1/hi/northern_ireland/3522434.stm.
73 Belfast City Council Policy and Resources Committee Minutes, 21 January 2005, B 3310, Appendix A: 'St. Patrick's Carnival Committee – Application for Outdoor Public Event 2005'.
74 *Irish News*, 5 February 2005.
75 *Irish News*, 18 March 2005.
76 *Belfast Telegraph*, 8, 9 November 2005; *Irish News*, 10 November 2005; *Sunday World*, 13 September 2005.
77 *Belfast Telegraph*, 5 January 2006.
78 *Irish News*, 5 January 2006.
79 *News Letter*, 5 January 2006.
80 Dominic Bryan 'Parades, flags, carnivals, and riots: public space, contestation, and transformation in Northern Ireland', *Peace and Conflict: Journal of Peace Psychology*, 21:4 (2015), 565–73.
81 Bryan, *Orange Parades*.
82 *St Patrick's Day Outdoor Event 2006: Monitoring Report* (Belfast: Institute of Irish Studies, Queen's University Belfast, 2006), p. 101; discussion of the report at Belfast City Council, Policy and Resources Committee Minutes, 23 June 2006, B704.
83 *St Patrick's Day Outdoor Event 2006*, pp. 58–9.

9

Shared space or divided future?

In the second half of the twentieth century Belfast, having suffered significantly from the bombs of Nazi Germany during the Second World War, had to adapt to continuing economic decline. Urban development had created suburbs and increased the size of satellite towns. The weakening of key industries saw the decline of working-class inner-city districts, which became dislocated from the city centre, particularly in the west and north, by the development of a motorway system. Those working-class estates, equally, became physically divided into Protestant and Catholic areas by violence and the building of interface walls.[1] Through the 1970s the remains of the Victorian city were further ravaged by car bombs and the building of security check-points at key locations in the city centre. The Grand Central Hotel on Royal Avenue, opened in 1893, closed in 1971, and became used as a British Army base. Major local stores closed down and the city struggled to attract outside investment.

The 1990s and 2000s saw significant redevelopments once again reorienting the city. On the site of the Grand Central Hotel was built the Castle Court shopping centre, opened in 1990. In time this would be superseded by the massive development of the Victoria Square shopping centre, opened in 2008, at the corner of Chichester Street and Victoria Street, opposite the old Town Hall. These covered shopping centres attracted international retail names, while leaving areas such as the High Street struggling. Custom House Square, the site of many political speeches and confrontations as the nineteenth century turned into the twentieth, was refurbished as a site for open-air events. This work was undertaken by the Laganside Corporation, which also developed the Waterfront area.[2] The Waterfront Hall, opened in 1997, and the neighbouring Hilton Hotel offered the possibility of Belfast hosting major events, as did the building of the Odyssey Arena, completed in 2001, in Queen's Island, the area of the old shipyard. Queen's Island as a whole was rebranded as the 'Titanic Quarter' with the building of the Titanic Experience interpretive centre – opened in 2012 for the one hundredth anniversary of the sinking of the great ship – and the construction of new buildings for the Public Record Office of Northern Ireland and Belfast Metropolitan College. More recently, in 2017, the magnificent, high-ceilinged drawing office in which Harland and Wolff vessels were once designed has reopened as the Titanic Hotel.

Limitations on access of cars to the city centre, a necessary security measure during the years of political violence, offered the possibility of a more pedestrianised city. The City Hall itself opened its grounds as a small area of welcoming space and a venue for a continental market at Christmas time. Meanwhile the run-down side streets off Donegall Street were redeveloped as the Cathedral Quarter, with long-disused warehouses finding a new lease of life as restaurants, galleries and entertainment venues. The café, serving a range of different types of coffee, became a dominant retail outlet in a city centre that required more than just shops in order to compete with easily accessible out-of-town shopping and shopping on the internet. Venues such as the massive IKEA, opened in 2007 on the eastern outskirts of the city, provided alternative locations with easy parking. Like so many urban centres in Ireland and Britain, Belfast city centre needed to be a place of leisure with events that attracted people by offering more than just work or shopping.

In the wake of the peace process Belfast also became a serious destination for tourism, with a range of new hotels being built. This required strategies that included the development of events and festivals with an international focus. The city needed to project an image of safety and welcome, while, with some senses of irony, the outward symbols of the conflict such as murals and interface walls became part of the tourist package.[3]

These new places, and renovated old places, have something in common. They have developed in the era of the peace process where the balance of political power has shifted and government policies reflect ideas of human rights, equality, 'parity of esteem', 'good relations' and 'shared space'. Many of the venues established rules which control the displays of flags or the wearing of sports shirts likely to define an area in sectarian terms. Driven by the commercial demands of tourism and the policy and legal demands of equality, the central areas of Belfast have been developed to tackle the sectarian divide, while its residential spaces, particularly the working-class areas, have remained divided. Belfast appears both more shared and more divided than at any other point in its history.[4] The tension created by this played itself out in the negotiating of the civic space and was never more manifest than during the dispute over the Union flag on Belfast City Hall in 2012.

The flags dispute

On 3 December 2012, after a majority vote in Belfast City Council comprising the representatives of Sinn Féin, SDLP and Alliance, the Union flag was lowered from its position above City Hall. The new policy was that it was to fly only on designated days, most of which are the birthdays of members of the royal family. That members of Sinn Féin, a republican party, were prepared to vote for a Union flag to be raised on royal occasions may appear odd. In fact it was a calculated symbolic strategy, communicating to many unionists that even their ability to control their own flag in Belfast was now limited. The principle of flying the flag only on designated days had been accepted in other councils, some with unionist majorities, but this was Belfast City Hall. This was the same symbolic arena from which People's Democracy had been excluded after its one sit-down protest on 9 October 1968. The coalition of votes became the majority when the Alliance Party, which had long pursued this policy as a sign of shared space in Belfast, was joined by Sinn Féin and SDLP councillors in voting for this option. This was a compromise decision, given that Sinn Féin had long argued that either both Union flag and Tricolour should fly over City Hall or no flags at all. The leader of the Sinn Féin group in the Council, Jim McVeigh, explained the party's rationale for voting to support the Alliance Party's designated days strategy. 'We will be voting tactically on this,' he said. 'It's time to close the circle … and bring an end to unionist supremacy. This is 2012 not 1912.'[5]

For many unionists, particularly sections of working-class Loyalism in Belfast, this was a step too far: although the Union flag still flew on certain days, Irish Republicans had been able to get it removed for the majority of the year. On that evening of 3 December the continental Christmas market, a feature of twenty-first-century Belfast, occupied the front grounds of City Hall surrounding the Christmas tree. As the vote on the flag took place, protesters were gathering in May Street at the rear of the building. There were no more than 2,000 protesters, but the rear gates of City Hall failed and the Police Service of Northern Ireland (PSNI), as it later admitted, was not in a position to protect the building adequately. Not only were fifteen police officers injured but so were two council staff and a photographer. As protestors headed back to east Belfast violence broke out around the Short Strand area and in other parts of Northern Ireland.[6]

Over the weeks that followed protests continued around the City Hall and across Northern Ireland. A number of Alliance Party offices and members' homes were attacked. Yet not only were Alliance Party members threatened, so were members of Sinn Féin and the SDLP and the DUP. Threats to the DUP probably reflect a sense of disenchantment within Loyalism at what was perceived as the failure of mainstream unionism properly to represent its interests. Between 3 December 2012 and St Patrick's Day 2013, the PSNI recorded 2,980 'occurrences' related to the flag protests.[7] Concern for businesses in the centre of Belfast was so great that the Belfast Visitor and Convention Bureau organised a campaign called 'Backin' Belfast'.

The first protests at City Hall numbered in the thousands but soon the routine Saturday morning protests had fewer than 100 people involved. The eruption of a dispute over symbols was part of a familiar pattern. But there is also evidence that the civic space in the centre of the city had changed. The scale of the protest was significant but it did not match the protests over the prohibition of Orange marches at Drumcree near Portadown in 1995 and 1996, the hostile demonstrations that greeted the Anglo-Irish Agreement in 1986 or the strike by the Loyalist Ulster Workers that brought down the power-sharing executive in 1974. While there were some protests that could be deemed illegal, as well as some violence, the scale was quite limited. Power had shifted both in the Council and in public space. The definition of that space, legally and through policy and practice, had changed. Belfast City Council has been proactive through policy and funding to dictate what takes place in the civic arena. The Christmas tree and continental market at the front of City Hall are just as important to consider as the flag protests. This final chapter will explore how the civic space is constituted in contemporary Belfast, considering in particular the policy of a Shared Future.[8]

Shared power, 'shared future'

At face value the 1998 Good Friday Agreement between the British and Irish governments and ten political parties, significantly excluding the DUP, appears to say very little about civic space in practical terms. The Agreement covers the political structures for devolved government in Northern Ireland, the relationship between Northern Ireland and the Republic of Ireland and the relationship between the United Kingdom and the Republic of Ireland. It also created a number of new or improved permanent bodies such at the Northern Ireland Human Rights Commission and the Northern Ireland Equality Commission, and it set up commissions to look at problems over the future of policing, the provision for victims of the conflict and the decommissioning of paramilitary weapons. Most controversially, it contains a process for the early release of prisoners. What the Agreement says nothing about is parades or anything, directly, regarding public space.

The reason there is nothing specifically about parades is because new legislation, the Public Processions (Northern Ireland) Act 1998, had come into force that year. Disputes over parades had been ever present since the foundation of the state but there had been periods of particular heightened tensions.[9] Confrontations over civil rights parades were central to the drift towards large-scale communal violence in the late 1960s and, as the peace process developed, a rebalancing of power became expressed through the PSNI taking a more hard-line view of Orange parades, particularly in residential areas perceived as Catholic. The route of the Drumcree church parade held on the last Sunday before the Twelfth of July in Portadown had been in dispute since at least 1985. As discussed in the previous chapter, Jack Hermon, Chief Constable from 1980–89, made known his distaste for the draining of valuable policing resources by the loyal orders, and in the 1980s the RUC undertook a tougher line on some parades.[10] In 1995 the RUC, to the surprise of both the Orange Order in Portadown and the Residents Group protesting, stopped the Drumcree parade from returning along the Garvaghy Road through a mainly Catholic estate. The dispute that followed would continue for two decades and cost, at least directly, five lives and many millions of pounds. Between 1995 and 2000 massive policing operations dealt with high levels of violence and disorder in both Protestant and Catholic areas. Other parading disputes in Derry, Belfast, Bellaghy and Ballycastle, and in a number of rural areas, at times seemed to threaten the peace process. The dispute in Portadown was so problematic that an inquiry into parades legislation was set up in 1996 which recommended that decisions on parade routes should be removed from the police and handed to an independent body.[11] The resulting Parades Commission had come into existence just months before the 1998 Good Friday Agreement. As a result, parades were not explicitly discussed in terms of the Agreement, although they certainly provided a significant backdrop to ongoing negotiations.

This was contestation over symbols of a magnitude that even Northern Ireland had not witnessed before. The reasons for this are clear. Republicans were entering into the political institutions, new and existing. They were to become senior government ministers, to take on ceremonial roles such as mayor and, after the St Andrews Agreement in 2006, to accept places on the Northern Ireland Policing Board. In such a shift of power the exclusion of symbols of Irish Republicanism from public spaces could not be sustained. Instead the Agreement made an explicit commitment to 'the principles of full respect for, and equality of, civil, political, social and cultural rights, of freedom from discrimination for all citizens, and of parity of esteem and of just and equal treatment for the identity, ethos, and aspirations of both communities'.[12] The public space was bound to reflect these changes. But this, in turn, would open up that space to very intense, sometimes violent, disputes over what could and could not appear there. Unsurprisingly, given the previous domination of the space by unionism, it was unionists who generally felt that they were losing out. It was unionists and Loyalists who experienced what they described as a 'culture war'.

Some of those changes would appear minor in retrospect. For example, just weeks after the Agreement, on 29 April, Sinn Féin held a meeting with African National Congress visitors at the Ulster Hall, historic venue for many past unionist rallies.[13] Others, more culturally based, and with economic benefits, were not particularly controversial, as when Belfast became a venue for the

Irish Dance World Championships in 2000 and in 2004.[14] During discussions on reform of the police, which led to the RUC becoming the PSNI, the symbols on the badge on police uniforms were a much discussed issue.[15] The St Patrick's Day event in central Belfast, launched in 1998, was annually the subject of disputes over its funding and context. Debates over the Union flag flying over Northern Ireland Government buildings, local council buildings and public services became more intense.[16] There was a review of the symbols that appear inside court-houses.[17] In short, the symbols and events that were seen as reflecting unionism were being questioned, while claims were being made that the symbols and events reflecting Irishness and Irish Republicanism should have their place in the public and civic life of Northern Ireland.

The only clause in the Good Friday Agreement that refers directly to practices in the civic space is a rather bland statement about symbols:

> All participants acknowledge the sensitivity of the use of symbols and emblems for public purposes, and the need in particular in creating the new institutions to ensure that such symbols and emblems are used in a manner which promotes mutual respect rather than division. Arrangements will be made to monitor this issue and consider what action might be required.[18]

Most pertinent is the enabling legislation that the British government brought forward as a result of the Agreement, section 75 of the Northern Ireland Act 1998. This imposes statutory duties upon public authorities, including, obviously, local councils. So, a 'public authority shall in carrying out its functions relating to Northern Ireland have due regard to the need to promote equality of opportunity- (a) between persons of different religious belief, political opinion, racial group, age, marital status or sexual orientation; (b) between men and women generally; (c) between persons with a disability and persons without; and (d) between persons with dependants and persons without'. But in addition, a public authority shall 'in carrying out its functions relating to Northern Ireland have regard to the desirability of promoting good relations between persons of different religious belief, political opinion or racial group'.[19]

The impact of both parts of this clause took some time to become apparent. However, in effect it makes a defining statement about the type of civic activities that are to be encouraged. Over the years that followed, the policies of local councils had to engage with the legislation regardless of the political make-up of the council. This does not lead to an immediate change in policies; indeed, on the issue of flags, some councils have maintained the existing policies. But all the political parties in all the councils have had to engage with the definition of civic space. The defence of an existing policy, or an attempt to change that policy, was undertaken in a new context and using the language of equality and good relations.

The flying of the Union flag on public buildings provides a good example of the impact of this legislative and policy regime. Key to the 1998 Agreement were political institutions that required coalition-style government between unionist and nationalist parties. This proved difficult to set up, after the election to the new Northern Ireland Assembly on 25 June 1998, due to a number of differences in the interpretation of the Agreement. But, late in 1999 arrangements were reached which led to a relatively short-lived Northern Ireland Government, with members of the four main parties taking up ministerial roles. The allocation of government departments left the UUP in control of three ministries, the DUP in control of two, the SDLP in control of three and Sinn Féin in control of two. Almost immediately there were differences over the flying of the Union flag on different ministerial buildings.[20] Unionist ministers ordered the flag to be flown outside their departments while Sinn Féin ministers ordered no flag to be flown. SDLP ministers ordered the Union flag not to be flown on the Twelfth of July. This produced heated controversy in the Assembly and eventually a committee was established to explore the issue.[21]

There was such contention that the then Secretary of State, Peter Mandelson, introduced The Flags (Northern Ireland) Order 2000. This 'notified' particular days on which the Union flag should fly on government buildings and designated the nine government buildings in Northern Ireland to which this would apply. The notified days (there were originally eighteen) in the main represented birthdays of members of the British royal family. Significantly, the list did not include the Twelfth of July but did include St Patrick's Day.

In October 2001, the Sinn Féin Member of the Legislative Assembly Conor Murphy challenged this Order in the High Court, partly on the basis that it was used for political purposes and, he contended, was 'not in keeping with the Good Friday Agreement'. The case failed, with the judge arguing that limited flying of the flag 'merely reflects Northern Ireland's constitutional position as part of the UK'. In addition, the judge argued that the flying of the flag did not breach section 75 of the Northern Ireland Act 1998.[22] The judgment of Kerr J in Re Murphy's Application for Judicial Review [2001] NI 425 suggested that:

> The Union Flag is the flag of the United Kingdom of which Northern Ireland is a part. It is the judgment of the Secretary of State that it should be flown on government buildings only on those days in which it is flown in Great Britain. By thus confining the days in which a flag is to appear, the Secretary of State sought to strike the correct balance between, on the one hand, acknowledging Northern Ireland's constitutional position and on the other not giving offence to those who oppose it. That approach appears to me to exemplify a proper regard for 'partnership, equality and mutual respect' and fulfil the government undertaking that its jurisdiction in Northern Ireland shall be exercised with rigorous impartiality on behalf of all the people in the diversity of their identities

12 City Hall, St Patrick's Day 2015. A PSNI officer keeps teenagers wrapped in Tricolours at a distance from 'flags protesters' wrapped in Union flags. Protests were held on a weekly basis after the decision by Belfast City Council on 3 December 2012 to fly the Union flag only on designated days. St Patrick's Day is one of those designated days, and the contentious emblem can be seen on the flag pole.

and traditions. I do not consider therefore that the Regulations have been shown to be in conflict with the Belfast Agreement.

Sinn Féin had argued that parity of esteem for the two traditions demanded that both national traditions should be reflected in the flying of official flags. The judge felt that by restricting the flying days to those practised in the rest of the United Kingdom the Secretary of State was making a distinction between the constitutional position of Northern Ireland and the rights of nationalists.[23] This argument has been repeated throughout the two decades following the Agreement.

The policy on when and where to fly flags on buildings controlled by district councils varied across Northern Ireland and was not covered by the legislation. Some unionist-controlled councils had the Union flag flying on the council buildings and other services, such as leisure centres, every day of the year. Other councils flew the Union flag on designated days, such as royal birthdays, and restricted the use of the flag to the main council building. Other councils, under nationalist control, now flew no flag at all, or used a flag designed to recognise the council area.[24]

In this context the balance of power within Belfast City Council became important both in the full Council meetings and in terms of key committees and their role in developing new policies. Unionist parties effectively lost control of the Council in 1997, and until the most recent election in 2014 the votes of the Alliance Party were required by nationalist and unionist parties to create a majority. The position of Mayor was rotated on an annual basis between the parties and committee chairs, as with ministerial positions in the Northern Ireland Government, filled using the D'Hontd power-sharing system. This meant that political parties within the Council were constantly engaging with each other to get policies through, which has required a degree of consensus building. And it is worth noting that in the City Council, just as in elections for seats at Stormont, the DUP has overtaken the UUP as the dominant force within unionism, while amongst nationalists Sinn Féin has supplanted the SDLP.

Belfast City Council, like other councils in Northern Ireland, was required to examine policies in the context of section 75 of the Northern Ireland Act 1998, which would include the policy on flags that flew on its buildings and at events that it organised and funded. This process started in 2002 and in May 2004 the Council produced an Equality Impact Assessment (EQIA), as required under the legislation, entitled 'Flying the Union Flag'. This assessment referred back to the legal advice on the case against flying flags on government buildings. But legal advice to Belfast City Council in this EQIA suggested that, unless the Council explored what was then the current policy of flying the flags every day of the year, then it would not be compliant with its equality policy.[25] After this consideration in 2004 the Council voted to leave the flags policy unchanged.

The evolution of policy and practice over the following ten years from 2004 was significant. The Council developed an Equality Scheme, a Good Relations Strategy (2003) and a Peace and Reconciliation Action Plan built around funding from the European Union. Indeed the Council updated its Equality Scheme under section 75 of the Northern Ireland Act 1998 in 2012. In addition the Council is duty bound to comply with work-place legislation which demands the provision of a good and harmonious working environment. In 2009 the Equality Commission produced the following guidance for the flying of the Union flag:

> The flying of the Union flag must be viewed in the context in which it is flown or displayed. Factors affecting the context include the manner, location and frequency with which flags are flown. The Union flag is the national flag of the United Kingdom and, arising therefrom, has a particular status symbolising the constitutional position of Northern Ireland. On the other hand, the Union flag is often used to mark sectional community allegiance. There is a world of

difference between these two approaches. Thus, for example, while it is acceptable and appropriate, in the Commission's view, for a local Council to fly the Union flag at its Civic Headquarters, the rationale for its display at every Council location, facility and leisure centre would be questionable.[26]

When organising events, Belfast City Council attempts to comply with policies that create a shared space. So, for example, on 8 May 2014 the Giro d'Italia bike race, second in importance only to the Tour de France, started in central Belfast. This was possibly the most high-profile global sporting event ever to have taken place in the city. For two days large crowds lined the streets of central Belfast and on the routes around the city. As with all events, conditions included the stipulation that 'flags, emblems or other paraphernalia of a political, sectarian, racist or partisan nature will not be permitted on site'.[27] This meant that, unlike at many national sports events around the world, there were no national flags (Figure 13).

The variety of policy documents produced by the City Council since the 1998 Good Friday Agreement reflected this context. The 2003 Good Relations Strategy looked to promote 'equality of opportunity in the discharge of the Council's responsibilities, taking into account the needs of persons of different religious belief, political opinion, racial group, age, marital status or sexual orientation, of men and women generally, of persons with a disability

13 Giro d'Italia, 9 May 2014. Great Victoria Street and other streets on the route through the centre of Belfast are cleared to allow the cyclists to pass.

and persons without and of persons with dependants and persons without' and 'to use the Council's influence as a democratically elected body, providing civic leadership to the City, to promote good relations throughout society'.[28] The list of priorities included the establishment of a Cultural Diversity Fund; the development of initiatives to promote the shared history of an increasingly diverse city; the development of initiatives on citizenship and civic pride, including exhibitions and events to reflect the different traditions in the city; the establishment of mechanisms to facilitate engagement with minority racial and ethnic groups; and a review of the criteria for the use of the City Hall to ensure equality of opportunity for all groups.[29] In examining the development of festivals in the city the strategy document suggests that funding for events should have criteria specifying 'that any event should be open, inclusive, non-party political and the promoters must be accountable in respect of the outcome'.[30] It also refers to 'Codes of Practice for supporting appropriate projects and events' named in the Community Relations Council's 'Guidelines for a Cultural Diversity Policy: an Advocacy Document'.[31]

The example of St Patrick's Day again proves interesting. The Council took over the organisation of St Patrick's Day in 2006 and the programme for the day specified that 'in line with all Council programmes we are committed to delivering an inclusive day'. The terms and conditions posted up at Custom House Square, where the staged part of St Patrick's Day was to take place, warned that 'Flags, emblems or paraphernalia of a political, sectarian, racist or partisan nature will not be permitted on site' and added the terse admonition 'No football Jerseys'. This effectively meant excluding the Tricolour and Celtic football shirts from the parade even if they were waved and worn by spectators.[32]

The 1998 Agreement did not specifically appear to deal with civic space but it provided a legislative and institutional framework that meant that public authorities produced policies, including the provision of public funds, that impacted, over time, on the civic. These policies form part of a broader government policy to create shared space. This was most clearly articulated in 2005 in the Shared Future policy produced by the offices of the First Minister and Deputy First Minister, the twin heads of the executive. The overall aim of *A Shared Future* is

> to establish, over time, a shared society defined by a culture of tolerance: a normal, civic society, in which all individuals are considered as equals, where differences are resolved through dialogue in the public sphere, and where all individuals are treated impartially. A society where there is equity, respect for diversity and recognition of our interdependence.[33]

Of particular concern in the document was the proliferation of flags on street furniture, such as lampposts, demarcating territory around Northern Ireland.[34]

There is a lot of evidence to suggest that, in terms of more residential areas, the first objective, 'tackling visible manifestations of sectarianism', has not been successful. There has been little reduction in terms of displays such as murals and flags. There have been projects to attempt to reimage murals and an inter-agency approach to reducing the numbers of flags that fly on lampposts, demarcating territory. While some paramilitary murals have been removed, new, overtly paramilitary images have been painted. And comprehensive research on the display of flags shows conclusively that there has been almost no change in the numbers of flags, or the length of time they are displayed, marking territory.[35] There is plenty of evidence that residential divisions have remained significant or become more distinct since 1998.[36] It might appear that neither the values expressed in the Good Friday Agreement nor the legislation nor the policies derived from it have had much influence. However, the centre of Belfast and the space around City Hall offer an alternative perspective.

Shared space

In 2014 Séanna Breathnach, an Irish Republican in Belfast and a former Volunteer in the IRA, picked out one of the aspects that had changed the attitude that Republicans might have towards the city:

> I think that the demilitarisation of Belfast city centre certainly made a big difference to how nationalists and Republicans felt about going in to the city centre, whether formally or informally. I think that events like Paddy's Day and the whole general sense of connection, not just with Irish people, but with the Irish diaspora, I think that was very, very big, particularly in the … whenever I came out of prison with the Good Friday Agreement in 1998, a couple of years after that, there was really a sense of buzz about the Paddy's Day and that things were really changing as well. I think it has relaxed a wee bit since then, which is maybe no bad thing.[37]

The St Patrick's Day events are again illuminative. From 1998 to 2005 they were organised by people connected to Féile an Phobail, the West Belfast Festival, and took the form of a series of feeder parades all starting in Catholic areas of Belfast and heading into the city. This was the type of performance of Irishness in the city centre that had not taken place prior to the Good Friday Agreement. It was a reflection of the political changes at City Hall, but it also marked a fundamental shift in the way that those considering themselves Irish could present themselves in this public space.

Interestingly, the origins of this development could probably be dated to 8 August 1993, when the main Republican Internment parade was allowed to gather in front of City Hall and Irish Tricolours were waved at and placed upon the statue of Queen Victoria.[38] The day before, a city councillor, Sinn

Féin's Alex Maskey, who would become Mayor of Belfast nine years later, discussed the possibility that the RUC would not stop the parade: 'the reality is that this is our city, and a substantial section of the populace here wish to march to the City Hall to give voice to their grievances'.[39] Speakers from the platform in front of City Hall included Gerry Adams, president of Sinn Féin, and representatives from independence groups in Catalonia and the Basque regions as well as from the Irish-American fund-raising group Noraid. The event ended up with the singing of the civil rights song 'We shall overcome' and chants of 'IRA, IRA'.[40] The following day, unionist politicians demanded an inquiry into the handling of the city centre parade, complaining about the 'flaunting' of Tricolours and the shouting of IRA slogans. Ulster Unionist Councillor Jim Rodgers argued that 'the police should have arrested those chanting pro-IRA slogans in what was clearly a breach of the peace'.[41] This was the first Irish Republican event outside City Hall to be allowed by the RUC and marked a turning point in the use of that important area of public space.

There is a more interesting and subtle process at work than just the access of Republicans and nationalists to the city centre, although this can of course be considered sharing space in the sense that everyone has access. It is the next phase that is as revealing, with the development of the St Patrick's Day event in 1998 and its evolution into a festival taken over by Belfast City Council in 2006 to become part of a list of civic events. Early evaluations of the event run by the Council in 2006 and 2007 suggested that the St Patrick's Day carnival did attract some people defining themselves as Protestant. A survey in 2006 suggested that around 17 per cent of spectators defined themselves as Protestant.[42] Since that period it has been noticeable that the political tension has gone out of the event. The St Patrick's Day carnival became one of the range of festivals and events on the calendar for the Council. The controversy that surrounded St Patrick's Day from 1998 had abated. But also noticeable was that involvement in the event seemed to reduce as well. By 2013 and 2014 the parades were shorter, with fewer community groups taking part. In 2014 the theme was time travel, with Beat Initiative producing excellent floats and some large models of Northern Ireland's three internationally successful golfers, three dance groups, none of them performing Irish dances, and a couple of bands on the floats playing music. The East Belfast Mission, based in a Protestant area of the city, did take part with its Irish-language group. The parade is now struggling for popular involvement. Gone are the groups that took part ten years earlier. No longer driven by the involvement of Sinn Féin and the West Belfast Festival organisers, but rather relying on Council officials and the Beat Initiative, the event is well organised, imaginative but small.

The appearances of the Tricolour throughout this period have been interesting. Excluded from the city centre for many years, it makes its first broadly legal appearance in the 1993 demonstration. It was prominent in the St Patrick's Day events which developed from 1998 loaded with expressions of Irish nationalism. But, as the event evolved and organisers looked to get funding from the Council it became more unwelcome. The Council is more interested in a civic event that reflects the values expressed in *A Shared Future*. In the St Patrick's Day events after 2006 the use of the Beat Initiative to develop a 'carnival' means the Tricolour does not appear in the parade. In that sense the Tricolour had been paraded in to the city, but then, like the Union flag, its use had to be moderated.[43] Popular displays by individual spectators could be tolerated, but in aspects of the event under the control of the Council the use of the flag was limited or non-existent.

Much more was taking place in the civic arena than simply the entry of a controlled version of Irish nationalism. Belfast Council funded and organised a series of events and festivals throughout the year in an attempt to attract people into the city. Events such as the Festival of Fools and Culture Night joined longer-standing events such as the Lord Mayor's Show and the turning on of the Christmas lights. From the 1990s Belfast hosted a significant Gay Pride event every summer (Figure 14). As already discussed, the Lord Mayor's Show was an early convert to the idea of carnival, through the work of Beat Initiative. In doing so, the events utilise a more global culture of music, dance and the use of masks. Although the history of carnival in many parts of the world is a story of resistance, in Belfast it has perhaps become a representation of multiculturalism, arguably ignoring local, more contested cultures and customs. In the case of the Lord Mayor's Show and St Patrick's Day it was not simply a matter of rebranding the events but of substantially changing and controlling the type of content.

This move towards the festival and the carnival was not lost on the more long-standing event. The Twelfth of July parade, discussed in the previous chapter, has made an attempt to rebadge itself as 'Orangefest' (Figure 15). In December 2004, under Alliance Lord Mayor Tom Ekin, a series of meetings were convened between organisers of the Twelfth of July in Belfast and the Department of Culture Arts and Leisure, the Community Relations Council and the Ulster Scots Agency. Meetings explored the potential for tourism at events and ways of drawing in a more diverse range of people to the city during the Twelfth of July.[44] In 2006, the same year that Belfast Council took control of running St Patrick's Day, £100,000 was made available by the British government to create events around the Twelfth of July to broaden its appeal under the title of Orangefest. Billy Mawhinny, an Orangeman from west Belfast, was one of those tasked with implementing these changes. In 2009 he commented: 'We've tried hard to make the Twelfth of July a more inclusive day of celebration. The city has changed, and we want to see everyone from all the different groups involved.'[45] Despite this attempt at

Shared space or divided future? 217

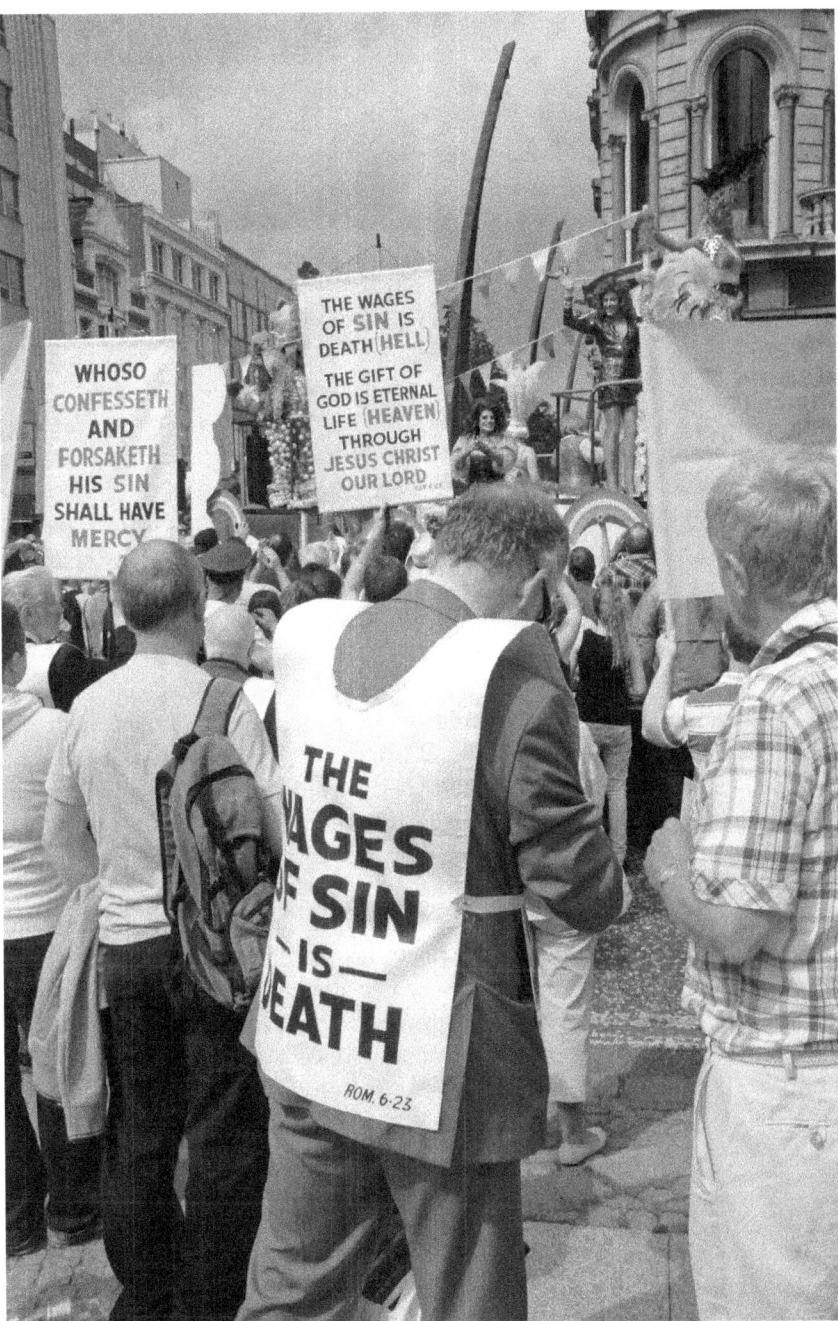

14 Belfast Pride parade, 30 July 2011. The annual parade makes its way down Royal Avenue, to be met by protestors with an alternative message.

rebranding, the parade itself, dominated by 'blood and thunder' flute bands, has not gone through a dramatic change. However, it is significant that the Orange Order feels the need to turn its Twelfth of July 'march' or 'walk' into a festival. Indeed, the Secretary of the Grand Lodge of Ireland was interviewed in the *Irish Times* under the headline 'From sashes to sambas?'[46] And in Derry/Londonderry during the same period the Apprentice Boys developed the Maiden City Festival to provide a new context for the city's major loyal order parade, marking the city's resistance to the Catholic James II during the siege of 1688–89.

In 2010 retailers in Belfast city centre, having for many years closed on the Twelfth of July, decided to open for business during the afternoon, while the Grand Lodge unveiled a new 'family friendly' mascot called Diamond Dan.[47] However, this shift by the Orange Order was not without resistance. The Reverend Stephen Dickinson, in 2008, told Orange brethren at the Ballyclare Twelfth of July parade, 'I notice that Peter Robinson and others have been saying in recent days we're about cultural tourism. This is about Protestantism, this is about Britishness – it's not about cultural tourism, Mr Robinson.'[48]

There is, at one level, no need to judge the success of these changes. What is interesting is they are being impacted on by a change in how civic space in the city is defined. Indeed, the Twelfth of July parades in Belfast in the second decade of the twenty-first century are still events at which considerable amounts of drinking take place, with rowdy crowds greeting Orangemen and bands, particularly around Sandy Row. And young spectators on St Patrick's Day will wander around the city with cheap Irish Tricolours hanging around their shoulders. It is possible to argue that there are more occasions when 'party symbols' enter the civic space. But they can do so only in the context of events that are at least attempting to create acceptability within that space. St Patrick's Day quickly moved from an event at which nationalists and Republicans could 'take' a city in which they had previously not be able to present their identity, to an event that would attempt to be open to everyone. The Twelfth of July, organised by the Orange Order, which by definition excludes Catholics, is nevertheless an attempt to create an event which reaches out beyond its shrinking, but still substantial, constituency.

The queen and Irish Republicans

One way of highlighting the complex and striking changes that have taken place in the civic arena is to return to the visits of the monarch to Northern Ireland and Ireland that have taken place across the period since 1970. As the fiftieth anniversary of the founding of Northern Ireland approached, Terence O'Neill's government began to plan for a celebration entitled 'Ulster 71'. Clearly, central to such an event would be a visit by the reigning monarch

15 Twelfth of July parade, 2010. Banners, partly sponsored by Belfast City Council, proclaim the parade, rebranded as Orangefest.

and it was hoped that Queen Elizabeth might open Parliament in June 1971 as George V had done in June 1921. But by 1969 it was clear that, with levels of violence steadily increasing, there were going to be some difficulties. McIntosh describes the slightly desperate and sometimes almost comic engagement between officials in Belfast and London as it became clear that the security situation was worsening through 1970 and into 1971. In February 1971 the Governor General, Lord Grey, conveyed to James Chichester-Clarke, who by then had taken over from O'Neill as Prime Minister,

> that the Queen realised that acceptance of the Home Secretary's reluctant advice against visiting Northern Ireland to open Parliament on June 22nd would come as a considerable disappointment to you and to me; but he hoped that in the circumstances we would agree that it was an inevitable decision. ... I think we must conclude that there is no possibility of a visit by any member of the Royal Family for this purpose.

The wide range of events that took place for Ulster 71 was not a total failure, with the main site at Botanic Gardens in Belfast opening on 14 May 1971. Official attendances were lower than expected and the visits from three opera and ballet companies were cancelled for security reasons. Although the use by the Northern Ireland Tourist Board on the slogan 'Come to Ulster' also seems somewhat desperate, in the circumstances it is interesting, and an echo of policies that would arise after the 1998 Good Friday Agreement, that the final government reports on the fifty-three towns and villages that held events concentrated on their success as 'community relations' exercises.[49]

Subsequent visits by the monarch have provided an indicator of the state of civic space. Queen Elizabeth had visited during her coronation year in 1953 and again in 1954, 1961 and 1966. However the failure to visit in 1971 meant that eleven years elapsed before she was next seen in Northern Ireland, at celebrations of her Silver Jubilee in 1977. On 10–11 August the royal yacht *Britannia* arrived in Belfast Lough. Extra troops had been drafted in for security. The queen did not visit Belfast, but instead flew by helicopter to her residence at Hillsborough Castle, twelve miles to the south. Next day the royal yacht made its way up the north coast to the seaside town of Portrush. The queen came ashore to visit the New University of Ulster at Coleraine, a small bomb exploding in the ground after she had left. Thereafter it was not until June 1991, a further gap of fourteen years, that she returned on a short, one-day visit which included a visit to the Lisburn barracks of the Ulster Defence Regiment. More frequent subsequent visits, in 1993, 1995, 1997, 2000 and 2001, reflect the lessening of security fears. In 2002, her Golden Jubilee year, the Queen visited Stormont for the first time since 1953.[50]

In 17–20 May 2011 Queen Elizabeth undertook an official visit to the Irish Republic. Amongst many notable events, she visited the Garden of

Remembrance in Dublin, dedicated to 'all those who gave their lives in the cause of Irish freedom', and Croke Park, headquarters of the Gaelic Athletic Association and the site where British soldiers in November 1920 had fired into crowds attending a football match, killing fourteen people.[51] Sinn Féin stood aloof from the visit, and as a result found themselves at odds with majority opinion in the Republic. However, the following year, during the Queen's Diamond Jubilee tour, Martin McGuinness, as Deputy First Minister, shook hands with her during an event at the Lyric Theatre in Belfast.[52]

Taken over time, these events indicate not only a reorientation of the place of the monarch in civic life in Northern Ireland and Belfast, but also a dramatic change in the status of Irish Republicanism. Throughout the violent conflict over three decades, potential visits from the head of state were difficult and clearly avoided. At the same time Irish Republicanism was effectively excluded from civic spaces, while its excursions into other public spaces, such as the annual commemorations of the Easter Rising on the Falls Road and Milltown Cemetery, as well as Internment commemoration events held in August, routinely involved clashes with the security forces.[53] In the new environment of the peace process, however, Republican events took on a new character. Internment commemorations in west Belfast, from 1988 onwards, became part of Féile an Phobail, the West Belfast Festival. The larger of the Easter commemoration parades on the Falls Road has taken on a different look since 1998, with some participants appearing in period costume and carrying replicas of early twentieth-century guns. As the events are outside central Belfast, policing has become light, with PSNI officers performing basic traffic duties during the march to Milltown cemetery.

These changes can be put in some perspective when compared to the dynamic of the events around the Twelfth of July. It would be difficult to think of another event organised in the United Kingdom which more specifically offers loyalty to the British throne. The Grand Orange Lodge of Ireland sends a letter to the queen expressing its loyalty before every Twelfth of July and receives a polite note of thanks from her secretary. This is read from the platform at the Belfast parade and at events all around Northern Ireland on the Twelfth of July. It is striking, however, that no visit by the monarch, or by members of her family, has included any direct engagement with these public displays of loyalty. It says much about the complex politics of civic events in Ireland that Queen Elizabeth II has visited the site commemorating the dead of the Republican uprising of 1916 in Dublin but not a Twelfth of July parade in Belfast.

Civic Belfast

On 15 May 2016 the Lord Mayor, Alderman Brian Kingston, opened an exhibition in City Hall, created at a cost of £1.3 million, exploring the history, culture and traditions of the city of Belfast. The narrative of the exhibition was agreed by the leaders of all parties in the Council.[54] Given the contested narratives attached to the city, this was no small achievement. It also followed a process of diversification of symbols within the City Hall, particularly through the addition of a series of stained glass windows. These include windows depicting the Famine (1999), the 1907 Belfast Dock Strike (2007), Celtic myths and legends (2012), the Spanish Civil War (2015) and the women of Belfast (2016), and additions to the RUC window (2006) and Ulster Defence Regiment window (2013). These of course joined a wide range of statues and windows that had adorned a unionist-dominated building since it opened in 1906.[55]

This book is full of examples illustrating the long-standing propensity to define civic life in Belfast in exclusive terms. Chapters have explored the complex power relationships impacted upon by dominant identities of class, religious and political ethnicity and gender that have demarcated the civic. Who is defined as 'the public', and what is described as 'respectable', changes over time. This can be analysed in two ways. First, one can examine who is given access to the city. On 8 August 1993 security forces first granted permission for Republican demonstrators to enter the city. Demonstrators brandished placards with 'Our City Also' on them and at City Hall they sang the civil rights anthem 'We shall overcome'.[56] Gerry Adams spoke to the crowd, claiming 'you have the right to your city, the right to your City Hall'.[57] Second, and the approach taken in this book, one can look at how the civic life is defined by the city and various agencies. How are the spaces and events planned and managed? What symbols and peoples and groups are representative of the city? The contemporary Lord Mayor's Show, or carnival, has come to represent diversity and, pointedly, avoids some of the sounds of the city, the marching bands, that might symbolise a less diverse or exclusive place. Laws, rules, policies, funding and procedures define how the space works.

The policy of shared space that has dominated Belfast in the twenty-first century has encapsulated the shifts in power and the struggle to redefine the civic space.[58] Nagle and Clancy have depicted the policy as an attempt, depending on which way you look at it, to find common ground and at the same time to give space that allows people to share but be different.[59] In a society with such political divisions those spaces are ones of risk and potential conflict. Nagle and Clancy offer the possibility that this space is one that, if successfully managed, allows for cohesion and difference.

Specific pre-conditions, wrought through engagements between sections of society, should be encouraged concerning how space is to be used by groups. Although this will not necessarily end conflict, it at least will provide room for groups to discuss their meaning of how their identities are expressed in public space.[60]

The issue of access to public space is itself inextricably tied up with ideas of citizenship and legitimacy. The use of public space, moreover, does not merely reflect perceptions of identity; it is also one of the important ways in which identity itself is performed. The potential of civic space in Belfast is through the performance of different aspects of citizenship before the relationship building takes place. When those Republican protestors in 1993 participated in a legal demonstration in front of City Hall their relationship to the city was inevitably changing. If their relationship to the city space was changing then, in a mediated way, and despite the anger of unionists, their relationship towards other people in the city had changed. So access and freedom of assembly, in allowing participatory citizenship, changes political relationships.

At that level it is not necessary to share the space together or through alternative identities. Yet that second version of sharing, one that is premised on performances of identities that fall outside or cut across the dominant ethno-political groups, is also vital. The policies that have defined the city since 1998 have not only impacted on the range of events taking place; they have demanded change in many long-standing events. The 'festival' and the 'carnival' have been the container through which so much takes place, even the Twelfth of July.

This renegotiated space that has emerged since the Good Friday Agreement has led to significant contestation. Nelson McCausland, senior DUP politician and Minister for Culture, Arts and Leisure from 2009 to 2011, has been among many within unionism who have seen what has taken place as a 'culture war'.

> The current political impasse came when Sinn Fein collapsed the Northern Ireland Assembly over their demand for an Irish Language Act. This highlights the fact that 'culture is upstream from politics' and that Sinn Fein has been running a 'culture war'.[61]

The changes identified in the later chapters of this book do represent a significant shift in power for unionism. While unionism does retain a substantial, maybe dominant, position in the symbolic landscape of the public space, there is no doubt, through the intervention of events acknowledging nationalism and through changes of definition of the civic, that this has transformed. This is identified by unionism as bringing a sense of loss, while nationalists have acknowledged and used the city in new ways.

A policy confined to adjudicating between the claims of opposing groups points towards a future not of shared but of partitioned space. Instead, this book provides material for a debate that takes into account the complex historical background impacting on the public spaces of Belfast, and that re-examines the whole idea of what constitutes the civic, and of what is to be permitted or encouraged within different types of public space. An examination of the historical complexity reveals significant shifts over time. It reveals complexity in power relationships that defy some of the stereotypes of the city of Belfast. And it suggests that, in a divided society, the civic space deserves care and attention.

Notes

1 Fredrick W. Boal, *Shaping a City: Belfast in the Late Twentieth Century* (Belfast: Institute of Irish Studies, 1995); Peter Shirlow and Brendan Murtagh, *Belfast: Segregation, Violence and the City* (London: Pluto Press, 2006).
2 Boal, *Shaping a City*, pp. 83–4.
3 Dominic Bryan, 'Titanic town: living in a landscape of conflict', in S. J. Connolly (ed.), *Belfast 400: People, Place and History* (Liverpool: Liverpool University Press, 2012), pp. 317–56.
4 Bryan, 'Titanic town', pp. 352–3.
5 'Moment vote passed inside, all hell broke loose outside', *Belfast Telegraph*, 4 December 2012.
6 Paul Nolan, Dominic Bryan, Clare Dwyer, Katy Hayward, Katy Radford and Peter Shirlow, *The Flag Dispute: Anatomy of a Protest* (Belfast: Institute for the Study of Conflict, Transformation and Social Justice, Queen's University Belfast, 2014), p. 75.
7 Nolan et al., *The Flag Dispute*, p. 52.
8 Office of the First and Deputy First Minister, *A Shared Future: Policy and Strategic Framework* (Belfast: Office of the First and Deputy First Minister, Good Relations Unit, 2005).
9 Neil Jarman and Dominic Bryan, *From Riots to Rights: Nationalist Parades in the North of Ireland* (Coleraine: Centre for the Study of Conflict, 1998).
10 Jarman and Bryan, *From Riots to Rights*.
11 *Independent Review of Parades and Marches* (Belfast: HMSO, 1997), available at http://cain.ulst.ac.uk/issues/parade/north.htm (accessed 23 May 2018).
12 *Good Friday Agreement*, Part 2 section (v).
13 *Independent*, 2 May 1988; Sinn Fein press release, 27 April 1998, www.sinnfein.org/releases/pr042798.html (accessed 22 April 2018).
14 BBC, 2 March 2004, http://news.bbc.co.uk/1/hi/northern_ireland/3525551.stm (accessed 22 April 2018).
15 Dominic Bryan and Gillian McIntosh, 'Symbols and identity in the "new" Northern Ireland', in Paul Carmichael, Colin Knox and Robert Osborne (eds), *Devolution and Constitutional Change in Northern Ireland* (Manchester: Manchester University Press, 2007), pp. 125–37.
16 Nolan et al., *The Flag Dispute*.

17 Criminal Justice review Group, *Review of the Criminal Justice System in Northern Ireland* (Belfast: HMSO, 2000), pp. 184–5.
18 *Good Friday Agreement*, point 5, p. 20.
19 Northern Ireland Act 1998, section 75.
20 *Guardian*, 2 June 2000; BBC News, 6 June 2000, http://news.bbc.co.uk/1/hi/northern_ireland/779415.stm (accessed 1 May 2018).
21 Northern Ireland Assembly, Ad Hoc Committee, Report on Draft Regulations proposed under Article 3 of The Flags (Northern Ireland) Order 2000, http://archive.niassembly.gov.uk/adhocs/flags/reports/adhoc1-00r-b.htm (accessed 1 May 2018).
22 Dominic Bryan and Gordon Gillespie, *Transforming Conflict: Flags and Emblems* (Belfast: Institute of Irish Studies 2005), pp. 17–20.
23 Nolan et al., *The Flag Dispute*, pp. 23–8.
24 Bryan and Gillespie, *Transforming Conflict*; Nolan et al., *The Flag Dispute*.
25 Belfast City Council, Policy on the Flying of the Union Flag Equality Impact Assessment – Final Decision Report, 2004, pp. 77–8, www.belfastcity.gov.uk/nmsruntime/saveasdialog.aspx?lID=2904&sID=1644 (accessed 6 May 2018).
26 Equality Commission of Northern Ireland, *Promoting a Good and Harmonious Working Environment, A Guide for Employers and Employees* (Belfast: Equality Commission of Northern Ireland, 2009), www.equalityni.org/ECNI/media/ECNI/Publications/Employers%20and%20Service%20Providers/Promoting_a_good_and_harmonious_working_environment.pdf (accessed 6 May 2018).
27 Belfast City Council, *Giro d'Italia Opening, City Hall, Terms and Conditions of Entry* (Belfast: Belfast City Council, 2014), http://sites.visitbelfast.com/assets/gallery/generic/TermsandConditionsofEntryGiroDItaliaTeamPresentationEvent8May14.pdf (accessed 6 May 2018).
28 Belfast City Council, *Good Relations Strategy: Building Our Future Together:* (Belfast: Belfast City Council, Good relations Unit, 2003), www.belfastcity.gov.uk/nms-runtime/saveasdialog.aspx?lID=2795&sID=2346 (accessed 13 November 2018).
29 Belfast City Council, *Good Relations Strategy*, p. 45.
30 Belfast City Council, *Good Relations Strategy*, p. 45.
31 Maurna Crozier, *Guidelines for a Cultural Diversity Policy* (Belfast: Community Relations Council, 2000).
32 Dominic Bryan, 'Parades, flags, carnivals, and riots: public space, contestation, and transformation in Northern Ireland', *Peace and Conflict: Journal of Peace Psychology*, 21:4 (2015), 565–73.
33 Office of the First and Deputy First Minister, *A Shared Future*, sections 1.2.1 https://www.niacro.co.uk/sites/default/files/publications/A%20Shared%20Future-%20OFMDFM-Mar%202005.pdf (accessed 6 May 2018).
34 Office of the First and Deputy First Minister, *A Shared Future*, sections 2.1, 2.2.
35 Dominic Bryan, Clifford Stevenson, Gordon Gillespie and John Bell, *Public Displays of Flags and Emblems in Northern Ireland: Survey 2006–2009* (Belfast: Institute of Irish Studies, Queens University Belfast 2010).
36 Peter Shirlow and Brendan Murtagh, *Belfast: Segregation, Violence and the City* (London: Pluto Press 2006), pp. 60–1.

37 Séanna Breathnach interview with D. Bryan, https://ugc.futurelearn.com/uploads/files/6a/ff/6aff563e-fde9-4696-91f2-a1aaab2b5954/Conflict_week_4_4_7_Seanna_Walsh_Interview_v2.pdf.
38 Neil Jarman, *Material Conflicts: Parades and Visual Displays in Northern Ireland* (Oxford: Berg 1997), pp. 150–1; *Irish News*, 9 August 1993.
39 *Irish News*, 7 August 1993.
40 *BNL*, 9 August 1993.
41 *BNL*, 9 August 1993.
42 Institute of Irish Studies, *St Patrick's Day Outdoor Event 2006 Monitoring Report* (Belfast: Institute of Irish Studies, 2006).
43 Bryan, 'Parades, flags, carnivals, and riots'.
44 Based on minutes of meetings attended by Dominic Bryan, 6 December 2004, 17 January 2005, 31 January 2005.
45 Peter Geoghegan, Culture Northern Ireland.org, www.culturenorthernireland.org/features/heritage/orangefest (accessed 20 December 2017).
46 *Irish Times*, 22 June 2006.
47 BBC News, 12 July 2008, http://news.bbc.co.uk/go/pr/fr/-/1/hi/northern_ireland/7503169.stm (accessed 13 November 2018). The Orange Order was founded in 1795 following a clash with the Catholic Defender organisation that came to be known as the Battle of the Diamond.
48 BBC News, 12 July 2008, http://news.bbc.co.uk/go/pr/fr/-/1/hi/northern_ireland/7503644.stm (accessed 13 November 2018).
49 Gillian McIntosh 'Stormont's ill-timed Jubilee: The Ulster '71 Exhibition', *New Hibernia Review*, 11:2 (2007), 17–39; BBC, 'NI's civic festival that was overshadowed by turmoil', 20 June 2011, www.bbc.co.uk/news/uk-northern-ireland-13839746 (accessed 28 August 2018).
50 BBC, 'Queen Elizabeth II in Northern Ireland', nd, www.bbc.co.uk/history/topics/queen_elizabeth_ii_northern_ireland (accessed 28 August 2018).
51 *Guardian*, 17 May 2011; *Irish Times*, 18 May 2011.
52 BBC, 'Queen and Martin McGuinness shake Hands', 27 June 2012, www.bbc.co.uk/news/uk-northern-ireland-18607911 (accessed 28 August 2018).
53 Jarman and Bryan *From Riots to Rights*, pp. 75–80; Kris Brown and Elisabetta Viggiani, 'Performing provisionalism: Republican commemorative practice as political performance in post-Agreement Northern Ireland', in L. Fitzpatrick (ed.), *Performing Violence in Contemporary Ireland* (Dublin: Carysfort Press, 2010), pp. 225–48.
54 Belfast City Council, 'A new £1.3million visitor attraction at Belfast City Hall', 15 May 2017, www.belfastcity.gov.uk/News/News-78902.aspx (accessed 13 November 2018).
55 Gillian McIntosh, *Belfast City Hall: 100 Years* (Belfast: Blackstaff Press, 2006).
56 John Nagle and Mary-Alice Clancy, *Sharing Society or Benign Apartheid: Understanding Peace-Building in Divided Societies* (Basingstoke: Palgrave Macmillan, 2010), pp. 73–5.
57 *Irish News*, 9 August 1993.
58 Milena Komarova and Dominic Bryan, 'Introduction: beyond the divided city: policies and practices of shared space', *City*, 18:4–5 (2014), 427–31.

59 Nagle and Clancy, *Sharing Society or Benign Apartheid*, pp. 73–5.
60 Nagle and Clancy, *Sharing Society or Benign Apartheid*, p. 100.
61 Nelson McCausland, 'The Good Friday accord gave preference to the Irish-Gaelic tradition over others', *Belfast Telegraph*, 12 April 2018.

Conclusion: public space – past lessons and future strategies

This book has explored the use and control of public space in Belfast across a period of nearly 250 years. It began with a period in which public space as understood today did not yet exist. The main streets of the medium-sized commercial town were the property of the middle-class and wealthy inhabitants who lived on them; the courts and alleyways crammed in behind were less formally under the control of the poorer classes whose homes they contained. For spaces open to all one had to go beyond the town, to the fashionable promenades along the Mall or the Long Bridge, or the rougher amusements of the Point Fields and Cave Hill. By the end of the period covered by the book, however, this spatial pattern had been inverted. The city centre is no longer a place where people live. It is instead a site for business, for consumption and for sociability. Beyond it, residential districts sprawl outwards in every direction. These are segregated, in a way that the old town centre had never been, according to social class and also, in the specific case of Belfast, by religious and political allegiance.

It is within this new urban landscape that issues of access to and control of public space became, and have remained, a problem. In the Belfast of the mid- and late eighteenth century the emphasis was on the preservation of what has been called 'polite space'. Urban elites deployed a combination of formal and informal means to protect areas set aside for their use from the intrusions of social inferiors. This was a world in which the town's proprietor, the marquis of Donegall, could make his gift to its citizens of an Exchange in which they could transact business conditional on an undertaking that unsuitable individuals would be kept away from the building; and where respectable citizens could appeal successfully to the local military commander to prevent the soldiers under his command from lowering the tone of elite promenading spots like the Mall by appearing there with their disreputable female companions.[1] In the anonymous mass society of the growing industrial town, where old forms of deference were breaking down, and new intermediate social groups proliferated, this type of overt exclusion of the non-elite became possible only in privately owned space – in the mansions and demesnes of the wealthy, in gentlemen's clubs or in the playing fields belonging to socially exclusive sporting organisations. Elsewhere, what developed was a whole culture of regulation governing the newly opened spaces created by urban improvement and the construction of a civic infrastructure. At the entrances to parks and public buildings stood notices itemising the behaviour required and not permitted, enforced by keepers and attendants. And on the streets and squares of towns and cities a hugely expanded police force sought not only to prevent crime but to regulate the movement of traffic and pedestrians alike, and to impose standards of decorum.

The first conclusion to emerge from this study is thus that history, whatever else it can contribute, confers no absolute entitlements in relation to the streets and squares of the modern city. Public space is not a timeless absolute. It emerged, in the form it is understood today, as a product of the changing urban landscapes of the nineteenth century. Claims phrased in the language of ancient, historically grounded liberties, or of inherent rights, are thus entirely without foundation. Nor has 'public' in this context ever meant free of restrictions. Instead the emergence of areas designated as public space, and the development of new forms of regulation and control governing what could and could not be done in that space, were two sides of the same coin.

What, then, can a study of theory and practice over time contribute to current debate on access to urban space in a divided society such as contemporary Belfast? The CRM was concerned with a range of issues around discrimination and political power, but the contestations manifested in spatial forms. It was the demand for the right to march in public space that required forms of policing that were to destabilise the state. Today, policy makers continue to struggle with uncompromising and often apparently irreconcilable claims surrounding the right to process through particular districts, to have access to sites of historical or political significance, to light bonfires, to fly flags, to erect memorials and impose place names. Can the experience of the past contribute anything to these ongoing debates?

Here again it is important to attend to historical context. The philosophy of government that shaped the rapidly growing towns and cities of the nineteenth century reflected the distinctive attitudes and values of the Victorian era. At its heart was a new belief in the potential of urban living: a conviction that the town, long seen as inferior to the countryside in morals and manners, could in fact be a centre of culture and civic virtue, as well as of wealth and commerce. To this was added a strong commitment to freedom. But it was a freedom conceived within the limits of nineteenth-century liberalism: rigorously individualist and negatively defined, in terms of freedom from external restraint rather than positive rights. That commitment, moreover, went along with an equally strong belief in self-discipline as the central criterion of respectability and social acceptance. From this starting point the elites that took over the management of Britain's towns and cities adopted two complementary strategies. In positive terms they sought to promote a sense of community and civic pride. The classical or Gothic outlines of expansive new town halls and other civic buildings proclaimed a kinship with earlier great eras of urban civilisation. Investment in museums, art galleries and concert halls testified that the industrial or commercial city could simultaneously be the home of high culture. Ceremonial events such as lord mayoral processions, the laying of foundation stones and the observance of local festivals invited all sections of the population to take pride in the status and achievements of their town or city. Where discipline was required, equally, it was applied along lines dictated by the prevailing political liberalism. Space was no longer 'polite' or socially exclusive. Instead streets, parks and public buildings became formally open to all. But entitlement to avail of this access depended on the acceptance of a wide range of restrictions and prohibitions, all justified by the principle that one person's exercise of freedom could not encroach on the equal rights of others.

Both of these strategies played a part in the management of nineteenth-century Belfast, though in each case with limited success. Its civic elite, liberated from the control of the Donegall family and empowered by municipal reform, enthusiastically promoted grand schemes of urban improvement, from the pioneering development of Corporation Street in the 1840s to the grandiose City Hall completed in 1906. The spirit of civic pride is evident, but the range of sympathies associated with it was distinctly narrow. Massive investment in prestige buildings and wider streets stood in contrast to the long-standing neglect of public health and other aspects of working-class welfare. Yet it is hard to believe that even a more broadly based vision of improvement could have done much to promote a sense of shared civic identity in a city so bitterly divided along lines of religious and political allegiance. It was only late in the nineteenth century, and in many cases with a degree of reluctance, that the city's elite gave their support to the annual rituals of the Orange Order. But long before that the ruthless maintenance of one-party rule at city level, blatant discrimination in the distribution of municipal employment and the partisan administration of justice all ensured that Belfast developed as a city characterised by a sense of proprietorship on one side and exclusion on the other.

Belfast's implementation of the liberal principle of access to public space was likewise flawed, though arguably not so completely so. Protestant and Loyalist events undoubtedly enjoyed a privileged status. Once the externally imposed restrictions of the Party Processions Act had been removed, they were assumed to meet the requirement for access, where Catholic and nationalist events were more easily deemed unacceptable. Yet, contrary to what is often asserted, Catholic and nationalist were never wholly excluded, in the period up to 1914, from access to the city centre, or even from the symbolic site of the Ulster Hall. Arthur Trew's attempt to assert a Protestant monopoly of public space was firmly rebuffed. It was only after 1920, when Belfast became the capital of a separate political unit, that access to public space came to be granted or withheld on explicitly political grounds. Nationalist demonstrations, now representing an unequivocal rejection of the legitimacy of the state, were confined, where permitted at all, to Catholic areas, while the Orange Order became more securely a part of the city's public culture. Yet even at this point liberal principles were not wholly abandoned. In 1934 the government resisted demands for the prohibition of the major public event organised by the Catholic Truth Society. In the changing political and cultural climate of the post-war years, moreover, there are signs of a further relaxation of policy. A court judgment secured the Ulster Hall for a celebration of the 150th anniversary of the rebellion of 1798. Later, in 1966, some open celebrations of the Republican military tradition took place, without interference, in west Belfast and elsewhere.

In contemporary Belfast questions of access to and control over urban space remain complex and contentious. Moreover, they must now be approached in a political and legal context quite different to that of the Victorian era. New definitions of human rights go far beyond the fairly narrow range of personal liberties that lay at the heart of nineteenth-century liberal thinking; contending parties formulate their claims in terms of collective as well as individual entitlements, demanding not just freedom from discrimination but the affirmation of group identity. A concern with promoting shared values now sits beside a recognition of cultural and ethnic diversity as legitimate, indeed as a positive asset contributing to a dynamic and creative society. Against this background politicians and policy makers have been required to adapt their approach both to the promotion of a civic identity and to the regulation of access to public space.

Where the first of these is concerned, the change has been far reaching. Official political ritual in Belfast prior to the 1970s, as in the Lord Mayor's Show and the staging of formal royal visits, was not overtly political. But it was implicitly British and unionist, and a celebration of hierarchy and commerce. Today, in contrast, the staging of St Patrick's Day and the revamped Lord Mayor's Show, as well as other officially sponsored events such as Pride, the Festival of Fools and Culture Night, are explicit celebrations of the coexistence of a multiplicity of ethnic and other identities, encouraging the sense of a city centre available to all. The emphasis on performance, humour and entertainment gives most of these events a carnivalesque tone. But the underlying purpose is to promote the development of a shared civic culture, where a sense of being part of a dynamic, diverse urban community will transcend, or at least reduce, long-standing divisions. It is an approach that gains credibility from survey data indicating that there is in fact a substantial part of the population willing to adopt definitions of identity that go beyond traditional polarities. In 2016, 41 per cent of men and 49 per cent of women in Northern Ireland declined to categorise themselves as either nationalist or unionist; significantly, the proportion rose from 30 per cent of those aged over 65 to 57 per cent of those aged 18–34. Since the early 2000s, equally, a significant minority, around one third, of the population have been recorded as choosing to describe themselves as 'Northern Irish' as an alternative to both 'Irish' and 'British'.[2] Wider political trends are also favourable. The recent establishment in a number of British cities of directly elected mayors with significant executive powers, after a century in which progressive centralisation has reduced local government in the United Kingdom to a cipher, opens up the possibility that the city can once again, as in the nineteenth century, become a unit of real political importance. Yet it has to be admitted that the emergence of a Belfast civic identity sufficiently well defined to bridge political and sectarian divisions will require significant progress from what is at present a fairly narrow starting point.

Turning to the second area of policy, acceptance of the legitimacy, and even the positive value, of diversity had obvious implications for issues relating to the granting or denial of access to public space. The opening of the city centre to previously excluded Republican groups is in part an acknowledgement of contemporary political realities both within the City Council and within the structures of devolved government in Northern Ireland. But it also reflects an acceptance, within the context of a broader definition of human rights, of new and stronger principles of freedom of expression and freedom of assembly. Such a rights-based approach, it can be suggested, represents a minimum requirement for the realisation of ideas of a shared society. Decisions relating to parades, protests and commemorations, touching directly on conflicting political allegiances and thus likely to lead to violent confrontations, have inevitably proved contentious, especially where elected politicians are involved. On the other hand, the potential of the ideal of a shared civic identity to itself act as a promoter of change should not be under-estimated. The prospect of achieving official recognition, and the funding that went with it, was enough to persuade the west Belfast-based organisers of a St Patrick's Day celebration to agree to the removal of its overt political trappings. The Orange Order, too, has felt the need to negotiate, if so far less successfully, for its own return from the sectional to the civic realm.

What further progress will be made remains to be seen. Ideally, continued dialogue will see a broader acceptance that public space is not a timeless and absolute category, conferring absolute rights of access and assembly, but a contingent concept to be constantly re-evaluated in the light of a changing environment. Ideally, too, progress will be in the direction of the ideas of shared space, based on recognition of the legitimacy of differing and diverse identities that underpin existing public policy. The problem is that the practical outcome of this policy is widely perceived as undermining its declared principles. In a society where one set of values, unionist and Protestant, has for several decades enjoyed uncontested dominance, any move towards greater equality can only take the form of a shift in the balance of power and advantage. Progress towards 'parity of esteem' has in practice meant that one side enjoys access to public space formerly denied it, while the other is forced to accept restrictions on formerly uncontested practices, such as Orange marches and the public display of the Union flag. Against this background there remains a real risk that what is presented as 'shared space' will in fact be 'partitioned space', with each side asserting absolute claims to what it sees as its territory, while every concession made to one within the remaining public space must be balanced by a proportionate concession to the other. Such a dispensation can of course be sustained, at least in the absence of acute political crisis. But the consequence would be that Belfast remains what it has been for most of the past two centuries: a city that hints at, but never comes close to realising, the positive potential of modern urban life.

Notes

1 See above, p. 30. For the concept of 'polite space' see Peter Borsay, 'The rise, fall and rise of polite urban space in England 1700–2000', in Andreas Fahrmeir and Elfie Rembold (eds), *Representation of British Cities: The Transformation of Urban Space 1700–2000* (Berlin: Philo, 2003), pp. 30–48.
2 Northern Ireland Life and Times Survey, 2003, 2016, www.ark.ac.uk/nilt/2003/Political_Attitudes/ID.html, www.ark.ac.uk/nilt/2016/ (accessed 3 May 2018).

Index

Note: page numbers in italics refer to illustrations

Adams, Gerry, President of Sinn Féin (1983–2018) 160, 171, 215, 222
Ancient Order of Hibernians 118, 129, 137
architecture 4, 25, 62, 68–9

Ballymacarrett 23–4, 42, 70, 80, 84, 109
Bates, John, Town Clerk and Town Solicitor (1842–55) 56–8, 70, 73, 77
Belfast Charitable Society 20, 27
Belfast Protestant Association 117, 119–20
Blackstaff River 23–4, 66–7, 79–80, 89n.15
British Association for the Advancement of Science 71
Brooke, Sir Basil, 1st Viscount Brookeborough, Prime Minister Northern Ireland (1943–63) 135, 147, 150, 151, 155n.15, 163
Bruce, Revd William 39, 42
buildings
  Albert Bridge 80, 123, 126
  City Hall 80, 84, 130, 133–4, 159–60, 176, 196, 198, 204–6, *210*, 213, 214–15, 216, 222
  court-house and prison 68–9, 98
  Custom House 68, 69, 116–17, 130n.5, 172, 197–8, 203, 212
  Exchange and Assembly Rooms 22, 29, 30, 51, 69
  Linen Hall
    Brown 19, 20
    White 22, 24–5, 30, 38, 39, 41, 45, 47, 71, 80
  Long Bridge 16, 18, 19, 63
  Poor House 20, *21*, 27, 73
  Queen's Bridge 63, 116, 117, 123
  Royal Courts of Justice 136
  Stormont, Parliament Buildings 138–9, 149, 150, 220
  Town Hall 18, 37, 78–9, 125
  Ulster Hall 69, 101, 117–18, 121–2, 126, 128–9, 130, 133, 140–2, 147, 156n.38, 208
Bunting, Major Ronald 170
Burton, Frank 181

Campaign for Nuclear Disarmament 162–7
Carrickfergus, Co. Antrim 16, 18, 38–9, 50, 69
Carson, Edward 139
Castlereagh *see* Stewart
Catholic emancipation 7, 49, 53–4, 55, 74
Catholics
  excluded from public life 73–4, 76, 87–8
  numbers 25, 74, 154n.10
  politics 73, 87–8, 118, 151
  religious life 7, 74, 100, 115, 140
  see also churches
Catholic Truth Society 140
Chichester, Arthur (1563–1625), 1st baron Chichester 19, 45
Chichester, Arthur (1695–1757), 4th earl of Donegall 19, 38
Chichester, Arthur (1739–99), 5th earl and 1st marquis of Donegall 20–2, 30, 36, 38–9

Index

Chichester, Frederick Richard (1827–53), Lord Belfast 124–5
Chichester, George Augustus, 2nd marquis of Donegall (1769–1844) 25, 41–5, 47, 54, 58–9, 63
Chichester, George Hamilton (1797–1883), 3rd marquis of Donegall (Lord Belfast to 1844), MP Carrickfergus (1818–20), Belfast (1820–30), County Antrim (1835–37) 44, 45, 54, 58, 61n.63, 75, 125
Chichester, Lord Arthur (1808–40), MP Belfast (1832–35) 56, 58
Chichester, Lord John 68
churches
  Catholic 26, 75, 115
  Church of Ireland 18, 20, 31, 35n.58
city status 70, 83, 127
civic ceremony 4, 37–8, 45, 46–7, 70–1, 125–6, 135–6, 138, 139, 220
  royal visits 70–1, 133–4, 149–50, 188, 219–21
  visits by Lords Lieutenant 39, 41–2, 56–7, 126
civic pride 3–5, 62–71, 87, 127, 189, 213, 230
civil rights movement 1, 158–9, 164, 167, 169–70, 174
Clarke, John, Mayor (1844–45) 75–6, 124
Conservative party 55–8, 67, 71–3, 75–8, 88, 107
Cooke, Henry 78, 94, 104, 125, 190
Cornwallis, Charles, 1st Marquis Cornwallis, Lord Lieutenant (1798–1801) 36–7
Craig, Sir James, 1st Viscount Craigavon, Prime Minister Northern Ireland (1921–40) 133, 136, 139, 140, 155n.15
Crawford, William Sharman 55–6
Cunningham, Waddell 38–9

Dawson Bates, Sir Richard, Minister for Home Affairs (1921–45) 137–8
De Certeau, Michel 11
Devlin, Joseph, Nationalist leader, 118, 122, 129
Dillon, John, Nationalist leader 121
Donegall family 17, 18, 19, 36–7, 54, 55–6, 58
  for individual members see Chichester; May

Drennan, William, United Irishman 41, 42
Drumcree, County Armagh 1–2, 206–7
Dunbar, George, MP Belfast (1835–41) 67

elections
  local 43, 48, 58
  parliamentary 9, 38–9, 44, 55–6, 57–8, 73, 93–4, 107, 147
electricity 81
Engels, Friedrich 4

Farset River 16, *17*, 23
Fenian movement 8–9, 74, 86, 104, 107
First World War 135–6, 138, 142, 150, 154n.10, 185–6
flags 2–3, 102–6, 147–9, 152, 185, 186, 194, 197–8, 204–6, 208–12, 213–14, 215–16

gas 4, 24, 28, 65, 81–2
Gay Pride 216, *217*, 231
Gellner, Ernest 173
Good Relations Strategy (2003) 196, 211, 212–13

Haliday, Dr Alexander 39
Hanna, Hugh 125
Hardwicke, Philip Yorke, 3rd earl, Lord Lieutenant (1801–5) 41–2
Henderson, James Alexander, Mayor (1873–75) 104, 107, 108
Hermon, Sir John, Chief Constable RUC (1980–89) 186, 207
Home Rule 74, 86, 107, 109, 114, 117, 128–30, 134, 185–6
house numbers 28
housing 17–18, 23, 65–6, 144, 167–71, 178n.60

Improvement Acts 63, 65–6, 77, 79, 89n.15, 97–8
industry 17, 143, 146
  linen manufacture 22–3, 83, 143
  shipbuilding 23, 83, 143, 163
Inglis, Henry 23, 25
Irish Republican Army (IRA) 1, 134, 137, 143, 146, 149, 151, 153, 180–2, 184, 214
Irish Volunteers 9, 129

Johnston, William, MP Belfast (1868–78), Belfast South (1885–1902) 102, 107, 108, 121

Kane, Revd R.R, Orange Grand Master 87, 119

Labour movement 88, 93, 117, 137–8, 171–5
 Independent Labour Party 117, 137
 Northern Ireland Labour Party 151–2, 164, 172–4
Lagan River 16, 22, 99
Lanyon, Charles 69, *116*
Lefebvre, Henri 11
Liberal party 49, 55–8, 73, 77, 78, *79*
libraries
 Linen Hall Library 22, 24, 41
 public library 80, 82, 126
local government
 Corporation and Sovereign 26–7, 36–7, 41–2, 43–4, 58
 Council 58, 67–8, 72–3, 78, 87, 88, 97, 144–5, 184, 196–8, 211–15
 Police Board and Committee 27–8, 31, 43–4, 47–8
 Lord Mayor's Show 166–7, 183, 187–93

McCausland, Nelson 193, 223
McCracken, Henry Joy, United Irishman 40–1
McDonnell, James 41
McTier, Martha 18, 27, 39, 40–1, 42, 74
Maginess, Brian, Minister for Home Affairs (1949–53) 148
Malcolm, Dr Andrew 71
Manchester martyrs 8, 109
marching bands 105–6, 108, 109, 140, 172, 183, 185–6, 187, 218
markets 21, 63–5
Maskey, Alex 159, 191, 196, 215
May, Anna (1774–1849), Marchioness of Donegall 42
May, Edward (?1751–1814), Sovereign (1803–6, 1809–10), MP for Belfast (1801–14) 42, 44, 45, 47
May, Revd Edward (c.1783–1819), Vicar of Belfast (1809–19), Sovereign (1807–8, 1811, 1818) 43, 49, 50, 54
May, Sir Stephen (c.1781–1845), MP for Belfast (1814–16) 44, 53

May Day 18, 171–5
Moore, Frank Frankfort 80, 106–7
Mulgrave, Constantine Phipps, 6th earl, Lord Lieutenant (1835–39) 56–7
Mulholland, Andrew, Mayor (1845–46) 61n.47, 66, 71
municipal reform 3, 58, 62–3
municipal trading 4, 81–2
Murphy, Conor, 209–10

Nationalist party
 (1882–1918) 87, 88, 118, 129, 134
 in Northern Ireland 144, 151, 152, 173
Nelson Club 46, 52
Northern Ireland Act (1998) 191, 196, 208, 209–10, 211

O'Connell, Daniel 77, 92, 94, 96, 102, 104, 108
O'Muilleoir, Mairtin, 193–4
O'Neill, Terence, Prime Minister Northern Ireland (1963–69) 151, 153, 163, 218
Orangefest 216–18, *219*
Orange Order 2, 45, 50, 54, 74–5, 86, 102–8, 141, 147, 185–6, 216, 218, *219*, 221, 226n.47

Paisley, Ian, Jr, MP North Antrim (2010–) 1
Paisley, Revd Ian 152–3, 174, 182
parks 5, 82, 228–9
parliamentary reform 38, 51, 53–5, 107
Party Processions Acts 86, 102, 108
Peel, Robert 44
 as model for Belfast Conservatives 76–7
People's Democracy 159, 166–7, 170–1, 174
police 28–9, 31–2, 48, 99, 108–9
 Irish (later Royal Irish) Constabulary 99, 120, 135
 night watch 28–9
 Police Service of Northern Ireland 205, 206, 208, 221
 Royal Ulster Constabulary 143, 148, 151, 166, 186, 190, 193–4, 207, 208
 Town Police 30, 76, 98–9
 Ulster Special Constabulary ('B Specials') 135, 143, 151, 158

Index   237

popular amusements 18, 101, 105, 117
  curtailed or suppressed 6, 97–100
population 3, 16, 23, 32, 83, 114
Preston, Sir John, Mayor (1877–79) 106
processions and demonstrations
  Lady Day 103–9, 111n.38, 118, 137
  legal restrictions 6–10, 86, 102–6,
      137–8, 146–7, 148, 207
  nationalist 109, 121, 128–9, 145–6,
      146–7, 152–3, 214–15, 221, 222
  religious 7, 74, 115, 120, 122
  Twelfth of July 74–5, 96, 102, 104–9,
      126, 137, 143, 151–2, 181,183,
      184–7, 206–7, 209, 216, 218, *219*,
      221
  see also marching bands
prostitution 19, 29, 30
public health 4, 66–7, 80–1, 144

Queen Caroline controversy 51–3
Queen's College (from 1908 Queen's
    University) 68–9, 71, 84, 123, 125,
    126, 150, 159, 166, 167, 189

railway 68, 71, 80
Rea, John 77, 95, 98
Redmond, John, Nationalist leader 121,
    129
Repeal movement 74, 77, 92, 94–5, 122
residential segregation
  by class 4–5, 24, 31
  by religion 25–6, 84–5, 114, 203, 214
riots 51–3, 54–5, 74–5, 85–7, 94–6, 103,
    109, 119, 138, 143, 152, 205
Rodgers, Jim 199, 215
Russell, Thomas, United Irishman 19, 41
Rutland, Charles Manners, 4th duke, Lord
    Lieutenant (1784–87) 39

St Patricks' Day 108, 109, 137, 142,
    193–9, 209, *210*, 213–16
sanitation *see* public health, water supply
sectarian animosity 26, 73–8, 84–8, 95–6,
    143, 160–1, 180–1
shopping 5, 80, 115, 203–4
Sinclair, Betty 172
Sinclair, William 21, 42
Sinn Féin 134, 144, 152–3, 182, 184, 190,
    194, 196, 204–5, 207, 209, 211,
    221, 223
sociability 18, 21–2, 204

Social Democratic and Labour Party
    (SDLP) 190, 196, 197, 204–5, 209,
    211
space 4–5, 85–6, 118, 181–4, 186–7, 190,
    198–9, 206
  exclusive and contested 1–2, 93–6, 117,
      159, 161, 182, 222–3
  future policy and prospects 222–4,
      231–2
  Good Friday Agreement 195, 204, 208,
      212–13
  'polite' 30, 228–9
  regulation 5–10, 28, 31–2, 92–3,
      97–100, 137–8
  sacred 12, 176
  shared 212–13, 218, 222–4, 232–3
  theories of 10–13
statues *81,* 104, 120, 124–5, 139, 142, 190,
    214, 222
Stewart, Frederick, Viscount Castlereagh,
    later 4th marquis of Londonderry
    76
Stewart, Major General Charles, later 3rd
    marquis of Londonderry 46
Stewart, Robert, Viscount Castlereagh,
    later 2nd marquis of Londonderry
    41, 46
street lighting 26, 28
street names 123–4
streets and localities
  Botanic Gardens 71, 82, 84, 101, 104,
      220
  Carrick Hill 115, 130n.1, 148
  Castle Place (formerly the Parade) 20,
      40, 47, 93
  College Square 24, 31, 190
  Cromac 24, 109, 118–19, 153, 170
  Donegall Place 20, 21, 24, 31, 52–3, 84,
      124, *183*
  Donegall Square 24, 69, *81,* 84
  Donegall Street (formerly Linenhall
      Street) 16, 18, 19, 20, *21,* 63–4,
      204
  Durham Street 85, 96
  Falls Road 66, 85, 109, 114, 121, 129,
      149, 152, 221
  Great Victoria Street 68, 102, 104, 123,
      212
  Hannahstown 103–4, 108–9, 118–20
  Hercules Street 25–6, 75, 80, 95, 100
  High Street 16–17, 20, 24, 31, 66, 75,
      203

streets and localities (*cont.*)
   Leeson Street 85
   Mall 18, 229
   North Street 16, 80, 115
   Ormeau Avenue 80
   Peter's Hill 21, 115
   Point Fields 18, 24
   Pound 25–6, 34n.37, 85, 96, 114
   Queen's Island 71, 101, 118, 123, 203
   Rosemary Street 24, 37
   Royal Avenue 79–80, 84, 118, 124
   Sandy Row 31, 75, 76, 85, 96, 152, 218
   Shankill Road 66, 85, 104, 114, 121, 140, 152, 185, 188
   Smithfield 21, 63–4, 85, 88, 115
   Victoria Street 63, *64*, 65, 69, 71, 78
   Waring Street 16–17, 20, 63
   York Street, *cover*, 24, 64, 68, 80, 172
suburbanisation 5, 13, 24, 31, 68, 84, 203

Tennent, Robert 50
Tennent, Robert James, MP Belfast (1847–52) 55, 57
Tennent, Sir James Emerson, MP Belfast (1832–45) 55–6, 56–7, 67, 75, 76, 78
Tennent, William 41, 50
Thackeray, W.M. 25
Tone, T.W., United Irishman, 19, 40
town meeting 27, 39–40, 49–53, 54, 94–5
Tracy, William, Resident Magistrate 96, 98, 99

trams 80, 81,
Trew, Arthur 119–21

Ulster Defence Association (UDA) 181, 182, 186
Ulster Volunteer Force (UVF)
   (1913–20) 129, 135–6, 138
   (1966–) 1, 153, 181–3, 185–6
unionism 1, 135, 136, 139–40, 142, 182, 205, 223, 232–3
Unionist Party 144, 145, 148, 153, 164, 184
United Irish League 117, 118
United Irishmen 40, 74, 93

Verner, Thomas, Sovereign (1819–23) 43, 45, 49, 50, 51–2
Verner, Thomas Junior, Sovereign (1841–42) 58, 63
Victoria, Queen 70–1, *72*, 124, 125–6
Volunteers 38, 39, 74

Warnock, Edmund, Minister for Home Affairs (1944–49) 146–7
water supply 27, 58, 66, 75, 80–1, 87
Watson, Revd Alex, chair NICND 162–3
Wesley, John 18
workplace expulsions 96, 119, 129, 135, 143, 171

Young, Robert 68
Young Ireland 94–5

EU authorised representative for GPSR:
Easy Access System Europe, Mustamäe tee 50,
10621 Tallinn, Estonia
gpsr.requests@easproject.com